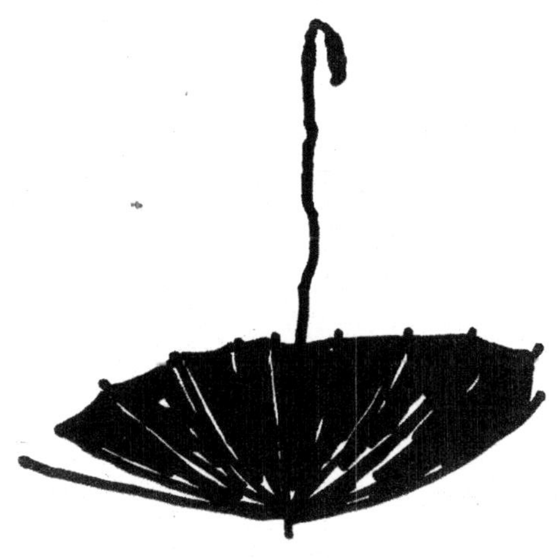

good deed rain

Near me,
there's a flutter of birds passing through heaven.
I'm singing in a silent place,
remembering my happiest friends.
I'm a stalk of grass
where the wind is blowing.
You have to
bend close to hear
anything at all.

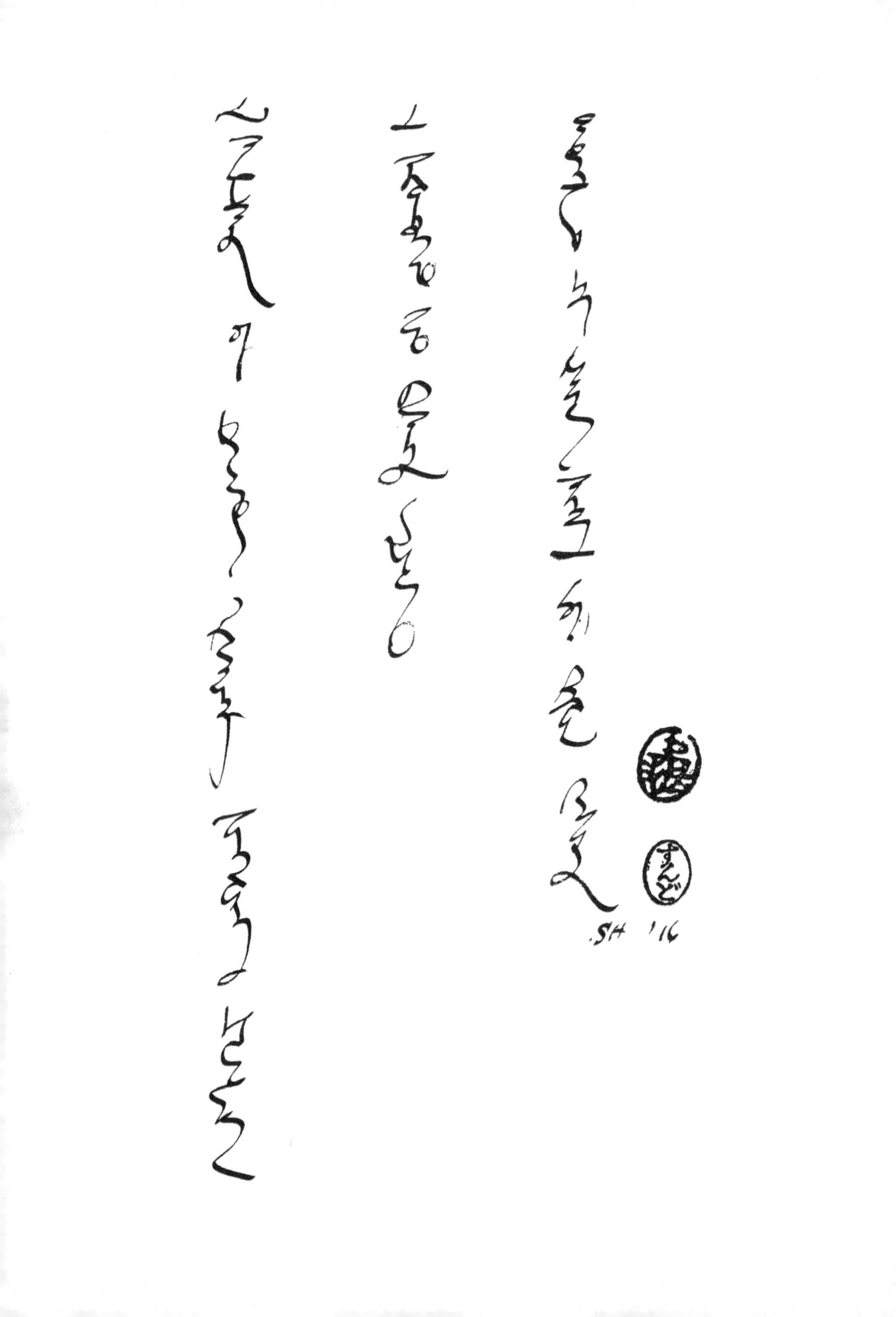

.SH '16

A Flutter of Birds Passing Through Heaven

A tribute to Robert Sund

Edited by
Allen Frost & Paul Piper

Bellingham, Washington
ISBN 978-1-944786-80-9
Edited by Allen Frost & Paul Piper
Cover "Shack Medicine" by Thomas Wood
Frontispiece and Title Page by Steve Herold
Back cover photo by Erik Ambjor
Production Assistance by Fred Sodt

The way this book seemed to build itself makes us believe Robert Sund had a hand in its creation. However this book is especially dedicated to the guidance and support of Tim McNulty and Chip Hughes.

INTRODUCTION:

Silence of water above a sunken tree:
The pure serene of memory in one man,—
A ripple widening from a single stone
Winding around the waters of the world.

—Theodore Roethke, from *North American Sequence*

This book is a tribute to Robert Sund, the poet and the man. It represents the contributions of many people whose lives were touched, in some cases shaped, by Robert. This community, as Allen and I got to know them through compiling this book, is a blessed group, and we have been honored to get to know them, in whatever small way we did. We hope this book will keep Robert's memory alive, and help resurrect his poetry to the stature it deserves.

Robert was a man of joy and grief. He lived in a world of words and images. Much of what he touched became magical. He was a true poet, which meant he lived the life of a poet. It was not a soft life, a life of privilege and ease. Robert was often homeless, and relied on the gifts of friends to stay afloat.

I first encountered Robert eight or nine years ago. Someone gave me his steelhead poem, published in *Poems from Ish River Country*. I was at the time a neophyte steelheader, and had caught very few, but I immediately recognized that Robert had captured the essence of both fishing and poetry in those simple lines. Place was precious to Robert, and his love of place, his simple well-suited language, often evoked these places (Ish River, Shi Shi, Taos) that lived in his heart and soul.

Steve Herold told me a while ago that Robert, who had studied with Theodore Roethke at the University of Washington, had taken Roethke's rhythmic impulses and integrated them into American language, the language of everyday people. Many of his poems are deceptively simple, yet like Blake's, contain the world or worlds. Steve also taught that Robert was the seed for poetry in the Skagit Valley, and as such, nearly everyone who wrote poetry in the Skagit after him was somehow indebted.

We hope that this book will contain familiar memories, photographs and poems, yet will also expose the reader to new anecdotes and parts of Robert's life. Several people told us that Robert traveled in a number of different circles. We hope we have represented those circles of friends in our book.

Paul Piper & Allen Frost

CONTENTS:

Robert Sund: Poem for Betty 1
Arthur Greeno: Recollection 3
Glenn (Chip) Hughes: A Dream of the Poet Robert Sund 9
Robert Sund: Letter to William Carlos Williams 10
Robert Sund: March Morning: For William of Passaic 13
William Carlos Williams: Letter to Robert Sund 14
Charlie Krafft 15
Joseph Stroud: From a letter to Tim McNulty 16
Mary Randlett: Photos 18
Charlie Krafft 22
KRAB FM 24
Robert Sund: Basket Bay, at Anchor Near Midnight 26
Steve Herold 27
Robert Sund: The Sullivan Slough Review 29
Charlie Krafft 31
Roller Barons, SC, La Conner 32
Glen Turner: The Roller Barons International Skating Club 33
Charlie Krafft: Portrait of the Poet Robert Sund 35
Praise for Bunch Grass 36
Robert Sund: Passages from the Notebook of Douglas R. Redwood 37
Jeff Winston 43
Bo Miller: Pen and Ink, Shi Shi 44
Arjuna Barton: Shi Shi Beach Rain Paintings 45
Steven R. Johnson: Photos of Shi Shi 46
Glenn (Chip) Hughes: Poem Given to Robert Sund at Shi Shi Beach 49
Gary Hickenbottom 50
Bill Slater: Two Bums in One Book 52
Robert Sund: Two Bums in One Boxcar 54
The Ish River Country Map 60
Robert Sund: Ish River 61
Gary Hickenbottom & Bo Miller 62
Glenn (Chip) Hughes: Robert Sund and the All-Time Poets Baseball Team 63
Robert Sund & Steve Herold: A Song to Celebrate the Summer 69

Maggie Wilder: Robert Sund 70
Robert Sund & The 6th Graders 71
Erik Ambjor 72
Joseph Stroud: I Remember Robert 73
Charlie Krafft: "The Famous Poet" Robert Sund 74
Frances McCue: Robert Sund (1929-2001) 75
Tim McNulty: Up Shit Creek 77
Finn Wilcox: Spare Change 78
Mike Price 79
Erik Ambjor 82
Michael Daley: Notes from Disappearing Lake Review 84
Riverrat Poems poster 90
Charlie Krafft & Erik Ambjor 91
Steven R. Johnson & Erik Ambjor 92
Jim Bertolino: Returning to the Poetry of Robert Sund 93
Kenneth Rexroth 97
Sam Hamill 98
Georgia Johnson: Ish River, September, 1982 99
Erik Ambjor: photography 100
Fred Owens: Robert Sund Soliloquy 107
Janet Saunders & Jim Smith: Robert Sund Anecdotes 110
Fred Owens 112
Sund for Mayor 113
Tim McNulty: By Heart 116
Sam & Sally Green: Memories of Robert Sund 120
Robert Sund: Our Fathers 122
Deshung Rinpoche & Robert Sund 123
Robert Sund: The Fishtown Woods letter 124
Christine Wardenburg-Skinner 128
Brad Killion 131
Barb Hathaway 132
Georgia Johnson: Robert Sund 133
Joan Cross 134
Robert Sund: A Painting Can Be… 135
Robert Sund: Unpublished Excerpts from the Taos Manuscript 137
Tim McNulty & Erica Pickett 140
Robert Sund: Wind Letters 141
Robert Sund: Where the Animals Wear Shoes 148

Anacortes House 150
Erica Pickett 151
Andy McConnell 155
Mary Hedlin, Tim McNulty, Erica Pickett 156
Ann Spiers: You Say, "Remember Me." 157
Finn Wilcox: Not Letting Go 158
Robert Sund: Autumn Equinox 160
Sam & Sally Green: Saturday, September 29 162
Glenn (Chip) Hughes: In Robert Sund's Shack 164
Father Pat Twohy: Invocation 166
Paul Hunter: As Migratory Birds 167
Chuck Easton with Autumn Scott 168
Bob Rose 171
Bill Yake: For Robert Sund 174
Michael Daley 175
Robert Sund: Prayer for Dana Richardson 177
Pat Twohy 179
Robert Bly: Lunch Time 180
Gary Snyder 181
Wendell Berry 182
Ginny Greeno & Brad Killion 183
Boni Killion: Robert Sund 185
Brad Killion 188
Robert Sund: La Conner Main Street 190
Erica Pickett 191
Marisa Papetti 192
Arjuna (Diane) Barton: Recollections of Robert Sund 193
Le Kai Wen (Chuck Luckmann) 195
Georgia Johnson: Some Moon 196
Bill Yake: Animism, Buddhism, Friendship & Autoharp Melodies 197
Andy McConnell 199
Eowyn Greeno 202
Erik Ambjor 204

ROBERT SUND:

First published poem from 1953

Poem for Betty

I remember saying
your legs were moving
like a flight of geese
in a lovely storm

I remember geese
just before the dawn
flying in one direction
through a natural season

I remember centers
warm centers of old delight
I remember hoping
I would not need to remember.

ARTHUR GREENO: Recollection

Born on November 29, 1929, in Olympia, Washington to Swede-Finn parents, Robert Sund was adopted as a young child by Evart and Elsa Sund of Elma, Chehalis Valley, Washington. He grew up at the family farm on "Swede Hill," with his parents, grandparents, and brother.

Robert graduated from Elma High School in 1948. He went on to Pre-Med studies at the University of Washington. There, he met his future teacher and mentor, the poet Theodore Roethke, who took him away from Medicine and set him on his life's path. He recalled Roethke asking early in their relationship, "You have a musical voice; do you know languages?" And, of course, he did, treasuring fluency in Swedish all of his life. To pay for tuition, Robert worked summers in the woods at one of the last railroad logging camps in the Northwest.

Robert finished his B.A. in Creative Writing in 1954. In the late 1950's, he worked in the Alaskan fishing industry, mostly as a boat's cook. During this time, he filled notebook after notebook with poems and observations of the vast natural beauty around him. Of that unpublished work he has said, "There may not be much there… a lot of people have done better." He returned to graduate study at the University in Comparative Literature (English and Scandinavian) from 1957-1963.

He was briefly married to a fellow student of Roethke's in the early sixties, a woman named Ireland. "She was beautiful," he said, "but it was mistaken."

In 1963, while working in the wheat harvest near Walla Walla, Robert learned from the radio that his mentor, Roethke, had died. *Bunch Grass,* his first published collection of poems, was penned into notebooks that same summer. Among the University of Washington Press's most widely anthologized work ever published is the following poem from *Bunch Grass:*

In a landscape that desperately needs color
why do the flowers
stay
so close to the ground?
You meet them with surprise
hidden
in the pale grasses.

From 1964-1967, Robert was poetry program director for Lorenzo Milam's KRAB-FM in Seattle. There, he conducted live interviews with such poets as Robert Bly, Galway Kinnell, and Lawrence Ferlinghetti. In 1968, he published Bly, Kinnell, and Pablo Neruda, among others, in the first and only issue of the *Sullivan Slough Review,* an ambitious magazine that is now a collector's item.

The seventies found Robert living the life of an artist. He was often broke, but always true to his calling. He sold single calligraphed poems and an occasional work of art in Seattle, shot passionate games of pool in her taverns, filled notebooks with poems, and discovered the work of Karl Gustav Jung. Jung's archetypal imagery fascinated him and he began a long series of gouache mandala images on paper that were shown in several Seattle galleries, including Richard White, Second Story, Polly Friedlander, and the Seattle Art Museum.

During that same time, Robert discovered the Autoharp, which became his lifelong instrument. Most of his poetry readings included at least a few songs with Autoharp accompaniment.

On a trip to Shi-Shi Beach with artist Charles Krafft in the early seventies, a vision came to him of a pyramidal shaped cabin behind the huge log drifts at the mouth of Petroleum Creek. Over the next few years, he and many friends fashioned two-inch thick drift boards of teak, cedar, and fir into a beautiful shelter with a beach-stone fireplace. Many survivors of that era fondly remember the glorious isolated beach, the vegetarian cuisine and the high times. Later, in gratitude for those days and the place, Robert was active in the movement to incorporate Shi-Shi into Olympic National Park. After that was accomplished, of course, the shelter was dismantled.

But, his passion for wilderness was ignited, and he turned to an earlier discovery of abandoned gill-netter shacks in Fishtown, on the North Fork of the Skagit River. Krafft had already moved there, and soon there was a thriving community of artists, including calligrapher-bookman Steve Herold, poet-artist Paul Hansen and sculptor-architect Bo Miller. Robert opted for a remote shack just downstream on Ship Creek (which he called Disappearing Lake due to the tidal action at the mouth of the river). There, he crafted another aesthetically pleasing shack filled with the simple beauties of stone, wood, pottery, and paper art. It became the center for his work for the next eleven years. As always, notebooks filled up with poetry, and from those efforts came two beautiful chapbooks in collaboration with printer Rusty North of Sagittarius Press, Port Townsend (*Why I Am Singing for the Dancer,* 1979, and *How the Dancer is Carried Into the Hall of Light,* 1982).

In 1982, he hosted Kenneth Rexroth at a poetry reading in La Conner, and published another chapbook with one long poem for Rexroth, entitled *This Flower* (The Great Blue Heron Society, La Conner, 1982). Perhaps prophetically, he attached an addendum to this exquisite work entitled "One More for Good Measure."

Maybe exalted gestures will be
retrieved in our time.
Maybe our grandchildren will go through
our trunks and boxes
and be amazed.

The most profound statement of his years at Disappearing Lake was *Shack Medicine* (Tangram Press, 1990, and Poet's House Press, 1992). In "A Note on the Setting" from this book, he said, "Out on the river you know you are in the midst of a great creation. You see the old work and the new work side by side; the ancient migration routes of all the birds, and the slow building of silt and soil in the estuary; a small grassy island, for instance, that wasn't there last year and that, in a few seasons, will grow new willow for the blackbirds and the beavers."

Here, too, he discovered the old Chinese and Japanese "hermit poets," and produced new versions of finely honed poetry from other translations. Robert calligraphed many such poems on "wind letters" over the next two decades, a practice he followed until the end of his life.

In 1984, his book, *Ish River* (North Point Press, San Francisco, 1983), won the Washington State Governor's Award for best new book of poetry. Here are poems written longingly about his family, grieving, and sometimes bitter, reflections of life in the towns and cities of Washington State, and tender reminiscences of love celebrated and lost.

After a short hiatus and a private showing of new paintings in California, at the home of friends in Point Reyes and at Woodacre, he was diagnosed with diabetes. Soon after, another chapbook was published. *As Though the Word Blue Had Been Dropped Into the Water* (Sagittarius Press, Port Townsend, 1986), consisted of eight "healing poems," including "Like a Boat Drifting."

Like a boat drifting,
sleep flows forward
    on the deep water of dreams.
Drifts and drifts...
until, finally
the bottom falls out of knowledge.
In the fragrant mist of dawn
the rower wakes,
  picks up the oars, sets them,
    and begins to row.
All night
he labored in his dream
    to be born
like a song in the mouth of God.

Back in La Conner, after hospitalization, he found shelter with many friends: Jim and Janet Smith, Barbara Cram, Alan Olsen and Charlotte Underwood. There, Robert Sund was active in a group of artists, musicians, and poets who formed the La Conner Arts Foundation (LAF), which worked with the town to restore Maple Hall for use as a community center. He calligraphed flyers for art show openings, and painted posters for the film society's movies.

In perhaps the most memorable mayoral election in La Conner's history, Robert declared himself a candidate in 1984, and "stirred the political soup." He did not win, but the effort brought an eloquent voice into the arena, and the politicians to the edges of their seats.

Some of Robert's most joyful days were spent working with Washington's young people as "Poet in the Schools" at Skagit Valley College (1969), Seattle Public Schools (1973), and La Conner Elementary School (1976-77). He also worked with Christine Wardenburg in their "Patterns in Nature" summer camp series at Burlington Little School (1987-1989). This program won an award of excellence from the Washington Alliance of Art Educators in October of 1988.

The Nelson family of La Conner gifted him a small corner lot adjacent to their lumberyard, which he later traded for land on La Conner's hill. After selling that, he moved to Anacortes and lived on the monthly proceeds and social security income.

He found a tiny cottage in the middle of the Flounder Bay Boatyard, and kind landlords in Bob and Erica Pickett. Here, over the remaining years of his life, he created another charming retreat. The gardens held a surprise in every corner—an interesting rock and shell grouping here, a perfectly placed, carefully selected stone there, with lovely board fences, a beautiful gate, and pampered flowers and plants everywhere. Here, he wrote the Garden Poems, which will be republished in the near future as broadsides by the "Poet's House Press."

Robert found a musical soul mate and mentor in guitarist Brad Killion, and their guitar-autoharp duets were delightful to hear. Recently, he teamed up with calligrapher Ora Mae Cunningham to establish the Ink River Studio in old town Anacortes. They laid plans for workshops and classes there, and were about to embark on them when he fell ill this past spring.

Although he was private about it, Robert was a very religious man. He put great faith in the teachings of the Buddha, although he recognized the universal truth at the core of all religions. He revered his teacher, Deschung Rinpoche (deceased), cofounder of the Sakya Monastery in Seattle. In a letter to the Monastery just shortly before his death, he wrote, "In the early 1970's in Seattle Deschung Rinpoche gave me my Tibetan name. Ever after, I have tried to honor his being, his generous spirit, and his kindness to me."

Robert's last will and testament created a trust, with an eleven member board of friends, to care for his work, publish it, and someday build his dream "Poet's House," a place for visiting artists to live and create poetry, calligraphy and pottery.

Robert Sund passed away at 12:40 AM on September 29, 2001, in Anacortes, Washington, while his beloved Ish Rivers teemed with spawning salmon, their spent bodies littering the banks of small creeks where they've not been seen in years. Family, and a grand circle of friends throughout the nation survive him. His thoughts for them were put succinctly in an unpublished poem from the Shi-Shi years:

Friends make us fuller.
When friends leave, their light stays behind.
It is like the blue sea
that supports the white breakers
that come and go.

No matter how far I go
I long to return and be with friends.
It is never the same fire I left,
but beneath it are the ashes
of all our meetings that have gone before.

GLENN (CHIP) HUGHES:

A DREAM OF THE POET ROBERT SUND

On a rocky shore, I open my other eyes.

This is the small cold rain of Puget Sound.
And there, on the promised water, in a skiff, is Robert.

He rows up onto the land, through woods.

He steps out, I join him, and we dance a two-step
there on the forest floor,
weightless as time, drunk on the greenish drifts.

ROBERT SUND: 1954 Letter & Poem to William Carlos Williams

Sund corresponded with many of the poets of his day, including Kenneth Rexroth, Gary Snyder, Robert Bly. At the time of this letter, William Carlos Williams was facing pressure from the U.S press, accusing him of being a communist. Because of these charges, his post at the Library of Congress was revoked. America's Red Scare pandemonium was at its peak. As Robert observes, "We're getting to the point where we refuse to be self-critical and are afraid to." Pulitzer Prize winning poet Richard Eberhart lived in Seattle and taught at the University of Washington. Sund kept Williams' reply framed in his cottage.

AFTER FIVE DAYS RETURN TO
Robert Sund - c/o Yvonne Youst
928 St. Ann St.
New Orleans 16, Louisiana.

VIA

Dr.
Nine
Ruth

PLEASE FORWARD

AIR MAIL
6¢
U.S. POSTAGE
NEW ORLEANS
AUG 27
1954
LA.
IA AIR MAIL
Dr. William Carlos Williams
Nine Ridge Road
Rutherford,
New Jersey.

August 27th '54
New Orleans

Dear Mr. Williams,

I've had this in my notebook for quite a while - and should have sent it to you long before this. Eberhart was out in Seattle directing the poetry workshop while Ted was gone on a Grant - we had a long talk when he (Eberhart) returned from sitting in as a judge for the Bollingen prize, I was happy with the decision finally made - but not so happy to hear about the Library of Congress deal and the stupid and blundering accusations made against you. I suppose they are actually to be pitied - the fools - and we can only hope that some day after all our little nudgings they'll awaken.

What is so pitiful about the world situation - about Communism - is not Communism <u>itself</u> only. It is what we're falling into. We're getting to the point where we refuse to be self-critical and are afraid to. Some thinking person comes along, says Here! here's what ails us, here's the fault with America - or one fault - and what happens? We're too lazy to think it out. We don't want to touch too close. So - you're talking like a damned Commy.

It's the old cry - and become an easy way out - an excuse for remaining sluggardly and unthinking.

Eberhart also said something to the effect that you weren't feeling too well - and then to have this kind of thing slap you in the face. I hope that you're well now, and a little more up to snuff. They still need to be taken aside - like evil children - and given a word or two.

MARCH MORNING is some kind of attempt - an expression - a reaction to this business. Probably not strong enough - a small voice, etc - but a voice anyway. I am sending it to Thomas Cole who published one of my poems last February in # 18. Maybe he'll print it, maybe not - if not he maybe someone else. At any rate I thought you might like to see it.

I've been in New Orleans since February (when - happily - I left the halls of academe) but am tiring of the phony French Quarter, the fat ladies from Willow Bunch, Michigan touring the antique shops of Royal Street - and their cigared husbands getting cheap masturbatory kicks out of the hoochy-kooch of Bourbon St. So in about three weeks I'm heading above the Mason Dixon, out of Jim Crow country, to New York City.

I'm growing windy - there's too much I want to say - and feel rather helpless via the typewriter - so will cut this short, hoping that this reaches you all right, and that I haven't been too presumptious.

Best Wishes -
Robert Sund

MARCH MORNING: FOR WILLIAM OF PASAIC

Out of my room. And down University Way
where it runs into Lake Washington, then East
toward the Cascade Mountains. The sun would rise
soon. All the clouds floated, orange-red
on their undersides. Beyond silent buildings,
across the frosted golf course, rousing all
the sea gulls - the field had taken wings!
hundreds of them! all wings flapping.
I moved along the canal under Mountlake Bridge:
framed in its arc the Cascades (like some
overgrown totempole) stretched over the land,
working a tremendous spell through all things.
No sun rose ever
before! and a fog rested over the lake-water,
whispy, angelic, nebulous, and all the ducks
moving out of their Moses reeds (let him be
born!) half awake, heads curled underwing.

And I thought of W.C.W. (waiting for some birth!)
and said: Here, Doc, here's a medicine; an answer
for the -Ist Boys. (Simple, direct): No one stands
on the mountain now, too far away, but that
big flaming belly rises still, burning, alive.

The Yahoos slept and snored, will sleep and snore,
through a million waiting alarms, while the sun
keeps swinging round.
And I remembered Baudelaire (Get drunk!),
perhaps saw him in the eye of a duck, misty,
then went home, fool again, to eulogize the sun.

Robert Sund
March 1953
Seattle, Washington.

Aug. 30/54

Dear Sund:

I appreciate as I enjoyed you verse which you have addressed to me. It is well put together - and distinguished in itself. It is part of that almost anonymous body of verse written by Americans nowadays that to me constitutes a distinctive style. It is a very good example of that style, cleanly made, you might even characteris it as athletic in build.

This is meant as praise. There is a sameness inescapable from a generic type that cannot be escaped. It is singing. To me it is ensemble singing - in effect. Some of it is distinguished . Most is a pious wish sing, the whole country thinks it has to sing, all the magazines and newspapers are full of it - with undistinguished results. If anything even mildly noteworthy comes of it everyone who can hold a pen thinks he is a poet.

I don't know what makes today a distinguished poem I certainly it is not by coppyig Villon or even Reiner Marie Rilke . The mass has to be transcended but . We may be sure that if a man or woman write well he will be read but not, widely, today. How will a poem such as hey have written in the present case carry much weight with an audience?

All I can say is that - it has a rhythmic feel to it that gives it unity, a unity that stands out as <u>not</u> copied from a book but stems from a sense of - a music that, to some extent, touches what is in all our minds. That's a good thing. The longish, somewhat irregular lines are unforced, in fact very sweet sounding in themselves; the phrases are in no case inverted. It's a very moving composition and subtly worded so that the "yahoos" may not suffer, God damn 'em.

Nice piece of work.

Sincerely

W. C. Williams

William Carlos Williams

9 Ridge Road
Rutherford, N.J.

CHARLIE KRAFFT:

I met Robert Sund in 1966 when he was still living in Seattle. I'd seen him sitting in coffee shop windows in the U. District in 1965 on my way home from high school, but didn't know who he was until a year later even though we were both involved with KRAB FM in '65.

I helped Robert go through the open window of the Seattle home of a girlfriend he was seeing when I first started hanging out with him. She was off at work and he wanted to end the relationship and grab some things inside without confronting her. He'd been married, but I never met his wife.

JOSEPH STROUD from a letter to Tim McNulty, December 6, 2013:

Robert has been on my mind a lot of late, not sure why, maybe it was turning 70 this year and looking back on old friends who have died. I first met Robert in Seattle, the summer of '66. I had come up to Seattle from San Francisco, and had a summer job with a construction company and was living in a boarding house near UW and near Robert's "little red house" (which you had to get to via a kind of cat walk). I was a young poet and knew no one in Seattle. John Logan had given me Robert's address so I looked him up and we hit it off immediately, and spent many evenings together (sometimes at Paul Hansen's house) reading poems, drinking, storytelling. One of the things we had in common was our love for Roethke's poetry. Robert had been, of course, a student of Roethke's, and I had become a friend of Beatrice, Roethke's widow, when she moved to San Francisco and was taking classes at SF State. I was also singing the praises of Kenneth Rexroth in those days, and I think I may have turned Robert in his direction. A few years later I became a student of Rexroth's in a graduate seminar at SF State, and Robert was always hungry for any impressions I could pass along. The following fall Robert came down to San Francisco, and was going to stay at my place for a few days, which turned into a few weeks, and then a month, 6 weeks...a pattern which was to repeat itself. I'm sure you're familiar with it. Robert was a great house guest, full of humor and delight, much laughter, many readings of poems. But I was a 'starving student' at the time, and worked busing dishes in the college cafeteria during the week, and as janitor in the library on weekends, cleaning toilets and mopping floors. Robert had no money, and it became difficult to feed both of us, buy the beer, etc. on my meager funds. So there were some strains and spats over the years. One memorable one was when I suggested some of his lines were moving into schmaltzy territory and because he had such a rich, textures, melodious voice he could get away with it when he read them aloud (he could read a want ad and make it seem sublime). He didn't like hearing that. And he could be thorny with me as well. But we always managed to patch things up. Robert did get to meet some of the San Francisco poets on his first visit, most of whom he was not particularly fond of or impressed with. He had a very strict parameter for what he considered good poems, and many of the SF poets didn't make the grade. But there was a memorable meeting between Robert and Jack Gilbert, who was a friend of mine, and I arranged an afternoon at my place where Robert was going to record an interview with Gilbert. I don't know if you know Gilbert's poetry, he's a fine poet in my view, and quite different from Robert, and with maybe an even stricter parameter for poetry than Robert's, and to see the two of them dance around each other was something to behold. I've often wondered what became of the tape of that interview. I do know that Robert was recording it for a radio program in Seattle, but I don't recall which station it was. Jack died last year. I would give anything to hear those voices together once again. After that fall, Robert and I stayed in touch for many years. I visited him in Seattle and La Conner a few times, and he came to San Francisco for a few visits. The last time I saw him was somewhere in the 80's when he came down to SF to do a reading at the Poetry Center alongside W.S. Merwin. We drifted away after that, I was building my house from the ground up, which took five years, and I was traveling a lot as well, but I've always kept his presence in a clear space within me.

MARY RANDLETT *photographs following pages.*

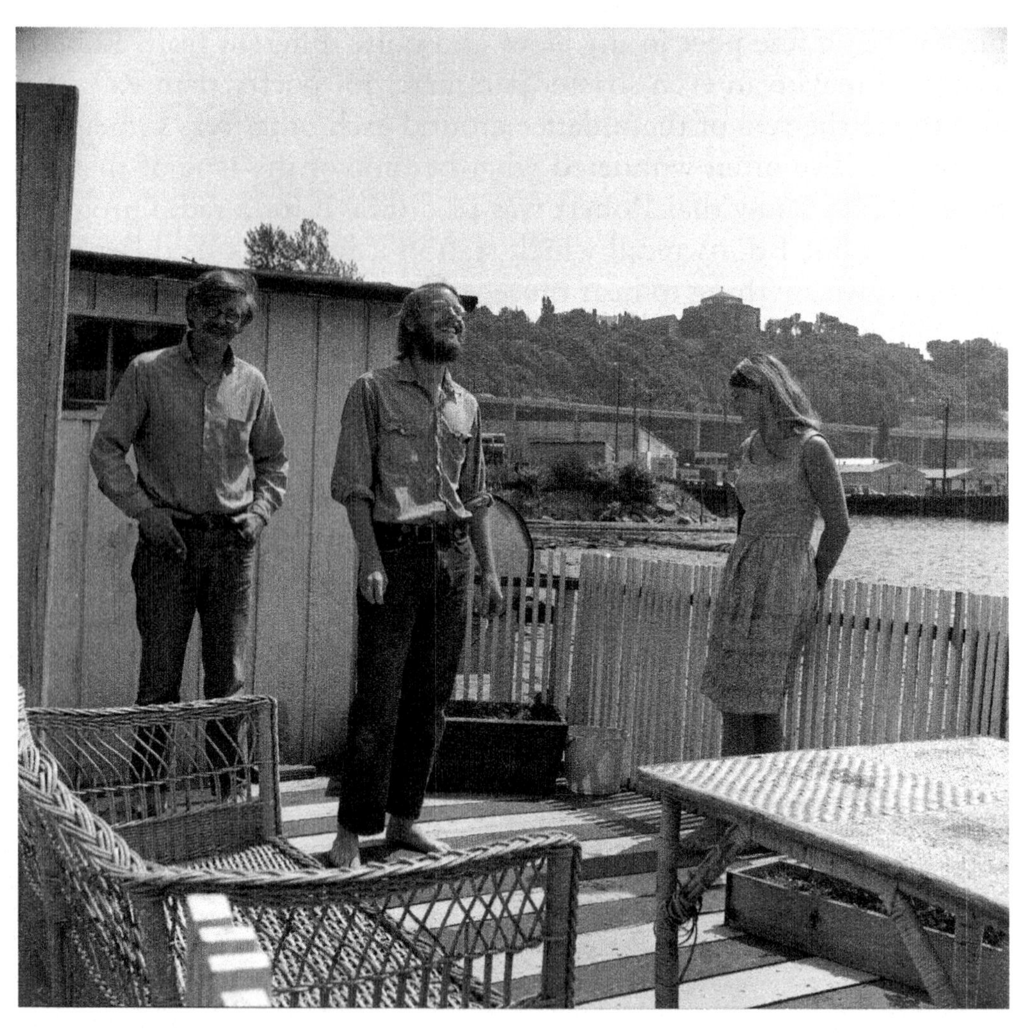

Robert Sund, Charlie Krafft and Arjuna Barton on Lorenzo Milam's houseboat, Seattle, July 1967.

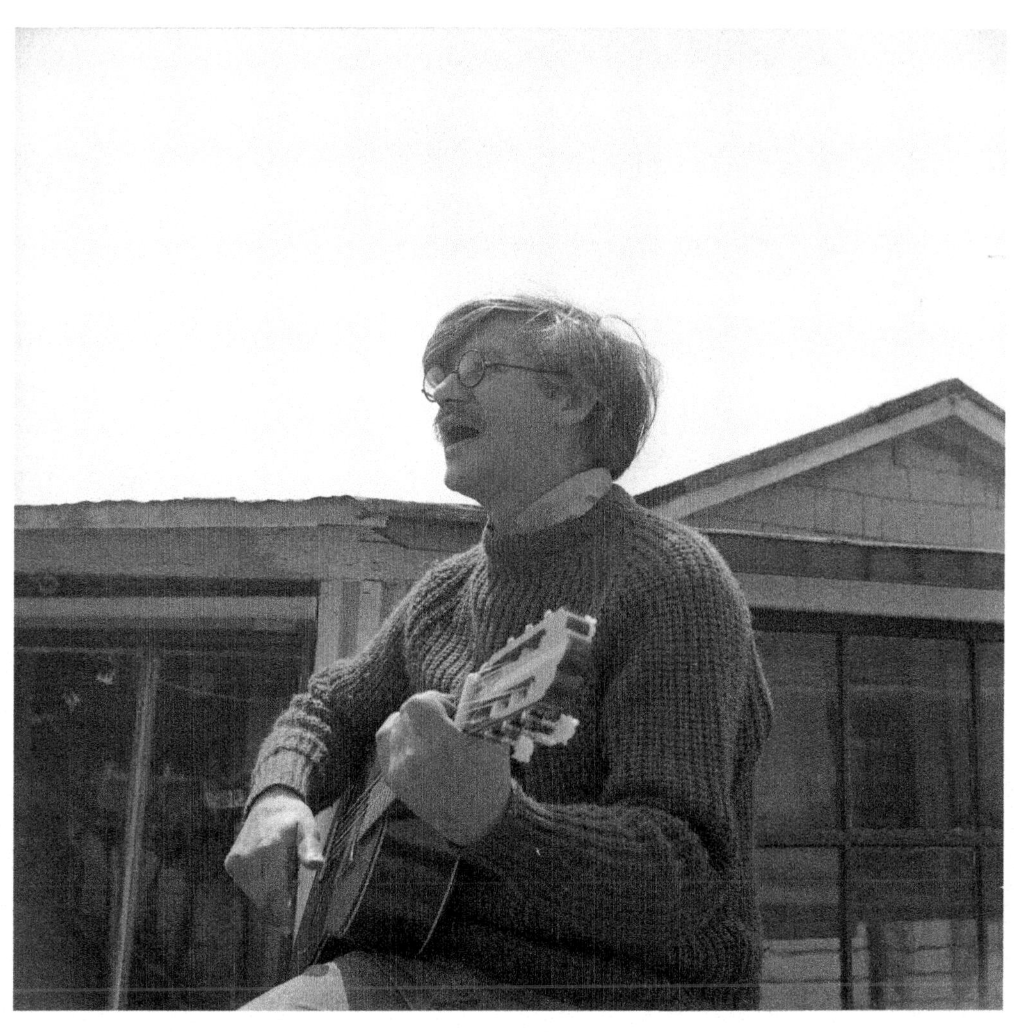

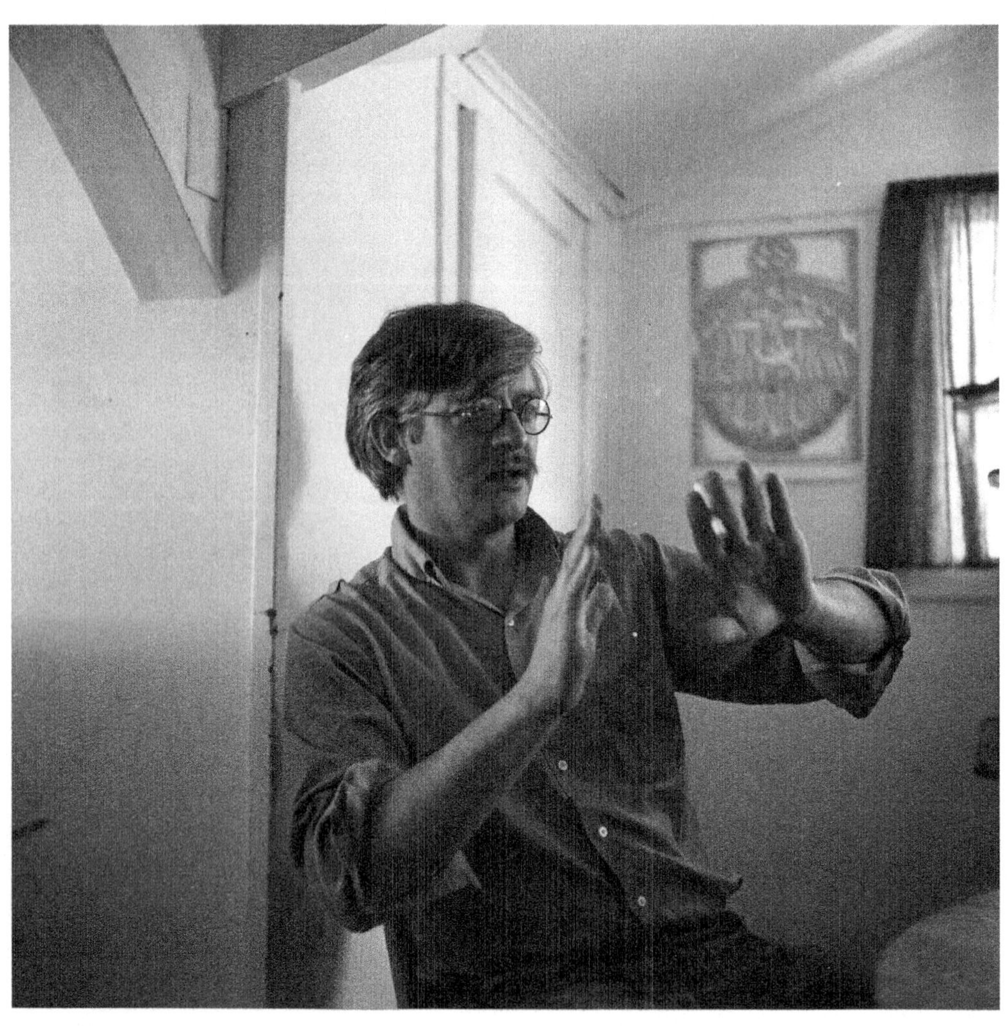

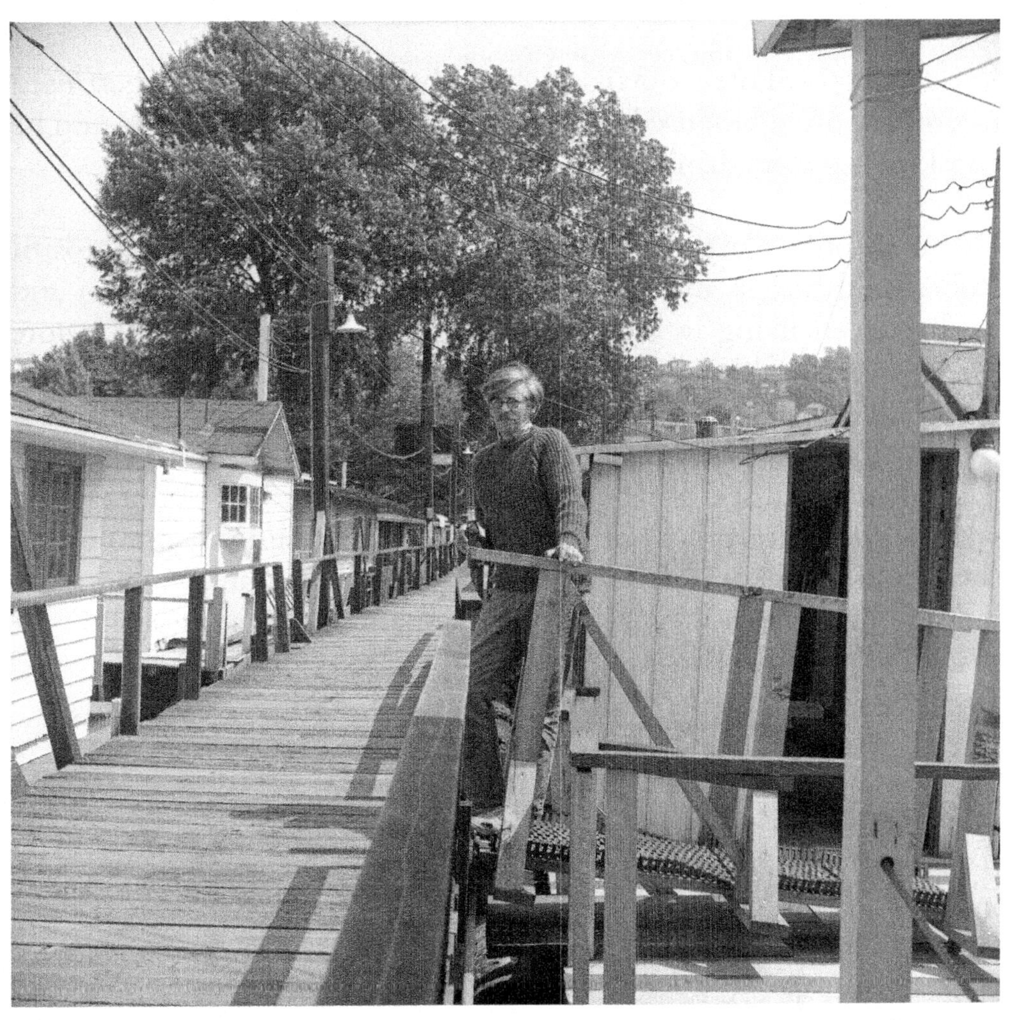

CHARLIE KRAFFT:

He and I drove to San Francisco once to ask Elizabeth Bishop to write a dust jacket blurb for his first book *Bunch Grass.* She declined. He was devastated, but undaunted.

I was living on Lorenzo Milam's houseboat at the time. Robert used to drop by often because he had a poetry show on KRAB FM and he and Lorenzo were drinking buddies.

Diane (Arjuna) Barton is the woman in some of Mary's photos of Robert and me on the houseboat. She was my girlfriend then and we had been living in San Francisco in 1967 and left right before The Summer of Love to live in La Conner, WA. Robert and I did a broadside while I was at the houseboat. The date on the broadside is 1967 so that must have been the year Diane, Robert and I drove to San Francisco to see Elizabeth Bishop because we had the broadside with us and I remember not having much luck selling them to poster shops and bookstores in SF and along the way home. We did sell a few and used the money to buy gas, beer and food with gas and beer being the priority purchases.

Student Co-Op Book News

Feature of the week: a "Broadside" featuring a poem by Robert Sund and drawings by Charles Krafft.

Finally—It's Happening, a portrait of the youth scene today is in.

Our latest acquisition in the Book Dept. is "Magazines." Comments on our selection of titles would be helpful.

It's time for Book of the Quarter selection for fall. Suggestions?

Our summer selection of children's books has some "Pop Ups," the "Tall" books and Dr. Seuss.

Western Washington University bookstore promoted Sund & Krafft's 1967 broadside.

Robert had a used Swedish car called an Isabella Borgward that he drove ever so slowly. We creeped down I5 to San Francisco and creeped back. One of artist Bill Cumming's eight wives had recently left him for Elizabeth Bishop who had been the Roethke Chair guest lecturer at the U.W. that year. When Elizabeth Bishop left Seattle, she followed her to San Francisco. Robert didn't know Bishop personally, but he knew her girlfriend and I believe he'd sent a copy of the *Bunch Grass* ms. (then tentatively titled *The Harvest Poems*) to her to pass on to Bishop.

The only thing I remember about the Foreword to *Bunch Grass* Robert never got from EB was waiting for him in the car outside of her apartment while he went in to retrieve his mss. He was in there for a while and when he returned to the car he was very dispirited. He told Diane and I that she'd declined to commit to writing a Foreword for him. I don't remember the reasons why. I only remember his disappointment over this and the extra long dedication pages that eventually ended up in the front of the book when it was published.

Robert had a circle of friends in San Francisco he'd met through John Logan. I don't remember much else about that trip there and back with him other than a vague recollection of meeting up with these people in a house in the Haight Ashbury, one of whom was a poet named Joseph Stroud whom we all thought was going to be the next Yvor Winters.

KRAB-FM: A Monday Night, Seattle, Spring 1968

"We're running a little over two minutes late now, so we'll go right in on into our next program with Robert Sund, KRAB's man of books, reading from Ring Lardner's collection of short stories, *Round Up.*"

Robert Sund:

"Well, I think this is going to be the last of the Ring Lardner stories for a while, unless there's someone out there in radio land who can't bear seeing the end of Lardner. I started this the beginning of winter when it was gray and wet out as usual, and a lot of people cooped up inside might like to hear these things. And I thought at the beginning of this whole thing that what might be some kind of private vice that I was indulging and I found out that there are a number of old Ring Lardner lovers scattered around the Sound area.

This is going to be the last story as I say. Spring's coming and we've got better things to do than listen to the radio at seven o'clock in the evening. Start barbequing out on the deck. This is a story called 'Travelogue' and it's one of those stories I think that's suitable to accompany *The Lorenzo Milam Railroad Cookbook.*"

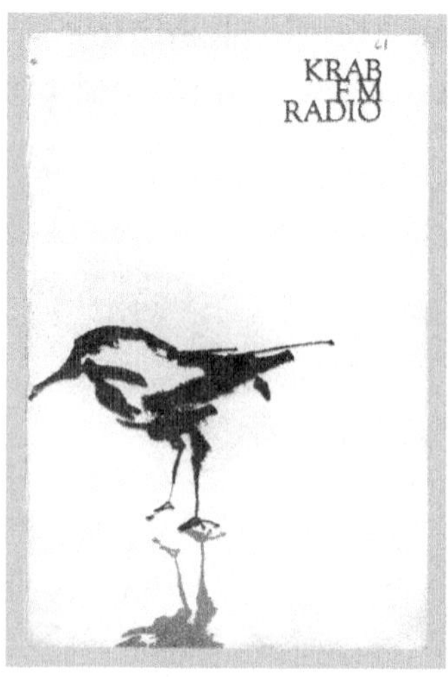

KRAB radio program guide for 1968, with the same **Charlie Krafft** *illustration that would appear on the cover of* The Sullivan Slough Review *in 1969.*

FROM THE KRAB RADIO PROGRAM GUIDES:

April 11, 1966 (guide 85) has this entry: "8:30 THE POETRY PROGRAM. Robert Sund reads some poems from his own "Ish River" collection."

March 10, 1969 (#161) "8:00 ROBERT SUND READS POETRY. If you enjoy this program and want more of them, please let us know one way or the other that you do. Bob did poetry programs for KRAB for three years before the old grey void got him down; I know there isn't an old grey void out there, not any more, and please, dear folks, open up your windows and give us a shout."

October 22, 1971 (#219): "8:20 THE MAJICK POET - Robert Sund, arriving at midnight last June with his poems and other musical devices. Additional music and dialogue with Nick Whitmer (guitar), Doc Spider (harmonica), and Phunky Phil Bannon."

CHUCK REINSCH:

I do remember that Robert frequently brought his autoharp when doing his show.

April 17, 1974 (un-numbered) "10: 30 ROBERT SUND TALKS WITH EDNA ST. DUM-DUM - A mock interview satirizing contemporary poetry. Edna St. Dum-Dum is a transvestite poet, publisher of several works, including the Clouded Horn, Your Camera and How it Works, A Half-Century of Accounting, and Swords and Ropes. From the KRAB Archives."

CHARLIE KRAFFT:

It used to be replayed during fundraising campaigns at KRAB fm. We did it at the donut shop studio one evening after we'd been drinking and had made a visit, for some reason, to the Eastlake St. Vincent de Paul's where we picked up a book called *Your Camera and How it Works* which I read from as if I were its poetess/author "Edna St. Dum Dum."

ROBERT SUND: BASKET BAY, AT ANCHOR NEAR MIDNIGHT

BASKET BAY: AT ANCHOR NEAR MIDNIGHT

The galley is cleaned up.
Near midnight again, the crew asleep an hour ago,
I go out on deck for the cool air.
At the head of Basket Bay
the Big Dipper seems cradled in the dark spruce ridges.
There is one small place where my body is.
Silence passes through me like light wind over water.
On the calm bay the boat scarcely moves.
Fish are milling out in the dark.
The taste of fresh water has maddened them, they are like
creatures of a joy which few ever see.
Restless, I step back into the galley.
My cup of tea is still warm.
I feel weary but don't want to sleep.
Like a fish my life is endless;
like a mountain range, huge powers shaped me.
I came out of the earth like dust,
I am blown on the wind like dust,
I rise up at the foot of prairie flowers
not like the dust which settles on people's faces and fills them
with grief,
I come like dust which has never been held in the hand.
I will be wrapped in the grey paper of a hornet's nest.
I will darken water
and leave it clear again.
Morning to morning, night to night,
to the faithful,
to those with wide black eyes of the haunted,
and to those who sing quiet songs,
to the forest termite,
to mountainsides in melting snow,
to cities in terrible chaos,
I will be visible, I will open my hands
and birds will fly out in all directions,
the dust falling from their wings like the air
of a winter morning.

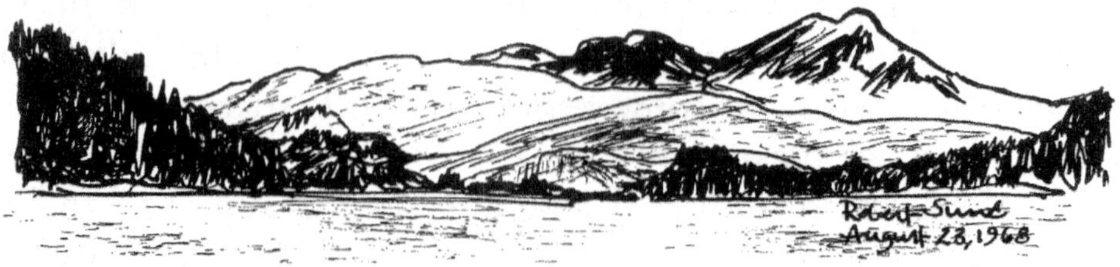

STEVE HEROLD:

Two 1969 items by Robert Sund from the *Nelsen House Journal*, that legendary manuscript from the early, formative days of both Robert Sund and the Asparagus Moonlight art movement. Robert was always reflective on his art and the nature of poetry, and his voice spoke for nature wherever he went. The first is one of a rare group of early poems from his time fishing in Alaska – all unpublished. The second one is typically Robert. Such conversational moments with Robert Sund were pure treasure with philosophy, art and poetry flowing onto paper in front of us to our utter amazement. For over 40 years we shared a private world of truth and beauty, and what things we made!

I.

Poem for Bud Blanchard, Cook on the Chinook

Faint wind from the straits.
At anchor in Funter Bay,
The Chilkats barely visible,
The blue sky disappears up into the stars.
Three hundred feet off our port bow,
The Chinook's galley lights go off.
The big dipper catches a falling star
And is empty again.

Robert Sund, Summer 1968

II.

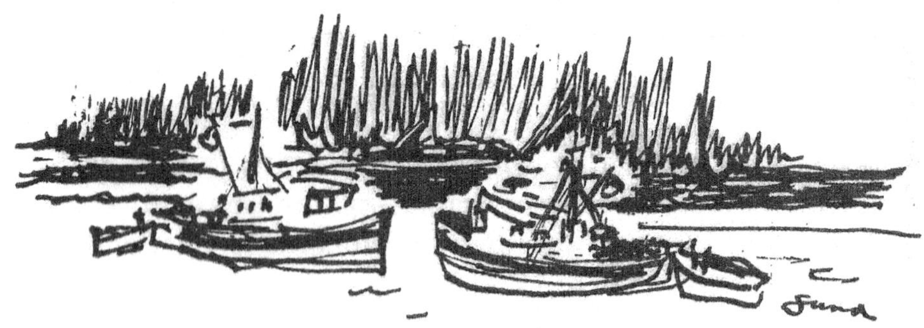

The beauty of language sometimes is that it is like a small town jail, the city fathers' beneficence is reflected even in the jailor's eyes. We sit inside, quote Neruda, and pour another drink; someone down the hall says from his cell: "Poetry is a garden full of verbs." In any enterprise worthy of our ancestors, the membership is generally small. About the size of a potato, the eyes drawn inward; white lands, glaciers, milk, bountiful…

In 1969, Robert Sund edited and published *The Sullivan Slough Review.* This single issue featured poems by Pablo Neruda (translated by Sund), Robert Bly, Paul Hansen, Joseph Stroud, Galway Kinnell, with art by Charlie Krafft, Morris Graves and others. Meant to be followed by further issues, it was a contentious project, and despite the collection's excellent quality, there were no further issues.

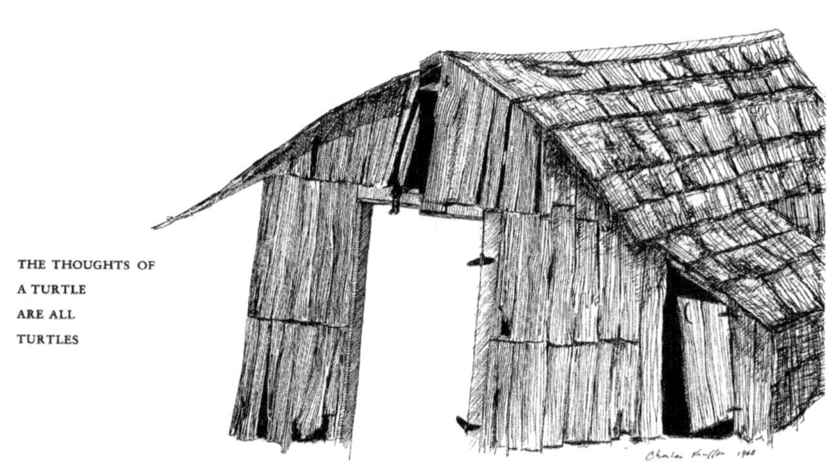

Image from Robert's essay in The Sullivan Slough Review. *The illustration by* **Charles Krafft** *is his woodshed in Fishtown.*

ROBERT SUND:

This is the first issue of
THE SULLIVAN SLOUGH REVIEW
An International Magazine
Devoted to Poetry

The poet is in love with silence. He wants to perfect all the outward sounds, in order to approach silence. And sometimes he has other good fortune.

The poet is like a man of the earth who falls in love with a sea goddess, and cannot rest. He enters the sea, without thought, and where the seaweed drifts free, and the sides of fish glow with many kinds of light, he finds that the silence of the sea is like a woman. After a time, he breaks away from her, crying into the long chambers of the sea, praises. Centuries later, if his cry was pure, we see that his bones glow like the wings of insects, like a mist hovering over mud. And we learn from his poetry, directly, that difficulty is blessed. Six hundred steps into the darkness, goodness grows radiant in the air around us. We witness the working out of a truth announced by Dylan Thomas when he said, "Song is a burning and crested act."

Poets are beginning to express these feelings. They come toward us with impatience, gentleness and joy. They face grief with dignity. They have clear voices, like birds. They know, as Keats knew, that "Fine sounds are floating wild about the earth."

The Sullivan Slough Review wants to publish this kind of poetry, poetry which is working out its own inner life and giving us fresh images of life.

The symbol of The Sullivan Slough Review is a solitary bird. It has passed from loneliness to solitude. The magazine is American, but we will also print the work of poets from as many parts of the world as possible, in translations that do not hamper the life of the original. We will print young poets, as well as well-known poets like Kinnell, Bly, Logan, Wright, and Snyder. Reviews and interviews will appear from time to time.

The editorial statement in this issue (THE THOUGHTS OF A TURTLE ARE ALL TURTLES) will clarify the intentions of this magazine. We are interested most in silence, and in great agedness.

We want to publish the work of poets who are like insects, free of dogma, fully a part of their world, alive, solitary members of the brotherhood of poetry, religious, thoughtful, full of clarity, and related to everything.
In prose comment, we want to discover or further describe what poetry is.
We invite comment on this first issue.
We want to hear from poets who have mud on their shoes.
—Robert Sund
Editor
The Sullivan Slough Review

CHARLIE KRAFFT:

You should know about THE ROLLER BARONS. Robert, Glen Turner and myself spent a year in La Conner around 1968 or 1969 concocting a mythology around a roller skating club we formed. We were semi-serious roller skaters and went skating most often at The Burlington Roller Frolic in Burlington. Robert was the leader. His name was "Col. Lubrication T. Bearins" I think. Glen Turner was "Francis Skate Key" and I was "Clutch Handrail." IRBC Glen and Robert did a KRAB fm show one afternoon about the fake history of THE ROLLER BARONS.

Roller Frolic to Close in Burlington

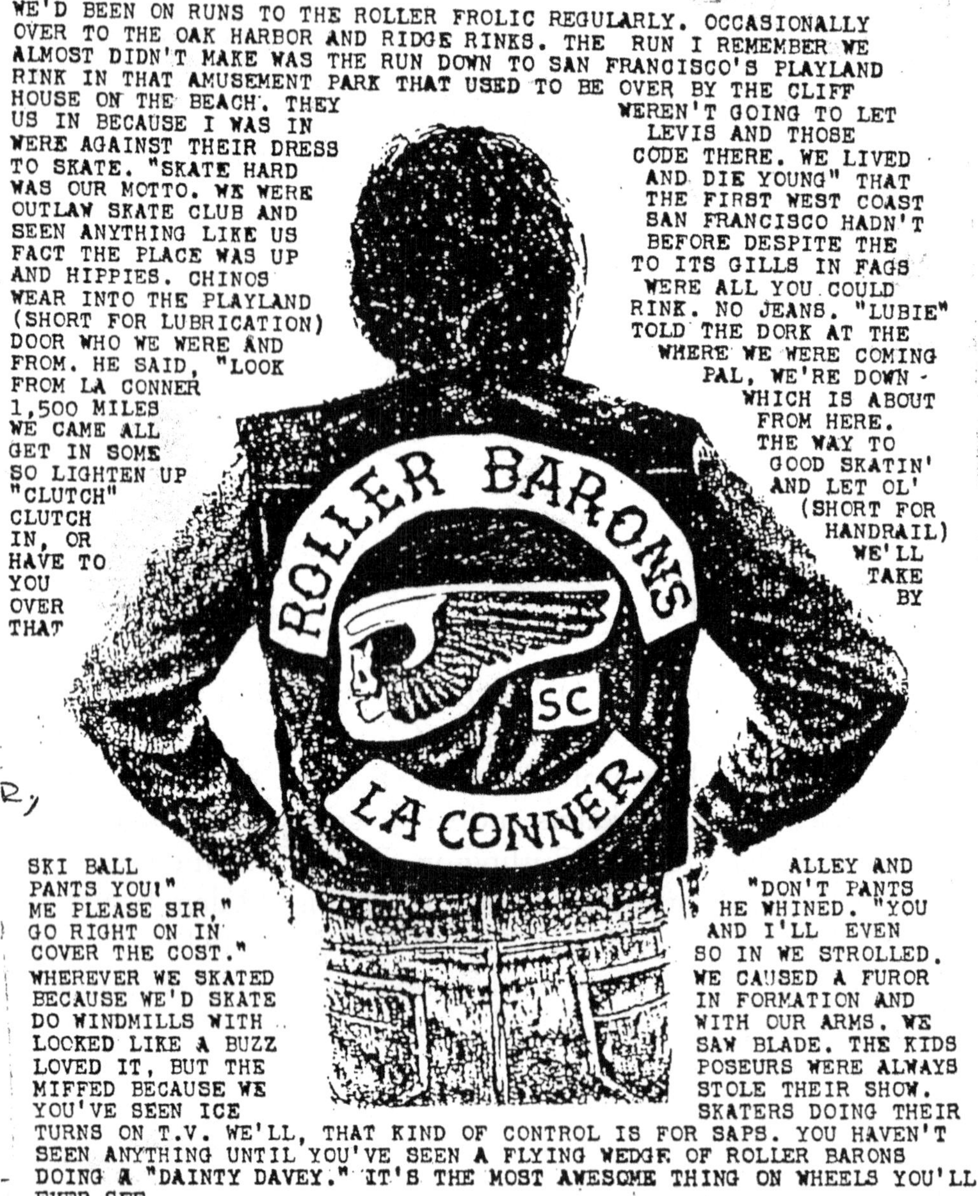

WE'D BEEN ON RUNS TO THE ROLLER FROLIC REGULARLY. OCCASIONALLY OVER TO THE OAK HARBOR AND RIDGE RINKS. THE RUN I REMEMBER WE ALMOST DIDN'T MAKE WAS THE RUN DOWN TO SAN FRANCISCO'S PLAYLAND RINK IN THAT AMUSEMENT PARK THAT USED TO BE OVER BY THE CLIFF HOUSE ON THE BEACH. THEY WEREN'T GOING TO LET US IN BECAUSE I WAS IN LEVIS AND THOSE WERE AGAINST THEIR DRESS CODE THERE. WE LIVED TO SKATE. "SKATE HARD AND DIE YOUNG" THAT WAS OUR MOTTO. WE WERE THE FIRST WEST COAST OUTLAW SKATE CLUB AND SAN FRANCISCO HADN'T SEEN ANYTHING LIKE US BEFORE DESPITE THE FACT THE PLACE WAS UP TO ITS GILLS IN FAGS AND HIPPIES. CHINOS WERE ALL YOU COULD WEAR INTO THE PLAYLAND RINK. NO JEANS. "LUBIE" (SHORT FOR LUBRICATION) TOLD THE DORK AT THE DOOR WHO WE WERE AND WHERE WE WERE COMING FROM. HE SAID, "LOOK PAL, WE'RE DOWN FROM LA CONNER WHICH IS ABOUT 1,500 MILES FROM HERE. WE CAME ALL THE WAY TO GET IN SOME GOOD SKATIN' SO LIGHTEN UP AND LET OL' "CLUTCH" (SHORT FOR CLUTCH HANDRAIL) IN, OR WE'LL HAVE TO TAKE YOU BY OVER THAT SKI BALL ALLEY AND PANTS YOU!" "DON'T PANTS ME PLEASE SIR," HE WHINED. "YOU GO RIGHT ON IN AND I'LL EVEN COVER THE COST." SO IN WE STROLLED. WHEREVER WE SKATED WE CAUSED A FUROR BECAUSE WE'D SKATE IN FORMATION AND DO WINDMILLS WITH WITH OUR ARMS. WE LOOKED LIKE A BUZZ SAW BLADE. THE KIDS LOVED IT, BUT THE POSEURS WERE ALWAYS MIFFED BECAUSE WE STOLE THEIR SHOW. YOU'VE SEEN ICE SKATERS DOING THEIR TURNS ON T.V. WE'LL, THAT KIND OF CONTROL IS FOR SAPS. YOU HAVEN'T SEEN ANYTHING UNTIL YOU'VE SEEN A FLYING WEDGE OF ROLLER BARONS DOING A "DAINTY DAVEY." IT'S THE MOST AWESOME THING ON WHEELS YOU'LL EVER SEE.

From <u>RINK KNEE, The Story of the Rise and Fall of The Roller Barons</u>, by Francis Skate Key

GLEN TURNER (aka Francis Skate Key):

THE ROLLER BARONS INTERNATIONAL SKATING CLUB

Robert Sund and I were sitting at the dining room table at my house in La Conner reminiscing about what we liked to do when we were young. We were about to found the Roller Barons International Skating Club, but we didn't know that yet.

We were just back from a run to West Mt. Vernon to get a bag of Jolly Rancher candy to assuage our attack of the munchies. Watermelon was, I recall, that week's favorite flavor.

Robert or I, can't remember which, suggested that we go roller skating. The further suggestion was made that we needed skating names.

Skates require roller bearings and they need to be oiled—lubrication. So Robert became "Lube" Baron (a play on bearings and hence the Roller Barons).

To become a member of the club, the one requirement was a name. Charlie Krafft was a lousy skater, so he became Clutch Handrail. His then girlfriend, Diane Barton, was Penny Gumm. My then wife, Eleanor, was Trixi Melodeum.

I volunteered to write the club anthem/fight song/ballad whatever.

I never wrote the lyric, but came up with the best composer/roller skating name: Francis Skate Key (no apologies to the "Star Spangled Banner" guy).

We hit the boards—skated in Burlington, Oak Harbor, and San Francisco. Then we decided to become the International Roller Barons by skating in Vancouver, B.C.

The only snag? We went to the amusement park in San Francisco to go skating. They had a dress code—khakis for men. We were in Levis. We asked for the manager.

While he was being summoned, the girls put some flowers in their hair. We hadn't really gone from La Conner to San Francisco to roller skate, but that was our story. We pled, entreated, exaggerated, and bald-faced lied for half an hour.

With Robert, Charlie, and I surrounding him, what chance did he have? So the International Roller Barons Skating Club became the first (and only?) skaters to ply their craft at that rink in San Francisco.

Thus the Roller Barons added a dress code coup to their skating legend.

Footnote: Robert and I could skate backwards; none of the other Barons could skate worth a damn. But they tried.

CHARLIE KRAFFT:

A cartoon portrait of Robert I dashed off one eve, pasted into one of my diaries.

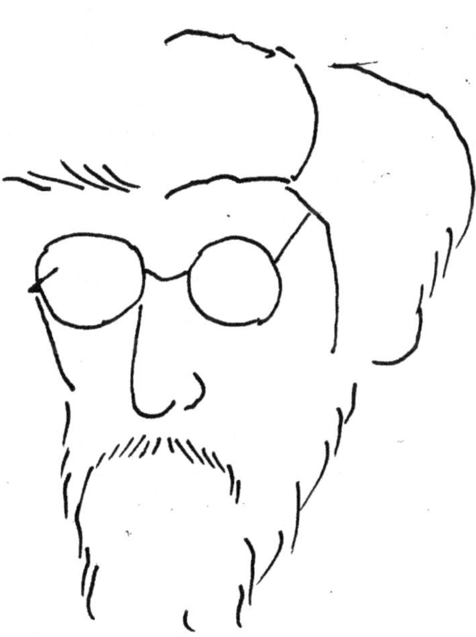

Portrait of the poet Robert Sund   July 9 69

PRAISE FOR BUNCH GRASS:

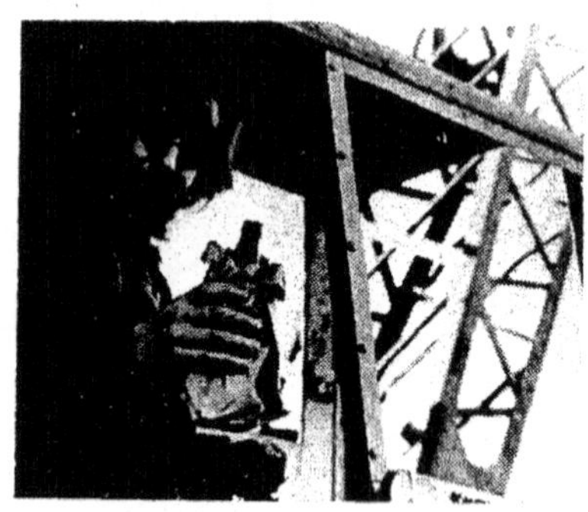

ROBERT SUND

Robert Sund, local resident and bon vivant, editor of The Sullivan Slough Review and poetry editor for THE NORTHWEST PASSAGE, recently published his first book, BUNCH GRASS. He is a graduate of the University of Washington where he studied under Theodore Roethke. BUNCH GRASS, published by The University of Washington Press, is dedicated to Roethke in memoriam.

Professor Frank Jones of the University of Washington says of BUNCH GRASS:

"This, Sund's first book, offers morning words for man's desire to receive and enjoy life just as it is. The Washington wheat country becomes a cosmos, and the poet a discoverer . . . Listening, we remember, or learn, what it is to be part of a world where everything, including us, belongs."

In a recent issue of LIBRARY JOURNAL, Ben W. Fuson, of Kansas Wesleyan University, said:

"Sund's forte is unpretentious direct free verse, scrupulously pruned of affected metaphor . . . His poems are daring in their lack of prose, their sparse verbalizing, their sensory precision."

"He has a trained power of observation, not only for sights, but for sounds and for various atmospheres that are difficult to grasp. Not only flowers and plants, but insects, animals and the weather become memorable."

—Poet Laureate, Louise Bogan, from a letter to Don Ellegood, publisher of University of Washington Press, 1969.

"Sund is likely the finest poet now practicing in the Pacific Northwest."

—Tom Robbins in the *Seattle Post Intelligencer,* 1969

"I can think of poets who are little known—like Robert Sund, who has only one book out—who have cultivated a fine observation and ear and tuned it to daily life, work, people, scenes of the West…and who are unpretentious in the presentation of themselves, but who have very high-quality work."

—Gary Snyder in an interview in *East West Journal,* Summer 1977

ROBERT SUND: Passages from the Notebook of Douglas R. Redwood

September 18, 1969

Up in the Skagit Valley again.
Winter is definitely on our minds.
Nobody has put enough aside for the cold months
and we're wondering what it'll be like.
The big sport last week was going out
on vegetable runs after dark, or toward
midnight if you like …
Field up between Conway and Stanwood
for cauliflowers.
Conway to LaConner, carrots and broccoli.
Over towards Mount Vernon, on Best Road,
the sweetest corn you ever ate.

September 19

GRAVENSTEIN POEM

In the dry spell between rainshowers
all around the apple tree
windfalls in the wet grass.
In the side of an apple
(a few hot days last week before the rain)
here and there
wasps dug deep
seeds open in the cold September air.

SKAGIT VALLEY AUTUMN

Vine maples turning color. Low clouds,
steaming ravines, hillsides, alder leaves
tumbling down, bright silver
clouds off on the horizon up the Skagit.

Blue hills, green farms, wet roads, rain
swelling the streams.
The Skagit rose six feet last night.

September 21

BELLINGHAM SUNDAY

Back at Larry and De's from the White House.
Lots going on out there on the border.
Quiet now.
Long drive down in the night rain.
Driving down at a good speed.
Larry at the wheel, best driver around
this part of the country.
Headlights pale in the dark road.
Like sitting inside a lantern looking out,
the lantern swinging past trees, farms,
dark hillsides, farms with the last
lights on, rain, memories, good thoughts,
the night and the day come together
like a prophecy.

September 22

Invited to stay here, there is a room
upstairs. Going to live in Bellingham
now, there is a fine spirit coming alive
here, a warmth that is present from house
to house, casual friendliness but springing
from deep concern. This is a very large family.

Thursday, September 25

The sound of a boiling pot

the guitar in the living room,
the broom coming from the kitchen,
up over the rug
through the hallway to the front door.

Now the guitar is stopped.
In the kitchen
the end-of-summer pickles
scooped into shining green jars.

Friday night, September 26

WATCHING THE MIST

Moonlight tonight, misty
late September,
a broad gold band around the moon.
Thin white clouds.
The sky is like an oyster.

Across the way
above the full mists
the dark hill rests like an island.
Down there in the misty grass
forgotten spirits
are getting themselves together.
Beneath a clump of reeds
on the silver water
Daddy-Long-Legs make music.
The thin long legs
send their bodies rising into heaven.

Small drops of water
in the bent arches of dry grass.
This wild hay has not
been cut for years.
Snails in moonlight

go slowly through the tall wet grass
carrying themselves like chalices.

Thursday, October 9

BELLINGHAM

Skagit Valley boys
drive all day long
all night too.
Dolly Varden pumpkin smelt farts.
Samish River.
"I like those galvanized water troughs
on the store steps in Edison."
Blanchard.
Home made pie in the good restaurant
on Chuckanut.
The rose gardens of Fairhaven Park,
the white picket fences and arbors
glowing among the dark roses.
Around the corner,
the bridge,
one traffic light blinking in Fairhaven.
The Kulshan, beer and singing.

October 11

Mid October, coming out of the house
heading out to the Kulshan.
Saturday night.
Just after eleven o'clock.
The air is cold.
No cars.
Not even a dog bark in the quiet.
In the dark between
street lights,
look up,

the stars are shining.
The blue sky is like a woman knitting.
The night air
holds
a handful of leaves.

October 12

FEAST

The quick winds blew
down the road
the neighbor's locust tree was stripped
almost bare this afternoon
it happened so quickly.
Long streams of yellow leaves
into the vacant lot
across the street
blown into the weedy grass.

Tonight we have had a feast,
huge dinner with baked bread
and afterwards
chocolate pudding with whipped cream.
Later, French coffee
and brandy.
A couple of joints going round.
In the living room,
in candlelight
we have come together
like leaves in a fencerow.

I'd stay, but some spirit
has come to take me walking in its
    cold steps.
Walking in daylight along the road,
on the wet shoulder

a garter snake drying out
its opal belly
turned up to the heavy sky.
Part of me goes on alone,
thinking.
I'll make it back to the house
around two in the morning,
smoke,
heat up the tea,
scratch a line now and then,
fall asleep with the light on.

October 14

Chuckanut Drive.
A day of blue sky.
Below the cliff road
the afternoon sea
is purring like a cat
in warm sunlight.

JEFF WINSTON:

I had an uncle living in Bellingham who was an abstract expressionist painter and that seemed like a pretty good destination. So I started a little coffee shop called Toad Hall on the South Side of Bellingham, 1969. Along came this multi-arts festival at Western Washington University in May of 1970 and up until that point I had heard these rumors of this sort of guru-god, Robert Sund. I hadn't actually met him. What I was struck by was, Ken Kesey was there at our coffee shop, Gary Snyder was there, Ferlinghetti was supposed to show up, and there were a bunch of South Side hippies and various and sundry people there. This was a time in American history where a lot of AWOLS and deserters were bouncing off the Canadian border, so we wound up with a lot of interesting characters. So I'm sitting out in the vacant lot next to the coffee shop and Snyder gets up to recite the dog soldiers of ancient China and a couple of hardcore hippie types stood up and started razzing him about, "What does this have to do with our lives?" Kesey jumped up and saved the situation by cajoling everybody and talking about how even hamburger flippers can understand poetry if they really want to try. The situation went on, there was quite a little crowd in the sidelot and then the rumor came up that Robert Sund was going to be reading at a party somewhere else in the South Side and it was going to happen in about an hour and everybody perked up and they were going to make it over to this party. And it dawned on me: this guy must be the real deal.

BO MILLER:

Here is a pen and ink I did of Robert in the Spring of 1971. He had just introduced me to Shi Shi and I had gotten together a lean-to off the old Miner's Shack. With a fireplace, it was a comfortable space to hang out during wet weather. Robert here is painting the view of the Arches and beginning his series of 'rain paintings' which involved leaving fresh paintings out in the rain—sort of a collaboration with Nature.

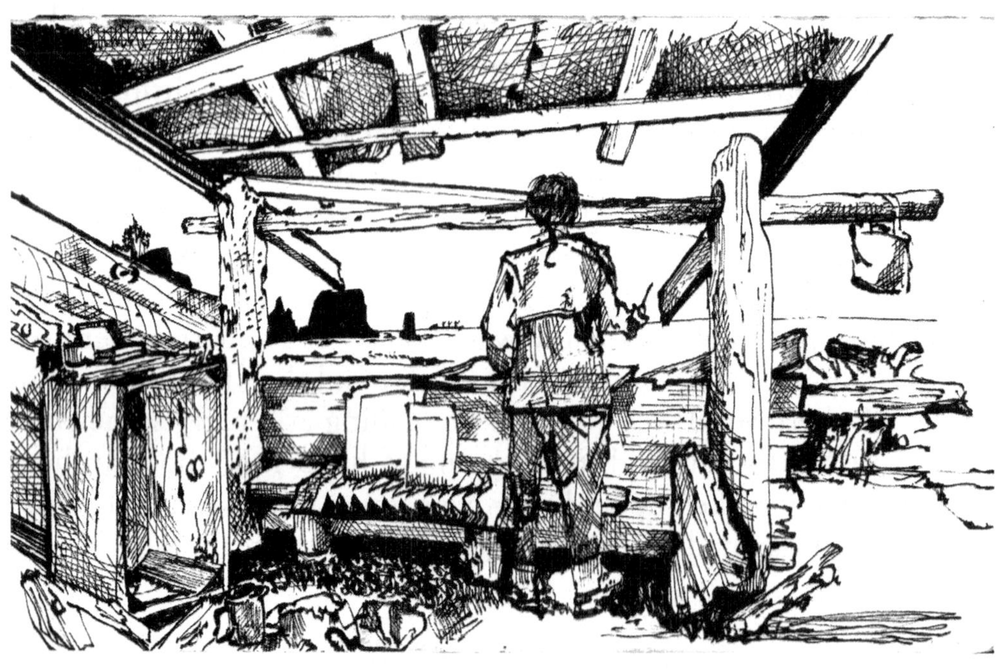

ARJUNA BARTON: Shi Shi Beach Rain Paintings

In early summer, near Solstice, we still wade through mud going above my ankles in the drier places along the trail. Robert's out here somewhere and I hope we are on the right path. Eventually we meet the coast and there stands a shelter, and Robert, and the beginning of this continent.

Early summer is squall season, and the rains come and go dramatically with heavy drops. Robert had arranged an artistic truce with the weather. He put out pieces of watercolor paper on the table outside the cabin and we would apply paint. Not knowing this art form, I did what looked good in the moment. Robert, of course, had mastered it. His color concentrates were splashed by the drops of rain to create a spiritually relevant and divinely significant piece of art!

Robert was always intent on as well as capable of producing magic. He was sure we didn't need to live in an ordinary world, and he gave himself over to reminding us of that. When the sun came out again after the squall, my paintings were like muted reminiscences of colors, like ghosts. Robert's were vibrant and fully alive.

Following photos by **STEVEN R. JOHNSON.**

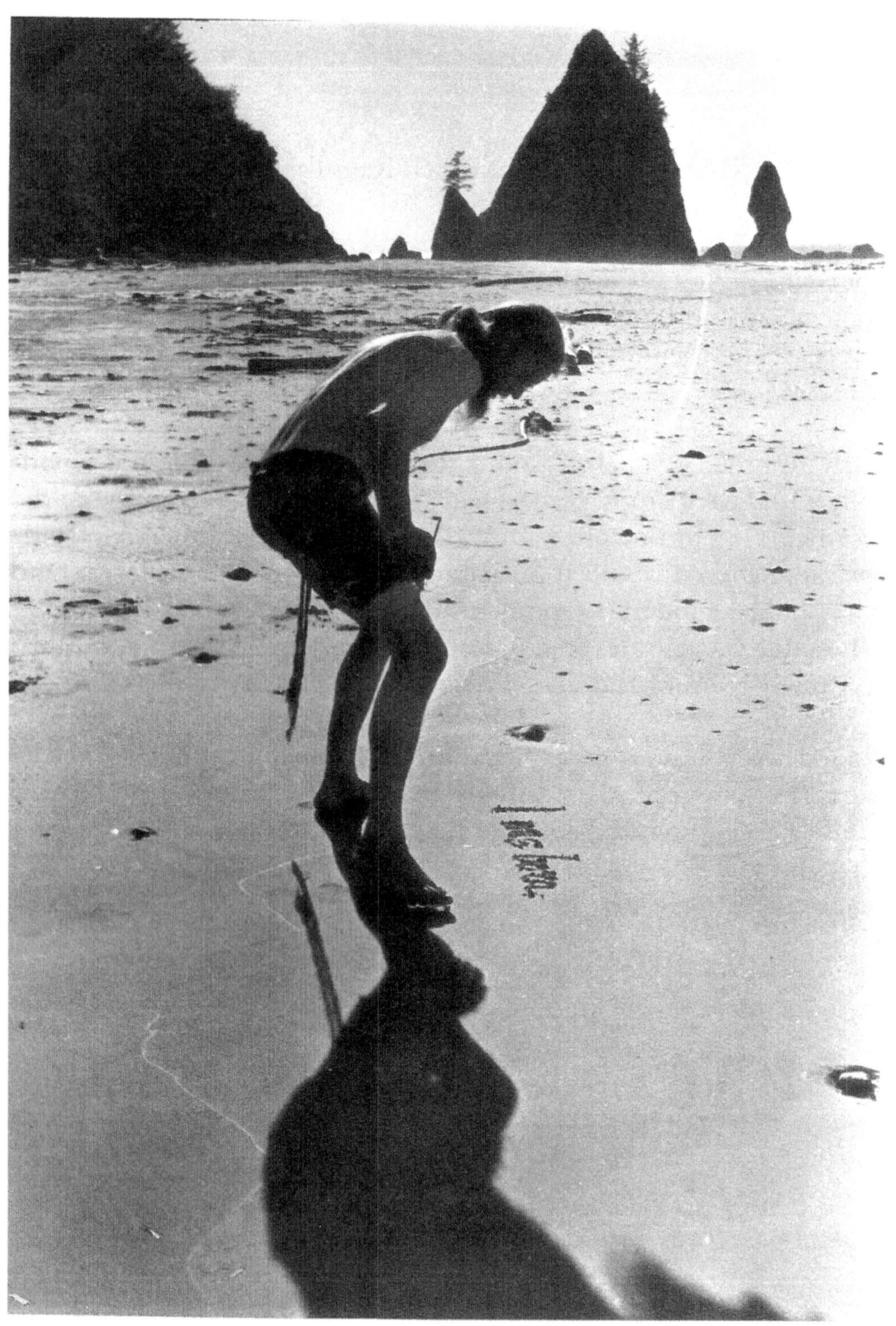

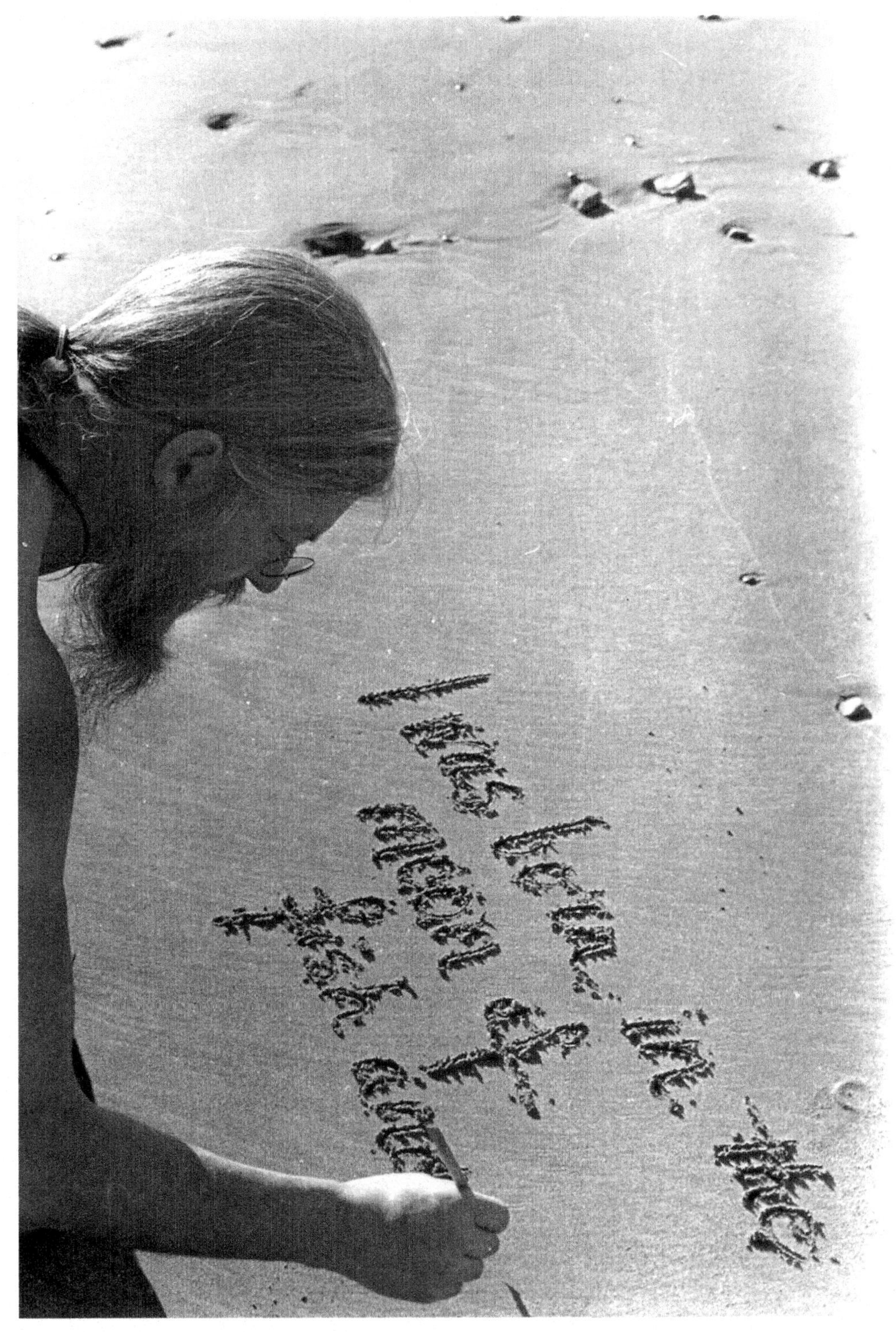

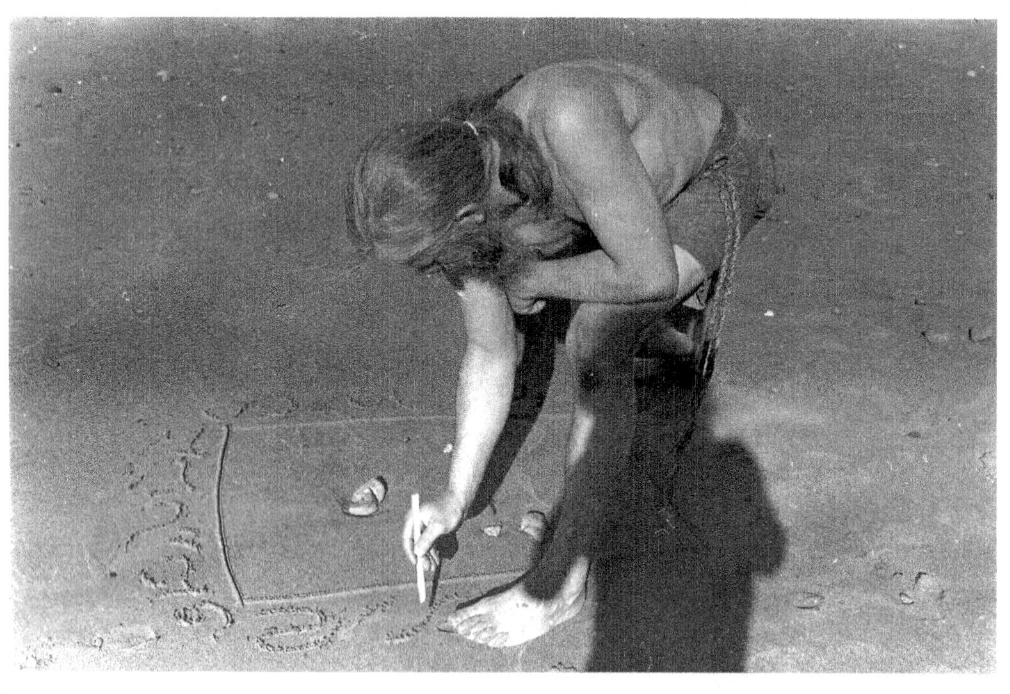

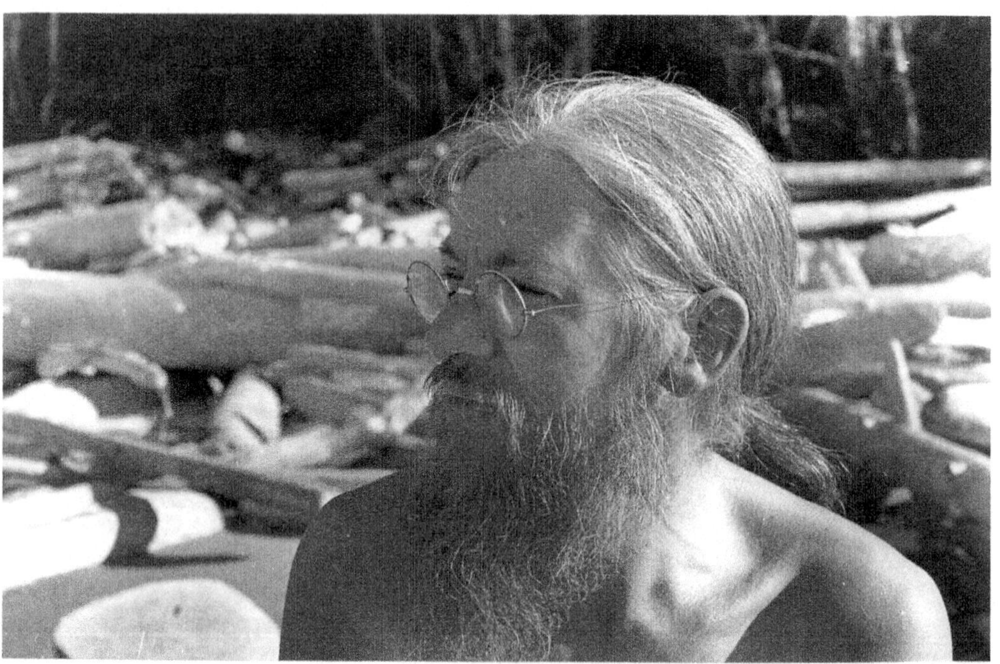

GLENN (CHIP) HUGHES:

I wrote this poem at age 20 when I stumbled across Robert for the first time at Shi Shi. I was camping with friends and RS was living in his Shi Shi tiny dwelling. I was entranced. We met up three days in a row. I had tea in his miniscule cabin. He read me some of his poems. When I left with my friends, I gave him a poem I'd been working on since I met him on day one—read it to him aloud and left him the piece of notebook paper I'd scratched it on. Then forgot about it. After Robert's death, when Tim was going through all of Robert's Shi Shi journals, Tim came across the poem—Robert had copied it into his journal!... with kind words about meeting me. So in 2001 I suddenly saw the poem again for the first time.

POEM GIVEN TO ROBERT SUND
AT SHI SHI BEACH, 1972,
SOON AFTER MEETING HIM

We carry
wood, build,
bury

and wet our food
at the ocean's throat,
and cut our noises
from its root
singing

ō
ā
the slow wave
shows us how to break.

GARY HICKENBOTTOM:

In the spring of 1972, we ended up in Boulder, Colorado together and Robert took a kelp horn with him. Robert blew that kelp horn to Gary Snyder, Robert Bly and Allen Ginsberg and everyone else attending at a special family table restaurant dinner. To get back from Denver, I rode the freight trains with Robert for three straight days. At one point on that trip, Robert stepped on his kelp horn. He threw the broken pieces right out the door, in the middle of Wyoming.

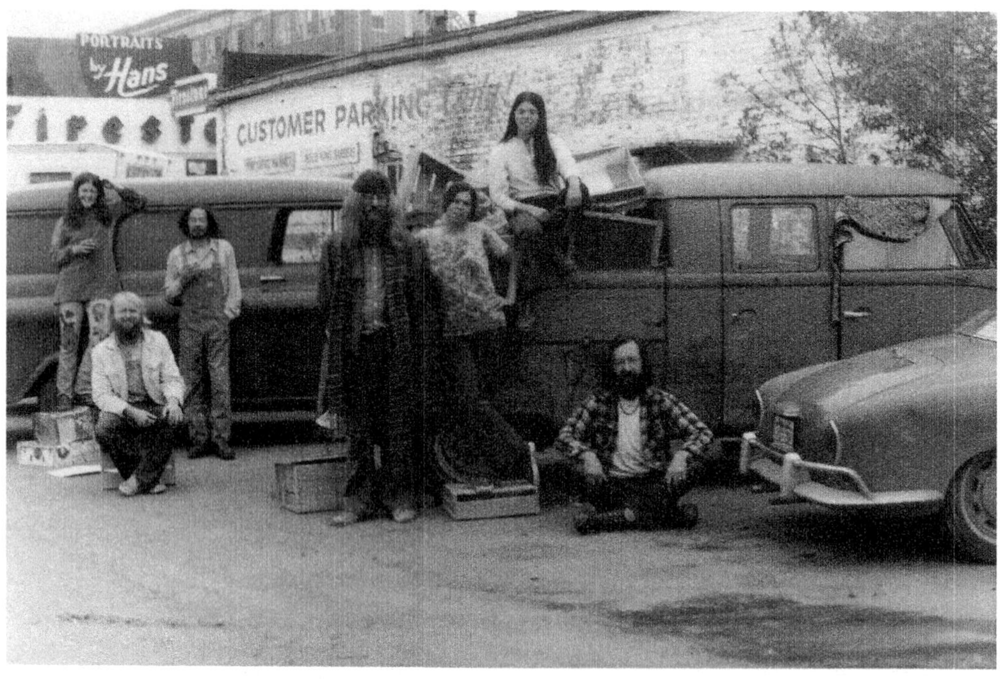

Boulder, May 1972 (left to right): Debbie Drown, Gary Hickenbottom, Douglas Spence, Robert Sund, Ginny Greeno, Colleen McKee, Arthur Greeno.

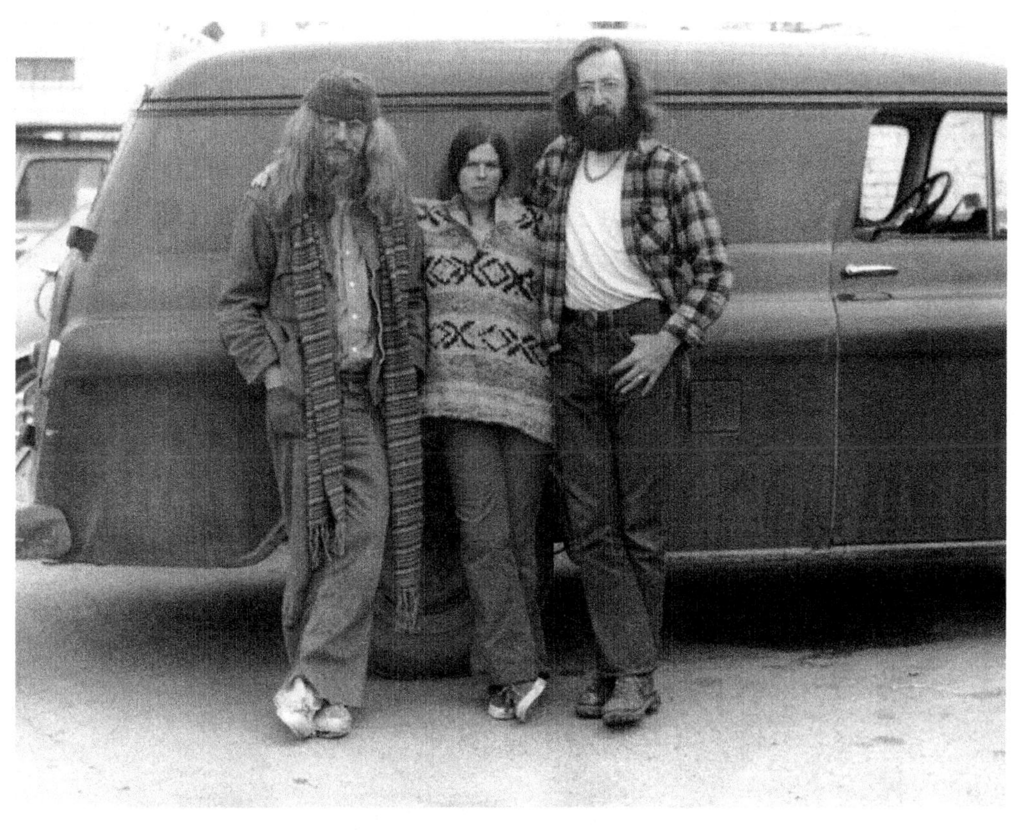

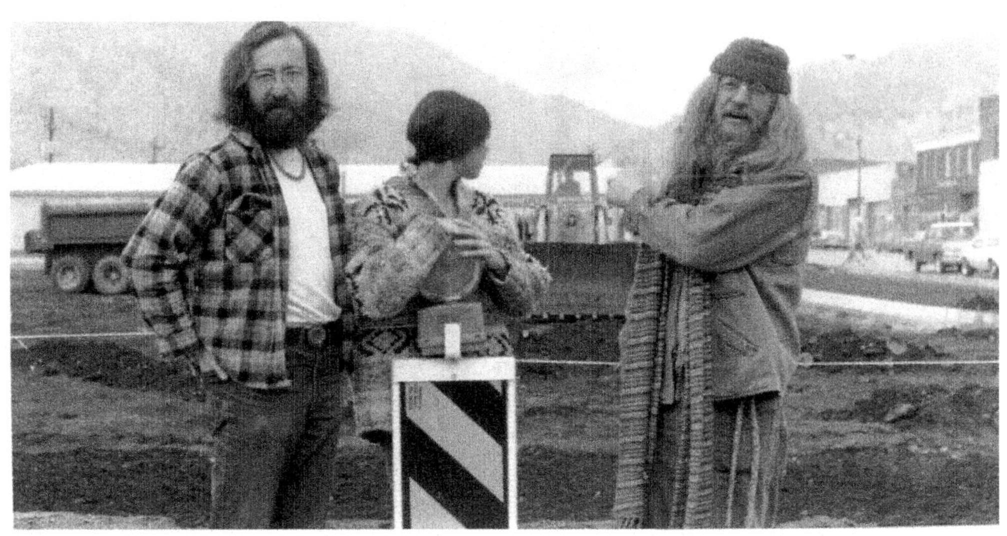

GARY HICKENBOTTOM:

Robert and I decided to visit Boulder while shooting pool late one night at the Central Tavern in Seattle. We found a ride on the HUB bulletin board at the U of W.... We spent almost a month in Boulder at Arthur and Ginny's helping at their restaurant 'The Family Table' and attending the reading which was awesome. And yes we did ride the freights back to Seattle. It was an adventure and we kept track in little notebooks. We put them together later and made a couple copies called *Two Bums in One Boxcar.* Robert sent a copy somewhere but no-one was interested in publishing.

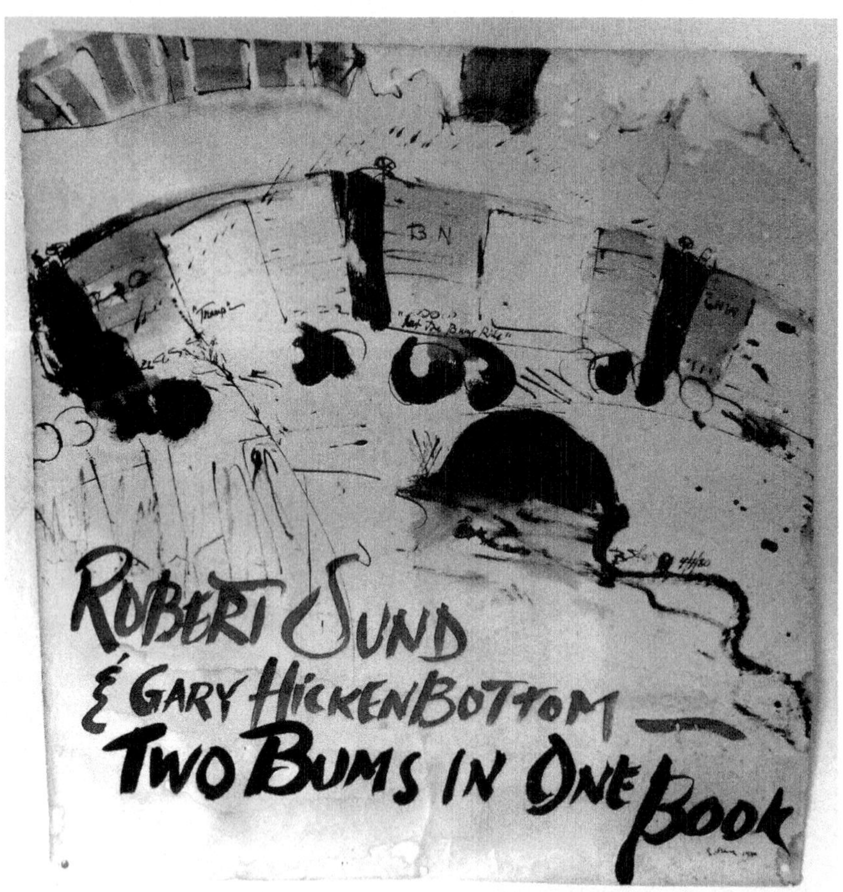

Poster by **Bill Slater.**

Two Bums in One Boxcar is an unpublished book of travel poems by Robert Sund and Gary Hickenbottom. Part 1, by Gary, is entitled, "LET THE BUMS RIDE." Part 2 is by Robert, titled, TRAMP. This is from the book's foreword, written by Robert Sund, ISH RIVER, Spring 1980:

In early May, 1972, I left Seattle in the company of my friend Gary Hickenbottom to visit friends in Boulder, Colorado; the first time I had ever seen that part of America. While we were there, a benefit was given for Karma Dzong, the Tibetan Center; poets Ginsberg, Trunpa, Sakaki, Snyder, Bly, all reading together. After three weeks Gary and I decided to head home. We had our packs, sleeping bags, a big sack of granola and some oranges, and each a jug of water. The last minute in Boulder we got 49-cent writing tablets and ballpoint pens; and that's where this book begins, eight years ago.

Robert's half of the manuscript is 35 typed pages, watching and listening, stops in little towns, hopping off in rail yards, talking with people in cafes and tramping with hobos like Billy the Hillbilly, whiling time on the long ride of passing land. What follows are excerpts from Sund's boxcar poetry.

ROBERT SUND:
Selections from *TWO BUMS IN ONE BOXCAR*

Ginny drove Gary & me from Boulder
this morning to the Denver freight yard.
We're sitting in the boxcar, both doors open,
waiting here, north to Cheyenne,
getting hotter, soybeans in the corner.
(A Mexican yard worker told us
which track to take, says it
goes to Butte, up through
"Wind River"...)
Kissed Ginny goodbye an hour ago
She's back in Boulder at The Family Table now, telling
    everybody
"They're on the train!"

Noise of the yard
    Engines, air brakes,
    Hum-and-grind industrial hogwallow
But even here, bird songs — lark —
rabbit running around
butterfly inside the car.
Creak and squeal of slow wheels, switching.
Ripple of heat, hours
before we get moving,
& finally the slow leaving
Denver about 2 pm.
At last we come out of the corner
and stand in the wide open
boxcar door.
The crossings go by,
slow rumble coming into a town
again — crash! car linked to car
    slams! and creeps on
    wheels clicking.

We wave at everybody,
    people in their back yards
    kids by the road.
Gary says: "I feel like a
Homecoming Queen!"

Fort Collins
Train tracks down middle of main street
going so slow
two Hippies on bicycles paddle
alongside rapping with us:
"Where you going?"
Seattle.
"It's supposed to be snowing in
Montana, snow and rain."

    Antelope in wide range land

Cheyenne by night
Switching for several hours in the dark
New moon shining on the steel rails.

Fitful sleep
Guts shaking
Wake off and on, look up
    country going by
silhouettes of trees
in the dark —
Trees!

Back at Casper the sagebrush was
    like rabbits huddled on the cold ground
Here the sagebrush stands up
and throws its
arms up into the sky.

Young cottonwoods fill the
stream valley, winding as
the river winds,
        river and tree.
The young cottonwoods
leafing out, a filmy clear green
O buy me silk like this
Let me
        run naked with silk
I'll leap up
into another world
And everyone will worship
        cottonwoods
        in early Spring
        end-of-May Wyoming!

Wild flowers on the slopes
foot of high cliffs
We go into a long tunnel
        black, black
Then out into the open
at Thermopolis — "WORLD'S
BIGGEST MINERAL HOT SPRINGS"
Spelled out in painted white
rocks in the high hill above town.

Out one side, upward slopes,
canyons, farms far back,
only part of a house or a
barn visible, as though
these people shied away.
Gary points to the huge
slopes of nothing but wild
blue lupin,

clustering and
sailing slowly outward
hundreds of acres
seven or eight miles
of lupin
and gold
black-eyed Susan.

Out the other door of the
boxcar we look down
on an immense valley —
a few painted barns and houses
— green tilled growing,
grass being worked hard.
And there, five miles
off — a giant mill
a beast of aluminum
and steel
high round chimney
spewing the sulfurous stench
of money
into this
perfect air.

High up we level off —
flat, narrow meadows full of
dandelions, small pools
buttercups
shine on water,
emerging between flowers
three white geese.

Our car is smooth! at last!
How lucky we are to pass
through here in the daylight.
Gary points to the high blue
mountains. We begin to

blend. (Where does Montana
    end
    and Idaho begin?)
Think about this.
Counties, states, nations.
No.
Continent.
Sea.
Mountain.
Desert.
Stream.
    Go everywhere
    without passport.

On we ride, slow
    we can look back
    and see the little
    green and white
    Burlington caboose following.

Downhill!
Willows, lots of trees!
High rock mountains
hazy with sharp
white snow ravines.

Far out past Spokane,
the Palouse country,
ponderosa, break in rock slab,
grass in dusky light
as though the earth
below sighed deep down
and slow time
brought up in its arms
    the silvery grass,
half moon

hidden in cloudy dark.
Big farms, little farms,
miles of land under plough.
Dark windows,
people asleep now.

Kelso-Longview,
A little misty rain in
Southwest Washington.
The frogs
      The fish
            The ducks
                  The evening winds,
The swallows
above the broad lowland
      Cowlitz swamps,
Crows
in the immense alder,
  Rain in the cottonwoods,
Rain-maidens gone mad.
Lush jungle is what this is!
THE ISH RIVER COUNTRY!

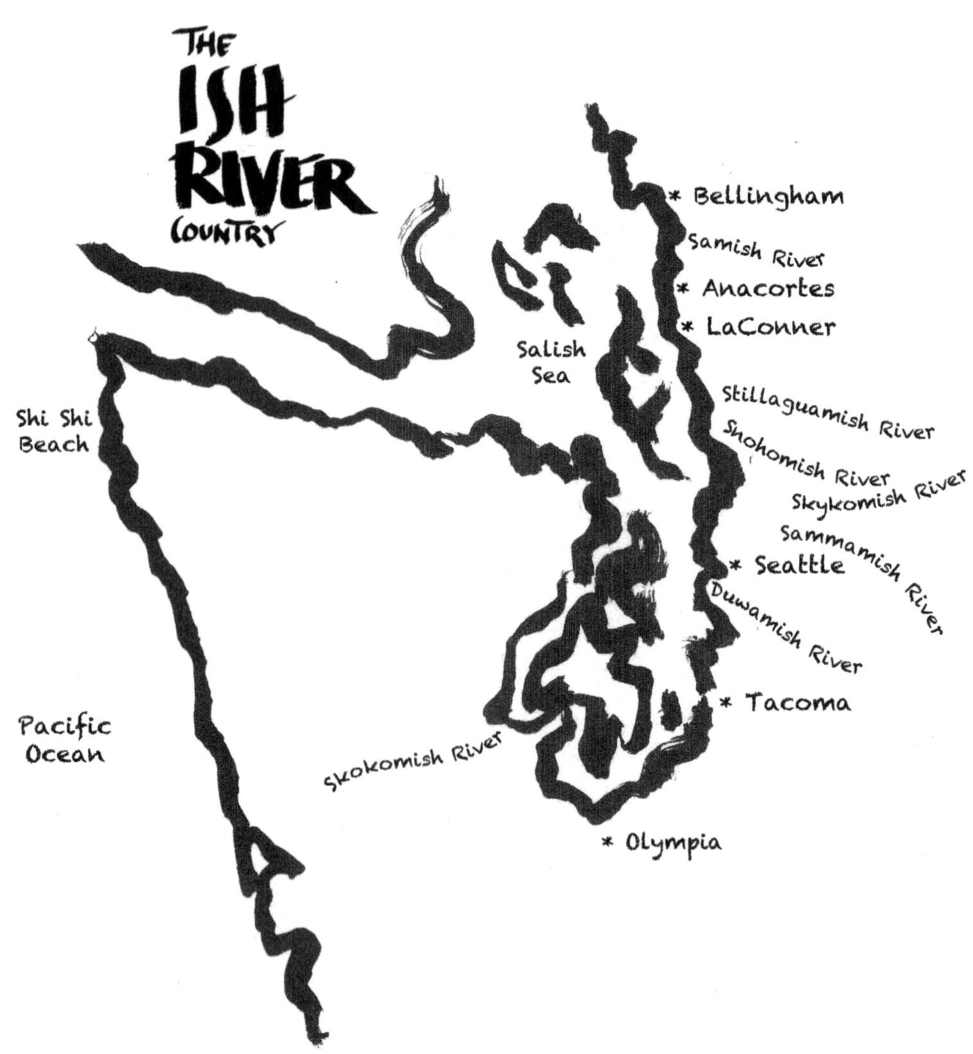
THE
ISH
RIVER
COUNTRY
Bellingham
Samish River
Anacortes
LaConner
Salish
Sea
Stillaguamish River
Snohomish River
Skykomish River
Sammamish River
Seattle
Duwamish River
Tacoma
Shi Shi
Beach
Pacific
Ocean
Skokomish River
Olympia

ISH RIVER

like breath,
like mist rising from a hillside.
Duwamish, Snohomish, Stillaguamish, Samish,
Skokomish, Skykomish ... all the ish rivers.

I live in the Ish River country
between two mountain ranges where
many rivers
run down to an inland sea.

Robert Sund

GARY HICKENBOTTOM:

Summer of 72, I lived at Shi-Shi most of the summer in the miner shack next to Robert. I remember lots of orange spice tea with Hudson's Bay 151, Rose Brand Chinese egg noodles and stir fry veggies. Robert would make really fine bread in his fireplace. We had lots of company. Late at night, Robert might tune up his autoharp. Even later would come poems, endless poems, like the waves which never stopped. To me it just seemed like magic, the whole summer.

BO MILLER:

This is a journal entry of mine involving a short discussion between Robert and Charlie Krafft.

10 June 72
1508 House Seattle
Misty Late-spring Afternoon

Silver-blue voice from the dim dining room:
"Charlie! Wanna shoot some pool down at the Central?"
"Nope? Well, that's one less quarter on the table."

GLENN (CHIP) HUGHES: Robert Sund and the All-Time Poets Baseball Team

In the summer of 1973, when Robert and I created—or discovered—the All-Time Poets Baseball Team, we had known each other for about a year.

I first encountered Robert in late summer of 1972 on Shi Shi Beach, when I was twenty. I had come there to camp for a few days with friends, and someone told me that upbeach, living in a tiny cabin near Petroleum Creek, was a poet who had actually *wintered* there. This seemed to me all but inconceivable, given the isolation of the place and its exposure to the Pacific Ocean in winter weather. The very notion struck me as mythic. I wandered upbeach to try to meet this person. He was glad, it turned out, to be met. Over a few days I spent some hours in his cabin, drinking tea, listening to him read his poems, talking about poetry. He was in his early forties; his hair was long and grey; he spoke with precision and grace. He read poetry beautifully. The poems of his that he read me—some published, some not—were evocative and lucid. I thought: "I've met a real poet!" When I left with my friends after three days, I trudged under the heft of my backpack toward his cabin; he came out; and I gave him a poem I'd written for him. Before accepting it, he said: "Read it for me!" I did, in a very nervous voice. I never expected to see him again.

One day the following spring, my mother, then an English teacher at Roosevelt High School in Seattle, told me: "You'll never guess who's coming to assist me next week in my poetry class: your 'friend' Robert Sund." *What?* "Oh, I remember him from my undergraduate years. He had a friend cheat for him to pass his Chemistry class."

Robert had received a small "Poetry in the Schools" teaching grant. I showed up for all three classes that Robert taught (during which I discovered, among other things, his high regard for a number of D. H. Lawrence's poems). Soon we were spending quite a few afternoons together, sometimes shooting pool and drinking beer in a near-deserted Central Tavern in Pioneer Square, with sunlight angling through the tall back windows to light up the dust and the old wood. During those days I discovered that Robert was a conduit for, and a great appreciator of, what could be called illuminations. Idly shooting pool with him, or driving up together into the Cascades to wander and sing and recite poetry near a waterfall, was, I discovered, how my own search for illuminations was best served.

Soon after summer solstice, on the evening of June 24th, 1973, we found ourselves in the house Robert was then staying at in West Seattle, accompanied by an odd-lot of three companions: the rascally Oregon poet Eugene Ruggles, a contemporary of Robert's; Jim Boster, a pal from my Shi Shi trip a year before; and my close friend and sometime bandmate, the banjo player Dave LeMargee. I recall that various intoxicants were imbibed and—it's possible—ingested. The conversation turned to poetry. The merits of various poets were discussed, the discussion turning both intense and hilarious. It was (unusually for Seattle in June) a bright summer's eve: and it was baseball season. Robert and I began considering which field position this or that poet was most suited to. Then everyone began chiming in with suggestions, and Robert produced an enormous sheet of paper, about 5' by 3,' and some gouache paints, and a small brush, and commanded me to draw a baseball diamond.

The discussion took a serious turn. Robert and I began overturning the ideas of the others, and hijacked the decision-making. While our companions kept up an interest and offered opinions, the two of us got down to the business of identifying with finality who should be playing—who had, indeed, in the metaphysical realm, *always* been playing—which position. Some fielding positions took as little as fifteen minutes to fill, after a careful review of this or that poet's character, qualifications, and achievements. Other positions remained vacant for some time, as we ruminated, considered, discarded. Lines recited from poems flew back and forth as evidence. The tone of our deliberations wandered from high humor to impeccable seriousness. Only once did we find ourselves in disagreement: I insisted that T. S. Eliot needed to be on the team, and Robert heatedly

Opposite Page
Pitcher: William Blake
First Base: John Donne
Third Base: Chaucer
Left Field: John Milton
Right Field: Gerard Manley Hopkins
Catcher: Walt Whitman
Second Base: E.E. Cummings
Shortstop: Dylan Thomas
Center Field: W.B Yeats
Bat Boy: W. Shakespeare

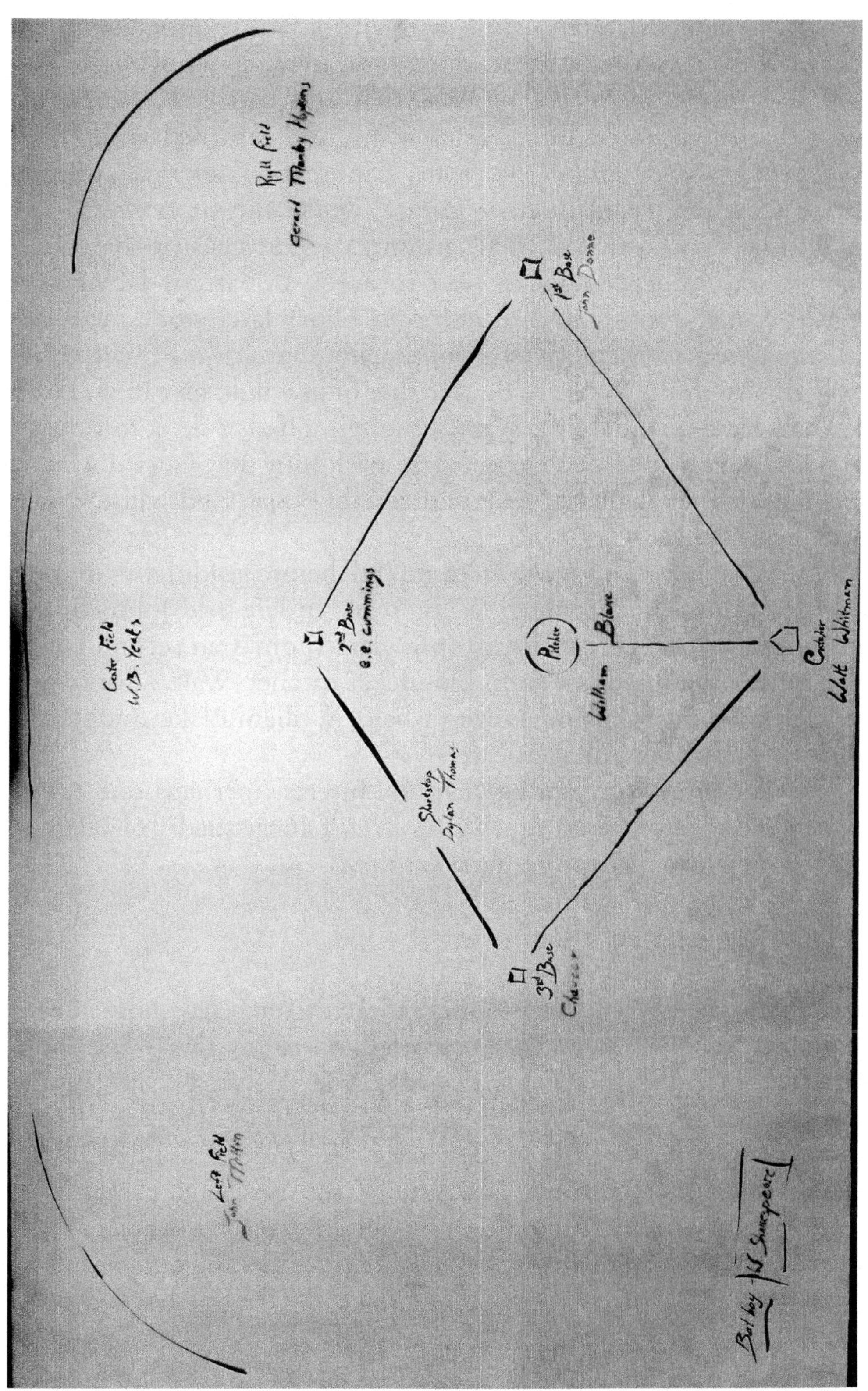
Right Field
Gerard Manley Hopkins
Center Field
W.B. Yeats
Left Field
John Milton
2nd Base
e.e. cummings
Shortstop
Dylan Thomas
1st Base
John Donne
Pitcher
William Blake
3rd Base
Chaucer
Catcher
Walt Whitman
Bat boy
W.S. Shakespeare

objected—objected, after a while, with vitriol. The team's constitution and my brushwork were interrupted for a long stretch while Robert waxed eloquent about the small virtues and many vices of Eliot's work. He disappeared into a back room and returned with Eliot's *Collected.* He read, gorgeously, from "Landscapes," a lyrical sequence that Eliot himself had labeled "minor" work, and pronounced that *that* was poetry—musical, rich, grounded—but insisted that Eliot's famous and influential poems were intellectual, barren, damaging. I argued that the music and meaning in Eliot's later work, especially in *Four Quartets,* was different but equally masterful. Robert waved away this assertion with disdain. Neither of us would give in on Eliot's baseball-team qualifiability. Finally, though, I had to defer to Robert's own status as a "real poet," and agree with him that Gerard Manley Hopkins, rather than Eliot, should suitably play (and will eternally play) right field.

The final positions were determined before midnight: in right field Hopkins; in center field W. B. Yeats; in left field John Milton; at third base Chaucer; at shortstop Dylan Thomas; at second base e. e. cummings; at first base John Donne; as catcher, Walt Whitman; as pitcher (pitching for all poets everywhere) William Blake; and serving as batboy, of course, Shakespeare.

Our three companions had lost interest; perhaps one or two had fallen asleep. Robert and I, however, felt satisfied in having recorded on paper truths of unique validity.

*

In January 1991, I wrote Robert a letter from a new home in San Antonio, where I had taken a teaching job, to say that I had found the sheet of paper presenting the All-Time Poets Baseball Team. It had lain rolled up among my possessions as they had been hauled from home to home, city to city, state to state. I reminded him of our discovery of the team, and listed who was playing each position. A many-sheeted response to my letter, dated January 29, 1991, written in Robert's typical correspondence calligraphy, included the following:

All-Time Poets Baseball Team
ADDENDA:

Take Whitman and let him be "the coach."
Neruda—Pablo Neruda—should be "catcher." (He could equally fill the pitcher's role.)

Is Roethke on somewhere in the first team? Brad [Killion] says, with what I feel is true inspiration, "He should be home plate umpire!"

[This is astonishing for how appropriate it is. NOTE: Sometime in the late Fifties, after the university and after wandering in America and coming home to the farm in Grays Harbor, and going back up to Seattle and some graduate work, I one day thought I should go back and do some serious study with Roethke. When I went to see him one afternoon, I walked into Parrington Hall when it was fairly quiet, the hallway nearly empty. He was coming out of his classroom workshop, with his big heavy overcoat and his loose-fitting suit, you could call it "baggy" but that would be missing the point: — His suit-coat was more like a comfortable cloak or robe.

Down the wide first-floor hallway he came, on his way to the English Department offices, lugging a cram-full soft leather carrying case. He rocked back and forth as he walked — his being was there, there was someone unforgettable — the weight of it helped him forward in that big body —

He had the heavy face of a brooding uncle; he had the uncle's laughter, too, and his own teeth showing a looney happiness to the world near at hand.

His hands in the air, the one holding the book, the one dancing to the words of the poem emerging into our lives — every poem has a first time in the world!

———

He comes walking down the hall . . . headed toward the office and Dorothy Bonwic the department head's secretary in the back office — you'd walk past desks of several secretaries to get to the back office. She'd type things for Roethke's class work. Maybe help type from his manuscript of his new poems.

He was on his way, and when he turned the corner into the office hallway, past the mailroom and the restrooms, and I stopped him to ask if he'd let me sign up for his poetry class, I felt I could benefit by more study — and who couldn't — but he understood what he needed to say — and he shook his head no. He sometimes seemed to be exasperated by having to take on so much. He could be intimidating in his weighty consideration and feeling for a student.

He offered to read once, after his year in Europe, the poems I had written in his absence. He penciled his remarks and hints on the typed up poems — (were they poems? is this what poetry is like? can it be like this — ? what am I hearing in the woods? —) About poetry I scarcely knew what to think or hope for.

He turned and was about to go through the office double doors, then turned back, set down his heavy briefcase swelling with books and papers —
He got down, bent on one knee, the other leg braced out in front of him — like a baseball umpire — and crossing his arms and sweeping them out wide of him, he declared me "safe" at the plate!]

A Song To Celebrate The Summer

Out in our pasture the blueberries grow.
Come joys of heart!
If you want me for something, meet me there.
Come lilies & akvileja, come roses & salivia,
Come sweet summer mint, come joys of heart!

Pretty small flowers invite us to dance.
Come joys of heart!
If you want I'll weave a crown for you.
Come lilies & akvileja, come roses & salivia,
Come sweet summer mint, come joys of heart!

And then I will set the crown in your hair.
Come joys of heart!
The sun goes down, but hope rises up.
Come lilies & akvileja, come roses & salivia,
Come sweet summer mint, come joys of heart!

Out in our field there are berries & flowers.
Come joys of heart!
But of all these, you're the sweetest to me.
Come lilies & akvileja, come roses & salivia,
Come sweet summer mint, come joys of heart!

Folksong from the Swedish island of Gotland,
Translated by Robert Sund, August 1974.
Calligraphy by Steve Herold.

MAGGIE WILDER: Robert Sund

I met Robert Sund first in Seattle around 1975 at a Japanese restaurant in the University District. He was dining with William Slater. My companion nudged me and whispered, "I think that's Tom Robbins sitting over there!" I approached, having just finished *Another Roadside Attraction,* and offered to order sake for them in appreciation for the fun read. I blathered on at length, and when I finished, Bill said, as Robert chuckled, "I'm actually *not* Tom, but I do live nearby! I could deliver a bottle to him!"

A couple of years later, I'd moved on board my boat in La Conner. I had spent the summer months refinishing the 1929 Dream Boat, and was just learning to take naps, rocking sweetly under the Rainbow Bridge. Suddenly there was a horrible scraping, banging noise. As I stepped up to the wheelhouse I saw a raft with five men standing aboard, two of them with long poles, pushing the raft along my pristine hull paint, leaving a long scar. One tipped his hat, another mentioned with great optimism that they were headed up river.

I replied, "Well, you'd think with *five people* you could manage!" The tallest man, the one with long beautiful silver hair and wearing a faded blue shirt with billowing sleeves, suddenly stopped his effort, rose a good two inches taller and announced "We are doing the best we can with what we've got!" I recognized him then as Robert Sund, the man laughing quietly at my buffoonery years earlier. Some months later it occurred to me that his remark was, perhaps, not an apology. And it was years after becoming his friend that I understood that this was indeed Robert's art and craft, doing the best he had with whatever life presented him. His best was often stellar, whether it was crafting a gorgeous domestic space out of what seemed like nothing, making a wind poem with yarn and paper, or cobbling together words that let us know why we so love the place where we live, here in the Ish River Country, words he crafted and left behind for us to use.

ROBERT SUND & THE 6TH GRADERS:

"In 1976-77 I taught writing in the La Conner School, through the Artists-in-the-Schools program funded by the Washington State Arts Commission. On the last day, my sixth graders in Nancy Lovell's class gave me the following farewell poem which they all wrote together. I'm not sure I deserve it all, but it shows how they felt about me."
—Robert Sund

TO MR. SUND—OUR THANKS:

—for spending your spare time with us
—for helping us with the pitfalls
—for giving your all
—for unconfusing our words
—for combining our poems for the book
—for coaching our poems to the best they could be
—for guiding us through the seasons of poetry
—for your opinions
—for your patience
—you are a gentleman
—for your consideration of people
—a tingling, lively, exciting person
—for being interested
—the man with a bag of poetry
—some magical "power" to pull it out of us
—for letting us make our own decisions
—for understanding feelings even when they were not your own.

ERIK AMBJOR:

I met Robert in 1977. I recently had gotten out of the Army, and completed a year of junior college and moved into a group home of fellows there in the Seattle U-District. After housemates Chuck Easton & Autumn Scott left for Boston to finish his music studies in the winter of '77, Robert moved into their basement room. Robert had a wonderful Zen-like aesthetic, which he brought to every place he ever lived. His sense of space was impeccable. The place would never be the same, nor would I. The host of characters that paraded through the house were from all walks of Robert's life. I was lucky to be part of many of those conversations, reliving fond memories with his old friends. That began a long and impactful friendship that influenced my life by expanding my appreciation of poetry, art and much more. His poetry like his many stories were brought to life by his resonant voice. He was a master of the reading. Roethke, his teacher, had instilled in him the discipline of memorization, which enabled him to get inside his poetry and give it much more dimension than other poets who were more well-known than he was. I was lucky to live closely to a real live poet and to experience his creative process of years until something finally felt and sounded right. The house was soon transformed after a Robert inspired cleanup and facelift into what became known as Cloud House. As Robert put it, "I sit here at the table, and things become clear, like breaking through the clouds." A common refrain became, "I live at Cloud House …right up from the Blue Moon and the Rainbow."

Editor's Note: The alley next to Cloud House was named Roethke Mews in 1995. It runs north, right past the Blue Moon Tavern, where Roethke celebrated receiving the Pulitzer and Bollingen prizes.

JOSEPH STROUD:

I Remember Robert

in a muddy field outside La Conner
leaning against a fence
stroking with one hand
the star-blazed forehead of a mare
in the other
holding out a windfall apple
odor of sweet clover in the air
Robert was happy in his Ish River country
Isn't it clear
he gestures
these single poems—
everywhere!
and pausing
looks down at the ground
Besides—
how can we lose
with mud on our shoes!

CHARLIE KRAFFT:

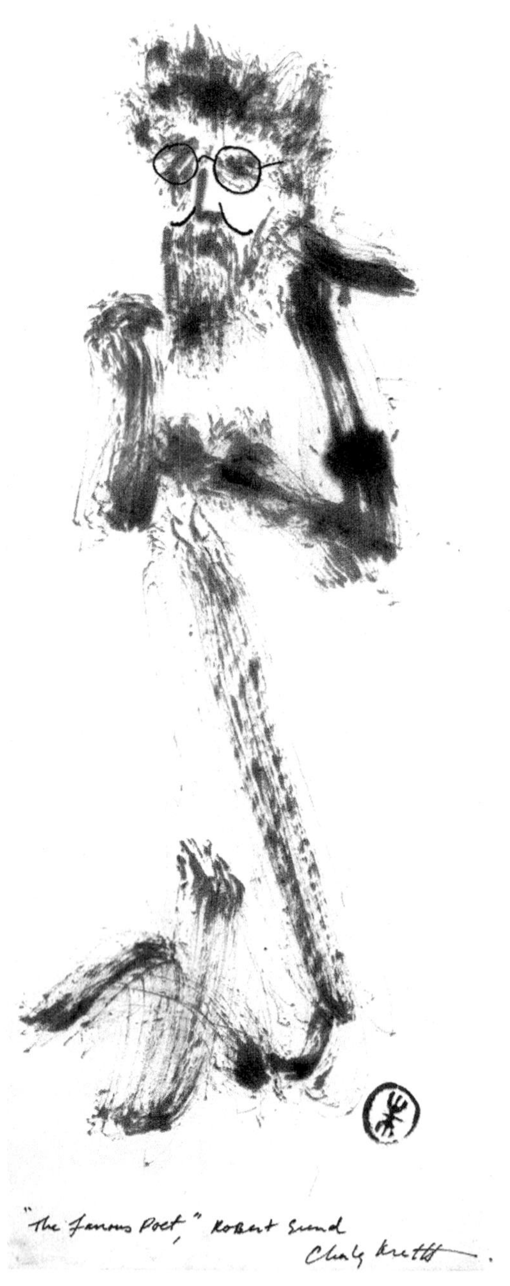

"The Famous Poet," Robert Sund (circa 1978).

FRANCES MCCUE: Robert Sund (1929–2001)

"Of all the poets I've met," Mary Randlett says of Robert Sund, "I could understand everything he ever wrote." Sund's clarity and musicality make his verse immediately approachable. A Robert Sund poem is about exactly what it says it's about, and you are pulled in, caught inside it:

Ten by Twelve

My shack is ten by twelve
    Two bottles of sake
    Under the bed.
    Hot soup on the stove,
    And bread in the oven.

My autoharp tuned up and ready.

When friends come rowing up,
How big this shack will get!

The poem's tiny cabin, filling with friends, is a perfect image for Sund's life and work. From the small shack downriver from Fishtown, a community outside of La Conner, Washington, where Sund spent his salad days, or the old houseboat where he lived on Lake Union in Seattle, or the cabins in La Conner where he took refuge in later years—each place became a hive where Sund wrote poetry, kept a robust journal, did calligraphy, played the autoharp, painted, and hosted other artists, writers, and neighbors.

During his lifetime, he published two collections of poetry, *Bunch Grass* (University of Washington Press, 1969) and *Ish River* (North Point Press, 1983), which won the Washington State Governor's Award in 1984. He also published nine chapbooks, beautiful small editions from local presses. Copper Canyon Press, then a small publisher, produced *The Hides of White Horses Shedding Rain.* After Sund's death, his friends gathered his journals and poems; three more books came out from Pleasure Boat, Shoemaker and Hoard, and Poet's House Press.

Although Robert Sund devoted himself to art, poetry, and music, he barely made a living. Sund sold calligraphy broadsides of his poems, one by one. He wrote poems; he painted mandalas in gouache and showed them at small galleries or at friends' homes. Still, the payments were small, and at different times in his life, Sund lived in places that other people had cast off or had donated for his use: the area downstream from Fishtown where he built a shack, or a corner lot in La Conner that a family gave to him. Sund came from days long gone, when small towns in western Washington were not overtaken with expensive vacation homes, days when a town might help support and embrace a resident bard. Looking after Sund, the poetic truth-teller, was what a number of La Conner residents did.

Originally from Elma, Washington, near south Puget Sound, Sund lived in close observation of both nature and language. As a young college student, Sund studied pre-med at the University of Washington until Theodore Roethke steered him toward poetry. He followed the great poet's advice and majored in creative writing. After graduating in 1954, Sund took work on Alaskan fishing boats, typically as a cook, and continued to fill notebooks with poems.

While some of the "Northwest School" painters attracted fame beyond the region, Robert Sund was a poet who stayed local. In a little shack near the mouth of the Skagit, a short paddle in a canoe from La Conner, he wrote this in his notebook: "Out on the river you know you are in the midst of a great creation. You see the old work and the new work side by side; the ancient migration routes of all the birds, and the slow building of silt and soil in the estuary; a small grassy island, for instance, that wasn't there last year and that, in a few seasons, will grow new willow for the blackbirds and the beavers."

TIM MCNULTY:

Up Shit Creek
—for Robert Sund

The low sun has settled
into the small fir trees of Bald Island,
and a cool upriver wind
has nudged back the heat of the day.

Out on the wooden dock
you wash up some greens
for supper.
A few leaves drift
on the incoming tide;
a cliff swallow glints overhead.

Not an idle bug lingers
over the dark water,
but a fish flops anyway,
like a hopeful poet
reaching into an empty pocket
for change.

FINN WILCOX:

"Spare Change" is a poem I wrote for Robert years and years ago. It's a poem he really appreciated and always teased me about, saying it sounded like Swedish zen.

SPARE CHANGE
Homage to Robert Sund

Your little poems I've collected
are beginning to add up.
Four lines a nickel,
six lines a dime,
an honest mistake
turned into mountains,
a shiny fifty cent piece!

Suddenly,
and without warning,
the soul steps forth,
pockets full,
headed for the liquor store.

MIKE PRICE:

I like poetry and visiting a poet sounds something like visiting a holy man or a shaman…Our adventure involved tossing a few supplies in the Volkswagen bus and heading up through Port Orchard and over the ferry and up towards Seattle in the night. We ran out of gas somewhere. We were walking around in the middle of the night looking for gas at 11 o'clock on a Saturday night. And we woke up in a tulip field in the Skagit somewhere. I woke up in the tulip field in the back of this bus, tulips as far as you could see, and James wasn't there and I got up and stretched and looked around and tried to figure out where we were. Then I could see James wandering towards me from the end of the field. He had two cups of coffee and a paper under his arm. And he got to me and he said, "Well, I got up early and I walked down and I think I can find him. I think I know where he's at."

So we end up driving into LaConner. Surprisingly enough, we find this gray haired old guy out in his garden and he was delighted to see us and glad to see James. They proceeded to talk at full speed and they were both smoking cigarettes then and I sat out on the porch while the cigarette smoke wafted over my head and listened to all this going on and looked through some of the poetry books. And we ended up running to the grocery store, getting a couple sacks of groceries and driving around in the countryside on these very bumpy roads while I'm taking directions and we ended up at a place where it looked like abandoned shacks with an old pier and some boats.

Now, I'm very interested in learning about poetry and one thing I learned right away was that there's a difference between what a boat is to you and me and what it is to a poet. You and I have boats, poets have metaphors of boats. So Robert was telling us stories about this great boat he had. I don't know when that boat was had, but it wasn't then. It sounded like this wonderful thing kind of like Neruda's harp of heaven where you break the bottle of wine on the bow and it gleams honey in the sun and everything. But this wasn't that kind of boat. This had about eleven inches of water, it was an old kind of rotten rowboat—you wouldn't even notice it if somebody didn't tell you to look into the water—and it was only held up by this old weathered rope. It was kind of like pulling an old fish out of the water. We found some oars in the weeds and we put the groceries in and I was probably the most reluctant to get in it. But I got in.

I found out that I was going to be doing most of the rowing. It was getting dark. I assumed he knew where we were going. There was no moonlight that night. Fortunately we were equipped with an old anti-freeze plastic jug with the top cut off of it. This turned out to be a lifesaver. And I began to realize the resourcefulness of Robert. Most details were taken care of. So as the water would rise up around my ankles, I would put the oars down and start bailing the boat, while these two were talking full speed, looking for cigarettes, telling poetry and they went on like this through the night. I would row, I would row and it would get dark and after a while, I could see no land. I'm going upstream. I don't know whether I'm going upstream fast enough or whether we're actually being carried out into the ocean. Water's cold, it's dark, there's some stars, all I can see is these two cigarette flames. This kind of cloud of white hair in the middle between them and they're just talking and I would say, "Come on guys. Look, I'll row but you've got to bail."

And they'd say, "Oh yeah, yeah, yeah," and they would take the anti-freeze can and they would go for a while and then Robert would remember another poem and pretty soon I could feel the water rise around my ankles. So this went on and we got further and further from land. This was one of those moments…how I got in that boat I don't know and I'm not as keen on poetry as I was earlier. And I'm not convinced that he was even paying attention to where we were going. The Skagit was very big. I just rowed and bailed and at one point we could see some firelight out there, I felt like I was rowing through time.

"Hey Charlie!"

"It's Robert, man! I'm going to my shack."'

"Hey, Charlie! Come here!"

"No, it's Robert!" He tried to stand up in the boat, "It's Robert! I'm going to my—"

"Shh! Sit down, Robert! Here, bail!"

And so he did somehow, but with very little attention, most of it on his friends and their poems, and we got to this place and he said, "Turn left."

It's completely black. I turned the boat and I row. I feel something large looming out of the dark, and then we hit the mud and we come to this abrupt stop. And there's this long silence. Then they started talking again. I don't know how long we're going to sit there. I didn't know what to do, but I thought I don't even have to stay with these lunatics anymore. So I got out of the boat and stepped into the mud and Robert, everything was a poem, 'One man steps out into the mud and the boat rises, and we're all going to make it.' What that meant was that with me out of the boat, it lifted enough that I could pull them. So I pulled on this old rotted rope and I just kept pulling up until I could see these pilings of the net shed rising up out of the dark.

This old decrepit shack, somebody had lived in there, apparently somebody from China, some refugee, who had papered the walls with newspaper and done calligraphy on them. *Nixon Resigns,* were the headlines, and they had been painted. And there were a couple glass jugs of beans and an old stove in the corner. We didn't sleep all night. I can see Robert now, standing there with his autoharp and a kerosene lamp singing at the top of his lungs. And he got down from the shelves a bundle of driftwood and he set it out in front of me. We had some beans cooking on the stove and he set out this bundle of driftwood and each one was a different length. It was a driftwood xylophone. You played it with two pieces of driftwood. And then he had the kelp horn, he had a whole set of them, graduated. And he had kelp castanets. Actually they were the same thing as the horns but they didn't have the holes in them and then you had a little jar of sand and you poured the sand in the castanet. I was not really good at any of this stuff. While he was playing autoharp, he would show me how to use the things, he would be reciting poetry and he would be doing each one at the same time to help me out. He was an exacting maestro. And we played music and poetry all night long.

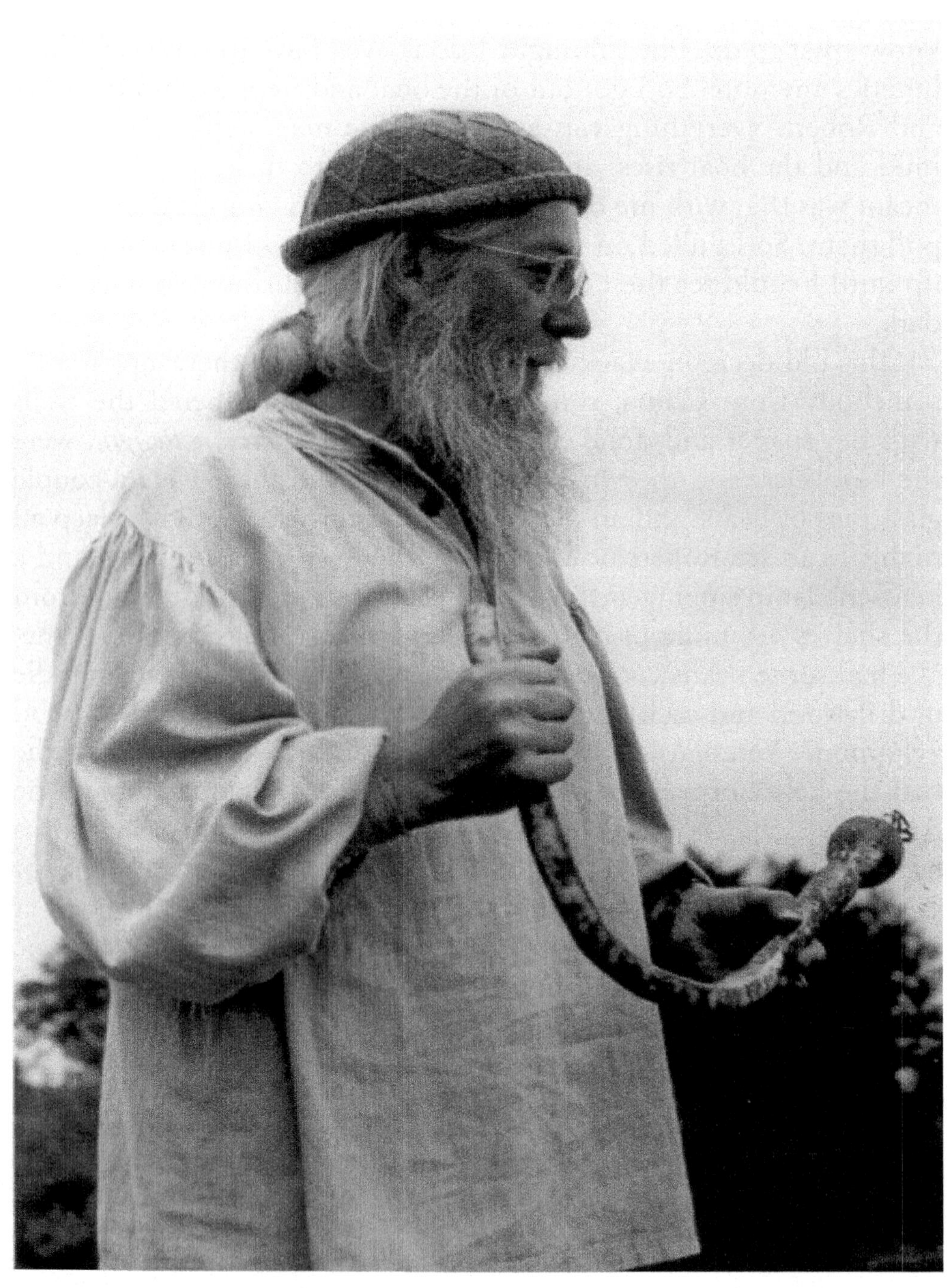

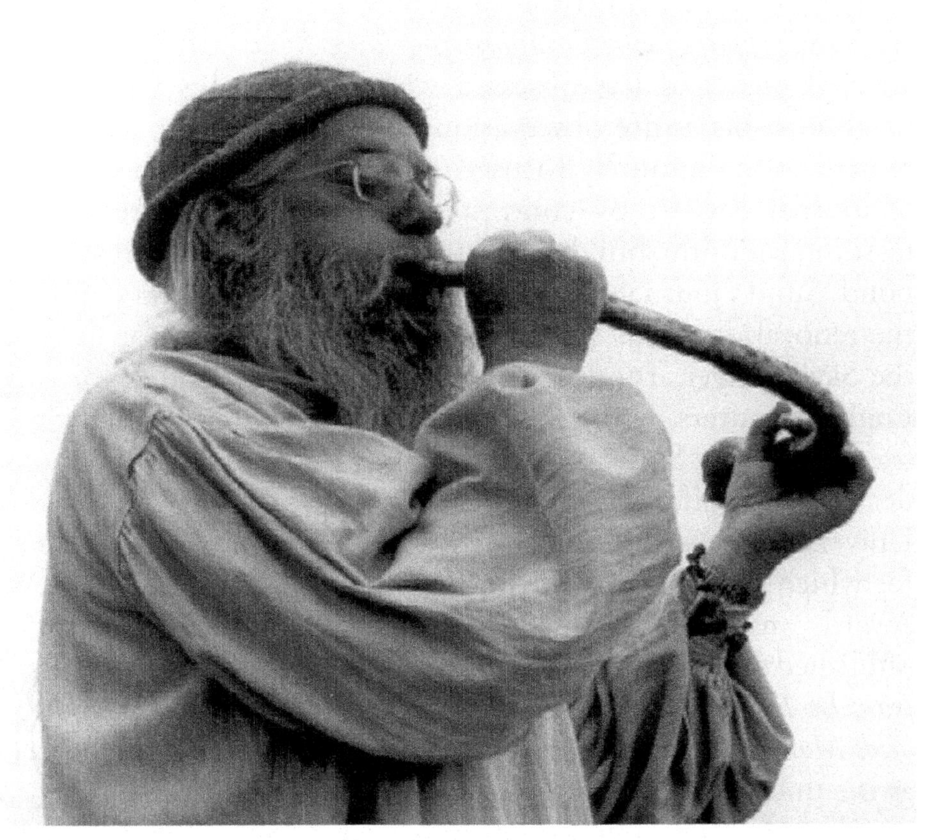

Photographs by **Erik Ambjor.**

On July 7, 1977, Robert Sund gave a performance of his poems to celebrate the saving of Shi Shi Beach as part of the Olympic National Park. The reading included songs by the Eternally Grateful Kelp Horn Band.

MICHAEL DALEY:

Notes from Disappearing Lake Review

For Henry David Thoreau's poems at Walden Pond read Robert Sund's *Notes from Disappearing Lake.* Had Thoreau been less of an explainer, and less obsessed with teaching his fellow men and neighbors, his astute observations in Walden might well have been refined to the minutely focused, musical poems Sund wrote by way of journal entries. By contrast, if Walden was Thoreau's response to several months building and then living in his own shack at the pond, Sund's journals span fourteen years of his life, and also include the renovation of his shack, originally the net shed for fishers along the Skagit River. Thoreau, however, did see it through for two New England winters, while Sund spent those winters in the town with friends. Robert Sund is on the way to publishing more books after death than in life. His first book, *Bunch Grass,* was published by the University of Washington Press in 1969, while his next, *Ish River,* for which he was awarded the Washington State Governor's Writing Award, was published by North Point Press in 1983. Although he published several chapbooks, his posthumous collected poems, *Poems from Ish River Country* (Shoemaker & Hoard), came out in 2004, and *Taos Mountain* (Poet's House Press) in 2007. He was widely regarded as the unofficial poet laureate of Western Washington.

Though *Notes from Disappearing Lake* is a collection of the best of daily entries over so long a time, culled and introduced by Tim McNulty and Glenn Hughes, it is fair to assume that entries not selected for this volume were also written as poems or prose commentary. The editors tell us, "For most of the 70s and 80s Sund spent part of each year at his shack in the tidal marsh and estuary of the Skagit River. His small shack was only a short row from nearby La Conner, Washington..." So, like Thoreau, he went frequently back to 'civilization,' and though sometimes in his hermitage, he did not lack the comforts of human contact, and did in fact, as evidenced in many of the entries, steep himself in the joys and lives of others.

There's something to be said for keeping a journal in daily or frequent poetic form. "The River Journals" represents, one would think, a practice of observation, emotion, and gestures; it depicts a life lived otherwise, away from the world, for there are no mentions of the news of the day— whose regime, which wars, the cost of gas, bread, wine, no intrusions by government and media. In his October 4, 1978, entry, Sund meets poet, painter and translator, Paul Hansen on a day when both made trips to town:

We look at the world —
something in the newspaper, maybe —
shake our heads and
break out laughing.

The image of Zen monks comes to mind as it does frequently in the book, hermit poets who removed themselves from the pace of the street, the influence of "the world." Two stanzas later, Sund issues first a gentle, prosaic comment on their laughter at news events defining the lives of others, and then with more precise, clinical detachment employs an image at once stinging and rife with the freedom of flight:

You could call it
ritual:
shaking off the
dust of the world —

Like the heron
picking lice out of
his wingfeathers.

Although there are some brief narratives in these journals—arrivals, travels and meetings with friends, encounters with mice, with a weasel, with swallows, and geese—*Notes from Disappearing Lake* reads like a primer in embellished lyrical form. Sund uses his front porch frequently, or the stillness at night, to capture the sound of migrations, of wind in marsh grass, of moon and cloud. The poems form an impressionist's gallery, evident from the name he gave the estuary he saw change with the years. It would be misleading to overlook the narrative—fourteen years in the life of a poet prepared for beauty, awaiting both a tidal and a personal change, is the story here, much as he did in *Bunch Grass* where Sund lays down his "songs" during the defined period of the wheat harvest in Eastern Washington. The book has several poems about gathering materials from "the lumberyard," that is, salvaging planks with "tarpaper still hanging" from another shack too far gone to restore, or about the pleasures of a roof that doesn't leak, of relocating mice and even trying to coax swallows to nest elsewhere. He speaks of being alone and in two poems combines missing someone with a change he notes in his own spirit. This entry, dated May 10, 1981, seems thematic:

If you're a friend of mine
and remember me otherwise —

It was the time I lost the light
and was stumbling on the way home.
. . .
Things change
        things change
and I see my life going for the better.

An ancient wave breaks over me.

And later, on May 23, of the same year, in one of the few titled entries, "Lily":

There is no use fooling myself.
Something is happening.
My old self and
        my new self
are having a long look at
                one another.
They are having long, long looks.

Months later, in October, Sund writes an entry precisely acknowledging his dedication to poetry and the cost he must pay for it:

Rowing upriver, I thought of you.
You are gone like the summer,
  and I am alone.

The oarlocks creak
    in the foggy silence,
  the river still and dark.

… … …
Both banks
    are foggy and dark.
I stay warm rowing my boat.

Sund records the changing years by recognizing his birthdays and that he's been on the river for ten years. Yet it seems changes he notices are not those we associate with aging, or maturity. It was a mature decision to enter into this life at forty-four, to step away from the call of academe, and the illusions of renown. Instead, he demonstrates a recognition of this value which, though it arose long before coming to Disappearing Lake, he articulates clearly on April 3, 1979. He calls it devotion. This may be one of the most didactic poems of the collection, yet it reminds me of a George Oppen statement. Certainly the least didactic of poets, Oppen kept a journal called "Daybooks". In an entry to his first Daybook, written in the early 1960s, he writes how the mind can be dedicated to poetry: "At least two kinds of devotion. The devotion to art, a sort of pragmatism of art which refuses to think anything which will not contribute to poetry. The other is a devotion which makes poetry of what the mind, the free and operating mind can know—know—and is going to know." I think of the way a computer or an electrical service can be referred to as "dedicated," and understand Oppen to mean something like this, that is, not so much in an emotional sense, one in which the mind must constantly attempt to persuade others, but the mind available, continuously, to its voluptuous art. Sund came to his devotion, and expresses it as a process, somewhat as Thoreau might have, if more succinctly:

The man who is not devoted:
he knows neither himself
nor what he has turned his back on.

The mysteries
are all words to him.
There is only a series
of cheap transactions
going on inside.

Before concluding, I hasten to remind readers that this book is composed of Sund's journal entries, and that the poems we find here, unlike those in *Poems from Ish River Country,* for instance, can easily be termed "less polished." True, some became drafts for *Shack Medicine,* and many entries were drafts to work on or discard, yet Sund's technical gifts are evident throughout. One example from *Poems from Ish River Country* illustrates a practice he employed frequently. In "Just Before Sleep, I Dream of my Grandfather returned to His Farm in the Early Spring," the line "he liked to tromp lopsided in a furrow" shows he knew his way around a vowel, the line packed then softened by alliteration or sibilance: "behind his horses…" He ends this poem using the same technique: a vowel driven rhythm, then alliterative with internal vowel rhyme, concluding with the matter-of-fact:

In the corner of the woodshed near the house
patches of powdery mold
are spreading
over his work shoes.

Shoes the poet no doubt wanted to fill. In *Notes* he shifts again between aural qualities, in this case in an undated poem, and the prosaic:

Winter weeds
outside my shack,
High water
in the windy morning.

The tops of marsh grass
stick up
above the 12-foot tide.

In the wind, bent grass
writes on the crests of waves.
I sit alone with
my first cup of tea.

The W sounds of wind reinforce what he was hearing so much so we are prepared for the grass like a poet who leaves nothing behind. I'm reminded of Chinese monks who left their poems strung from branches to weather, and Sund's own calligraphed "Wind poems." A lesser ear would have heard "rides" instead of "writes," and a dramatic poet, "writhes."

Robert Sund's *Notes from Disappearing Lake* is remarkable less for the fine work Hughes and McNulty have uncovered from his journals, and not even so much because his practice led first of all to his chapbook, *Shack Medicine,* in which Sund himself selected the very best from these journals, but the journals are remarkable because he wrote them seemingly without audience. A poet who chooses such a hermitage "turns his back on" not only the world, its "dust," its "lice in his wingfeathers," but on its ears and the aspirations he might have had to a public voice. He abandons the ever-present need for audience to devote himself to beauty alone; for this we can be thankful.

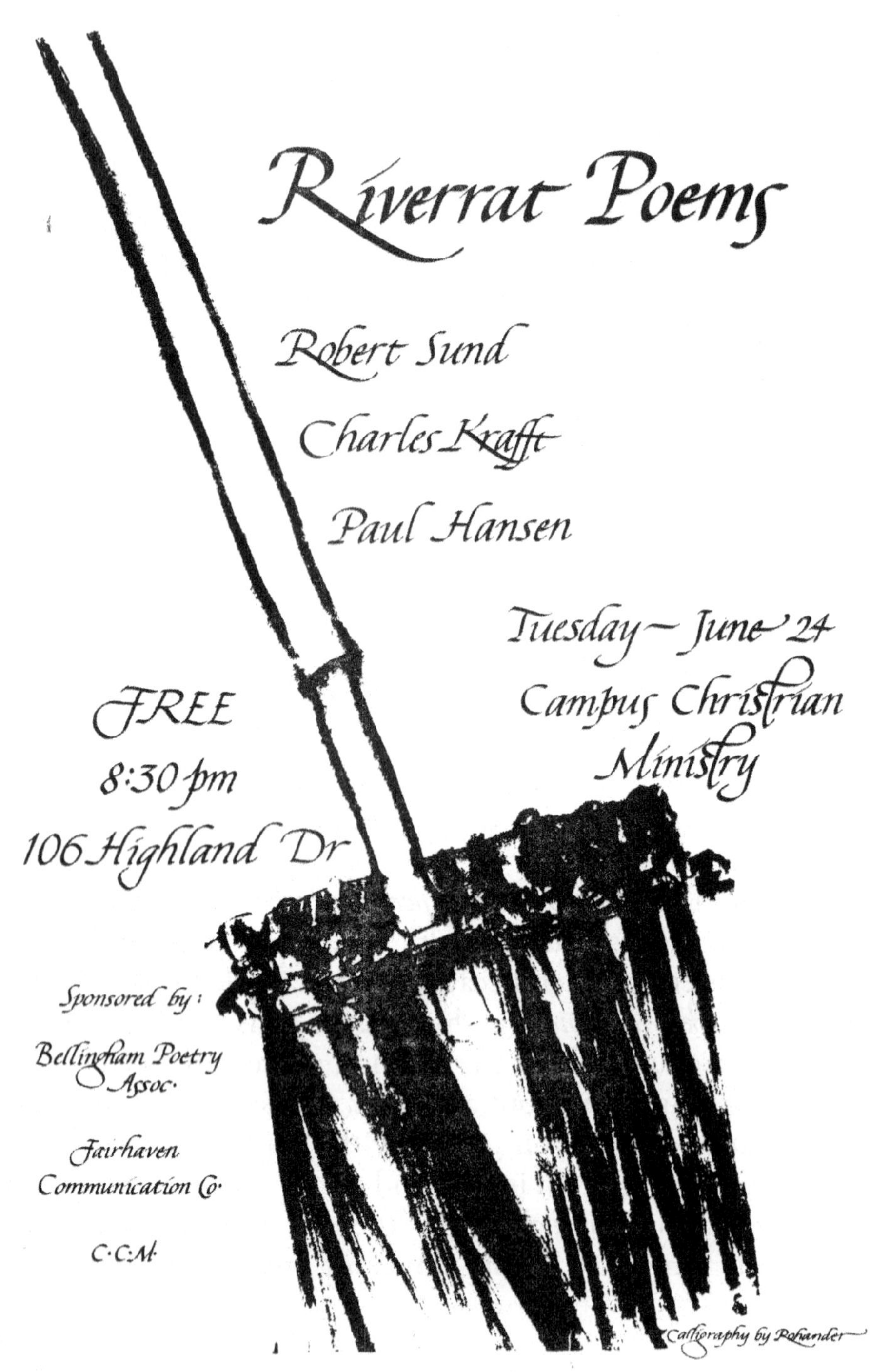

Reading at Western Washington University, Bellingham, 1978.

CHARLIE KRAFFT:

In La Conner Robert's circle was mostly male and we referred to ourselves as "The River Rats" because many of us lived on the Skagit River in shacks and float shacks, including Clyde Sanborn who had as well developed a sense of the absurd as Robert and often cracked us up with it. Clyde Sanborn drowned in the river one night on his way back to his shack on the river in a kayak. Clyde and Robert were the town poets with a capital "P."

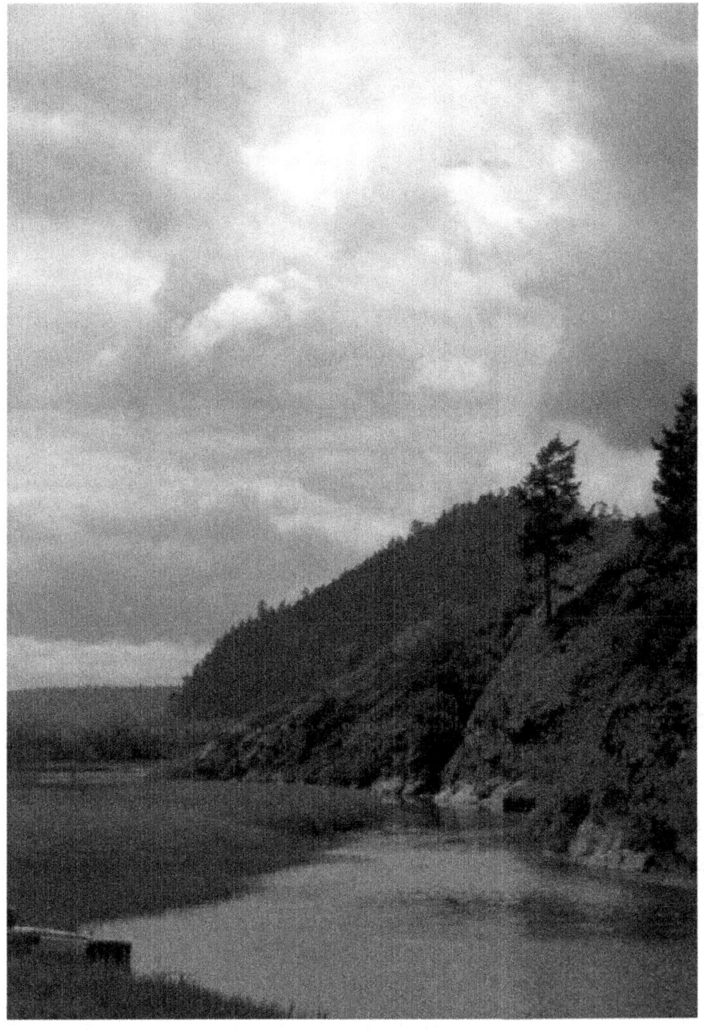

Disappearing Lake. Photo by **Erik Ambjor.**

STEVEN R. JOHNSON:

The locals called where he lived Shit Creek, and Robert never liked the name and he called it Disappearing Lake. A lake at high tide, and cat tails at low tide. He also called it "Swallow Heaven" with his elaborate Bird Palace, and the birds loved it.

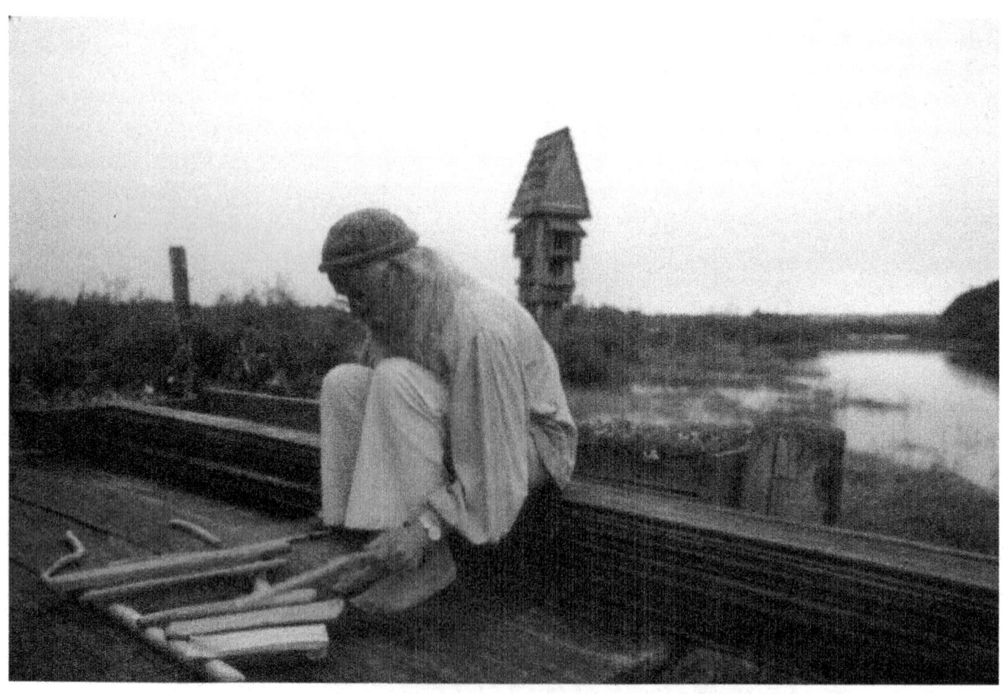

Robert Sund playing his driftwood xylophone at Disappearing Lake, with the Bird Palace in background. Photo by **Erik Ambjor.**

JIM BERTOLINO:

Returning to the Poetry of Robert Sund

Thanks to poet Tim McNulty, I own, and am enjoying, a book published by Pleasure Boat Studio in New York. The title is *Notes from Disappearing Lake,* and the subtitle is *The River Journals of Robert Sund.*

I knew Robert (you'd be wrong to call him Bob) back when he was still sometimes staying at his cabin on an estuary of the Skagit River, near La Conner, Washington in an area known as Fishtown. These journal entries are pretty much poems, and Sund has been widely praised, and recognized by key publishers, for his poetry. He is probably best known for his volumes *Bunch Grass,* 1969, University of Washington Press, *Ish River,* 1983, North Point Press, and *Poems From Ish River Country: Collected Poems and Translations,* 2004, Shoemaker & Hoard—which I used as a textbook when I was Writer in Residence at Willamette University, 2005-06, in Salem, Oregon. Robert died at age 72 in 2001, and that comprehensive volume was published posthumously.

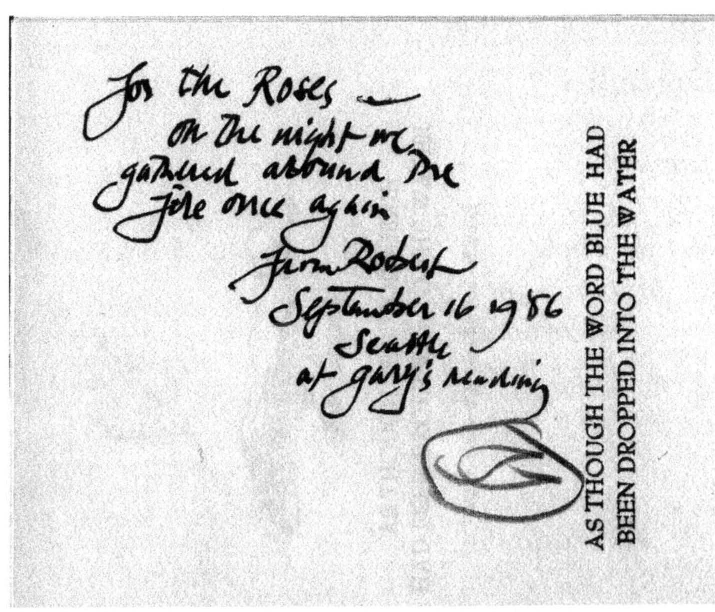

However important his volumes have been, those who know and love Robert Sund's poetry tend to treasure his limited edition chapbooks,

which include *As Though the Word Blue Had Been Dropped Into the Water,* 1986, and *Why I Am Singing For the Dancer,* 1999—both published in hand-set letterpress editions by Rusty North at Sagittarius Press in Port Townsend, WA.

His chapbook *Shack Medicine,* first published in 1990 by California's Tangram Press in a letterpress printing, then reprinted in 1992 by The Poets's House Press, is my own favorite of the smaller collections, and offers poems that are the most similar to those in *Notes From Disappearing Lake.* I should note that I found and was inspired by Sund's first book *Bunch Grass* during my initial year as a graduate student, which was at Washington State University. WSU is in Pullman, at the eastern edge of the Palouse wheat-growing region—which is where the poems are rooted. I took the good news of his poetry to my students and colleagues when I transferred to Cornell University in 1971 to work on an MFA degree.

Here then are some samples of the poems in the 2012 volume *Notes from Disappearing Lake:*

December, 1976

Some men
reap their harvest daily,
like ducks
swimming about the bay as
tide descends,
gobbling water plants
with feathery heads
down under
ripply water,
never realizing
their ass is skyward &
open to the wind.

This poem is a fine example of some of Sund's key characteristics as a poet: his detailed daily observations about the world around him, and his sense of humor. Also, like the majority of poems in this book, the poem carries the date it was composed.

He honored and learned from the great Chinese poets, and learned traditional calligraphy to enhance his own poems. He often embellished his poems with tiny drawings of mountain and island landscapes. *Notes from Disappearing Lake* opens with a reproduction of the calligraphy of a poem titled "October 12, 1973," and it is punctuated by an image of mountains and an island watercourse.

In this next poem he not only identifies the date, but the time of day. He must have felt that composing a poem that early in the morning, the hour should be noted:

April 24, 1977 4 A.M.

In the excited mind
words fly.

The night is still, the water still —
& suddenly, in the mind

(as on the night river
a beaver
breaks the silence)

the first ripple of a poem
swims almost invisible by the river bank.

Blades of grass standing in the river
feel the waves rise and
pass through them.

Here Sund finds an appropriate metaphor for his own poetic process, which implies that not only does he draw his inspiration from the environment, that environment physically experiences his poems. It should also be noted that he employed the ampersand (&) rather than the word "and"—in the process endowing his poems (even in print) with an aspect of calligraphy, as well as the minimalist clarity of the Chinese poetry he loved.

I will complete this gesture of appreciation for one of Washington State's great poets, who had the grand good fortune to have studied with Theodore Roethke while a student at the University of Washington, with this beautiful observation:

July 20, 1985

After a hot day
cool night comes —
dark out in the marsh
dark on the island.
In the nightwind the
young shoots of willow
cry against the windowglass,
as the branches
bend and
spring back.

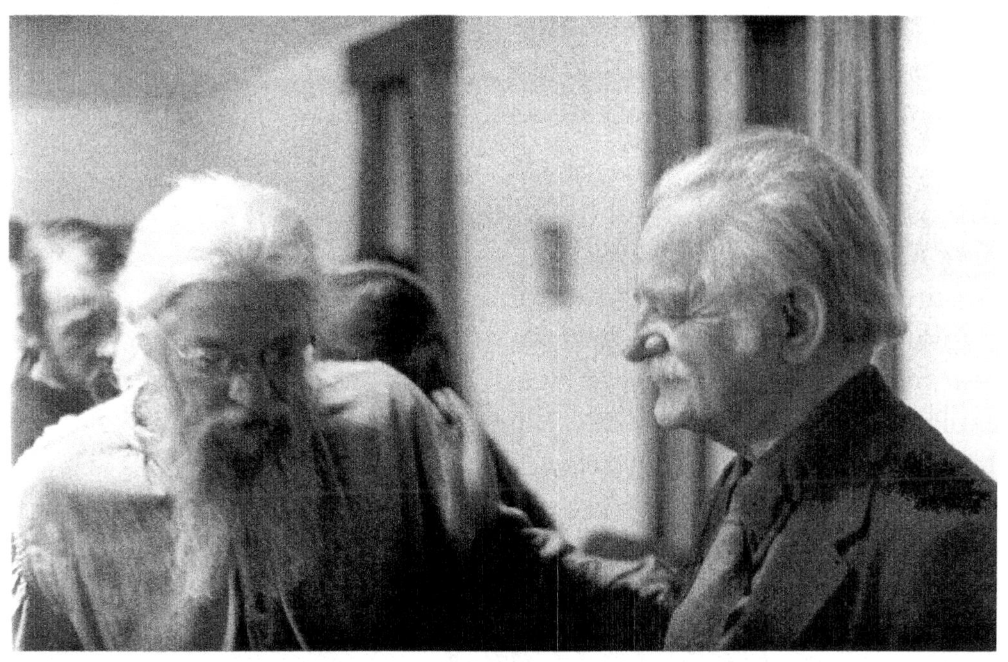

Robert Sund and Kenneth Rexroth at the La Conner Community Center Poetry Reading, Labor Day 1980. Photo by **Erik Ambjor.**

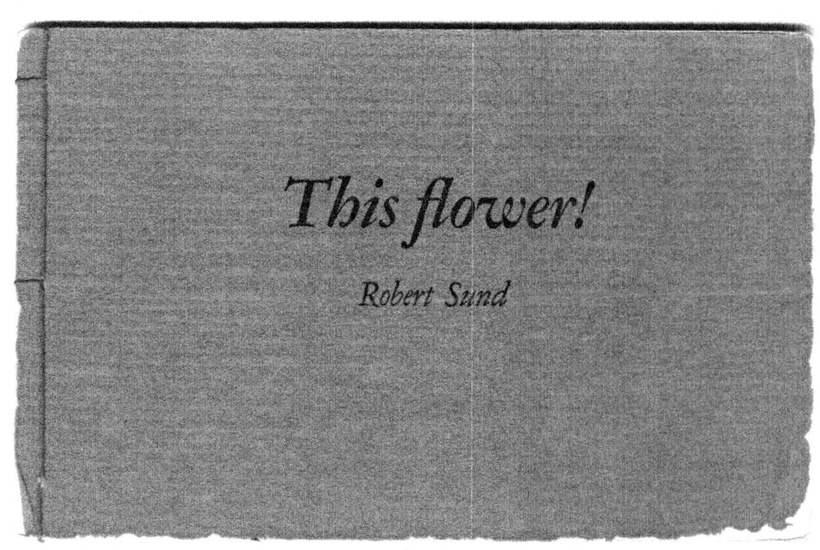

Cover of This flower! Poems dedicated to Kenneth Rexroth, published 1982.

SAM HAMILL:

Although I printed and published Sund's *Hides of White Horses Shedding Rain,* we were not close.
A Sund story: When I came home from a stay in Japan, where I translated Bashō and Issa, I went to visit Paul Hansen. We went to visit Sund. Robert was doing "versions" of Bashō and Issa and began explaining haiku to me. It was highly entertaining.
He of course knew no Japanese.

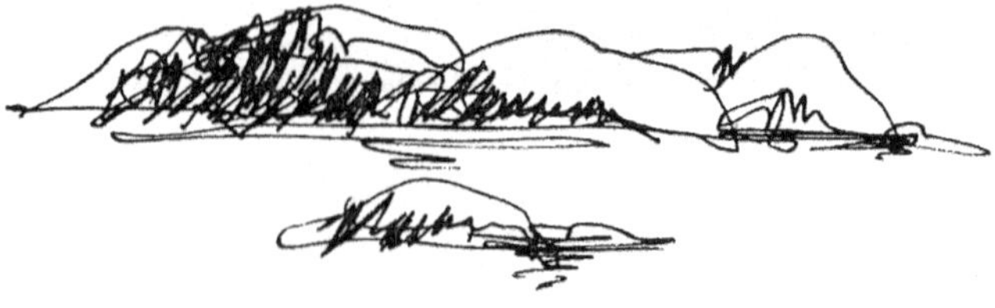

This book is one of an edition of three hundred copies printed on Arches wove paper and signed by the poet. The type is Bembo, and takes its name from Cardinal Bembo, whose *De Aetna* Aldus Manutius published in 1495, and for which the type was designed, probably based upon the same Neo-Caroline handwriting upon which Nicholas Jenson modeled his types. The printing was completed at the closing of the year 40080 in Ish River Country.

Robert Sund

From colophon page of The Hides of White Horses Shedding Rain (1981).

GEORGIA JOHNSON:

Ish River, September, 1982

For Robert Sund and Bud Johnson

If shit creek had drained into the Stilly
at island crossing,
or my dad's favorite drift spot had been below
Al's landing on the Skagit, Bud and Uncle Bob might have
met up one fine day.

One standing in waist deep waters, home made fly rod in hand
as shadows lengthened over his hole,
the other rowing for all he's worth up towards home,
singing an old Swedish folk song.

Bud would have spoke up first,
admiring the hand crafted dory, "Svalen",
Uncle Bob probably inquired politely about luck and
the contents of the creel.
There would be agreeable remarks on the color of the river
how the salmon were running, perhaps that beside the
eight pounder was an almost full pint.

They both could stop time, slow the river down, make the
sun pierce an alder grove along the dike like jewels.

Removed to the bank, elbows propped on knees,
They're sipping and jawing, like boys.

This is where my poor poem fails them,
as one would mention the war, any damned war
and the other declare that socialist intellectuals are selling
out the country.

And me? I am out on a far bank, separated by river, unable to
believe that their love of place, or me, might overcome all other.

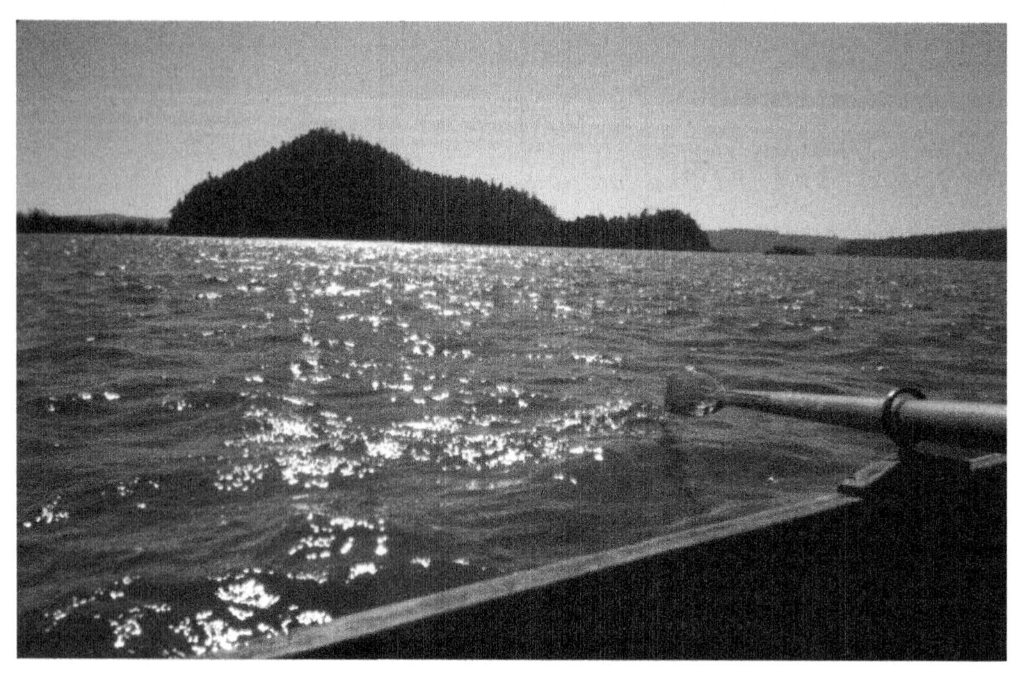

ERIK AMBJOR *photographs. Robert Sund rows to Disappearing Lake.*

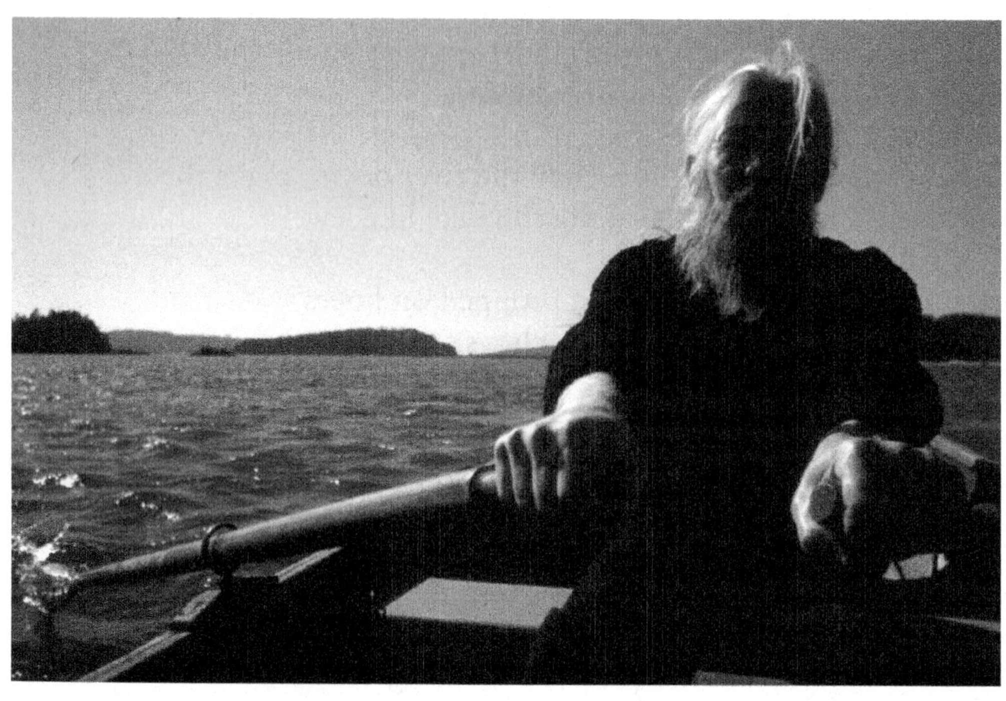

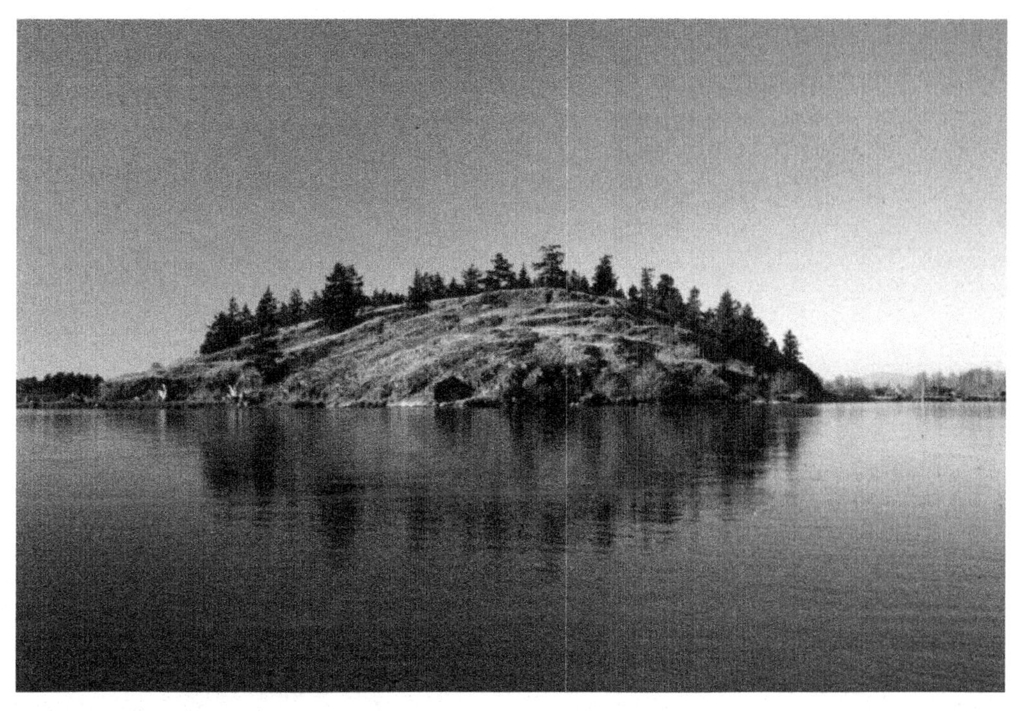

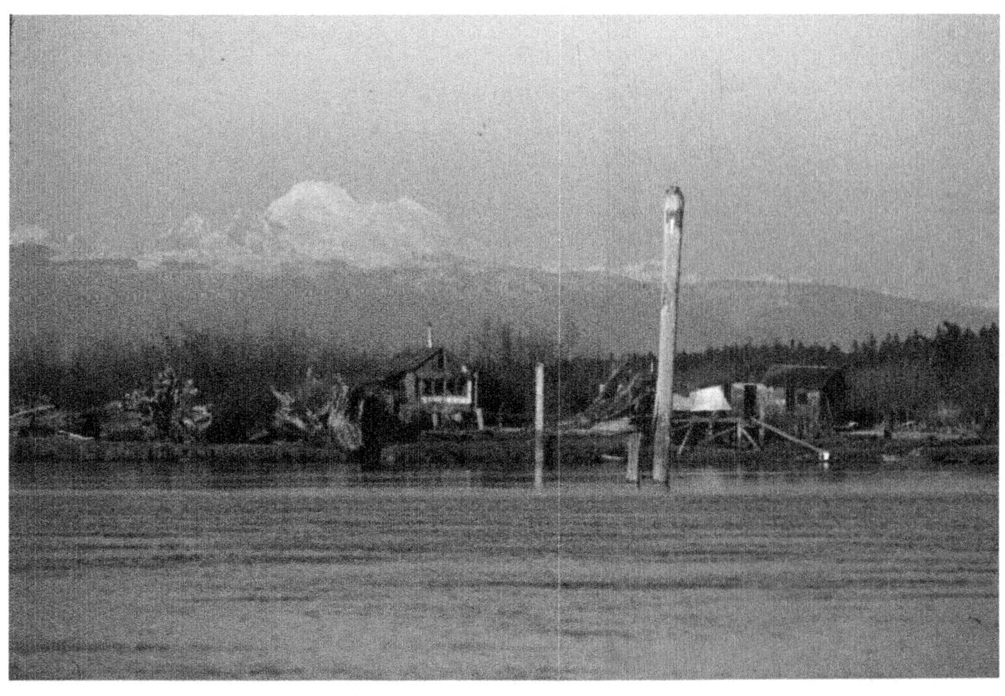

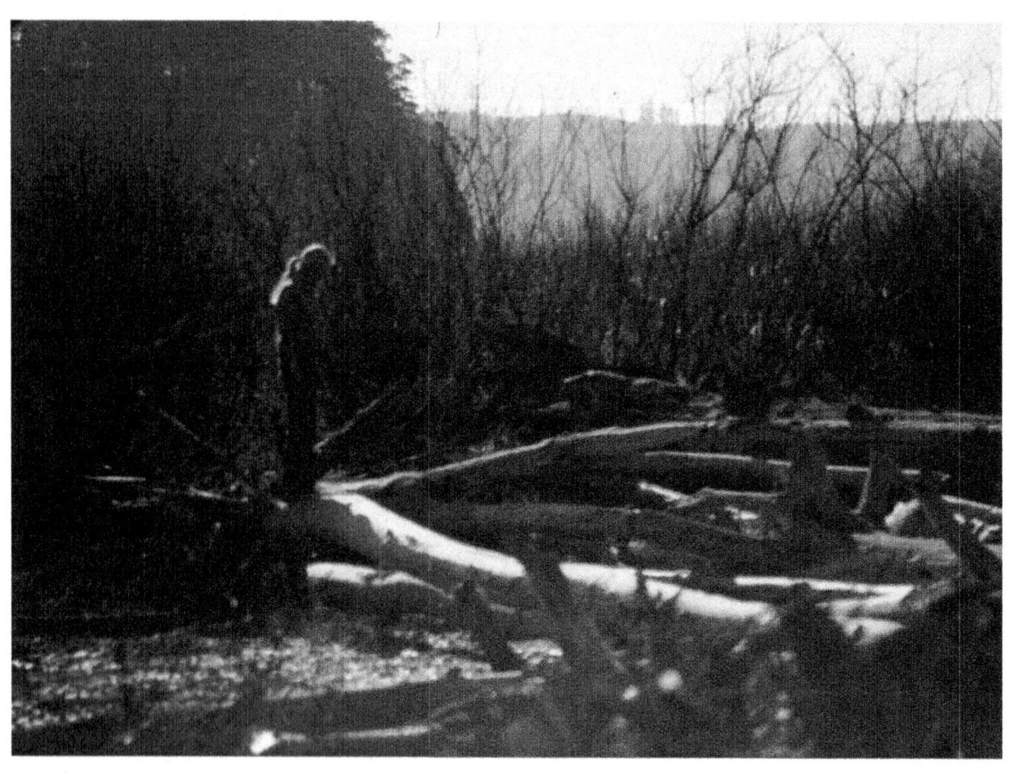

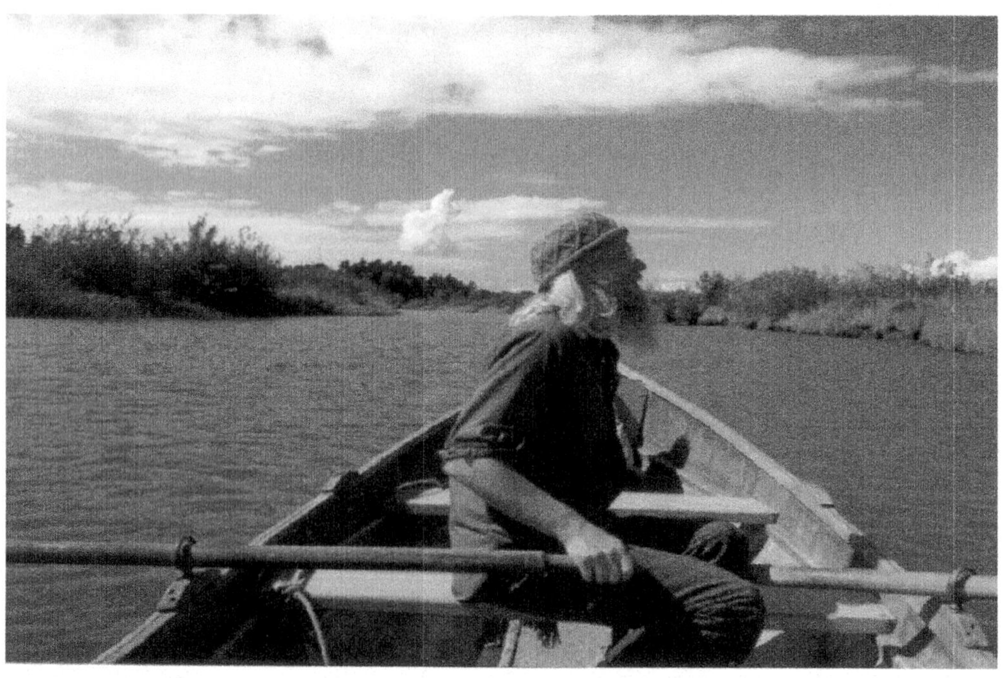

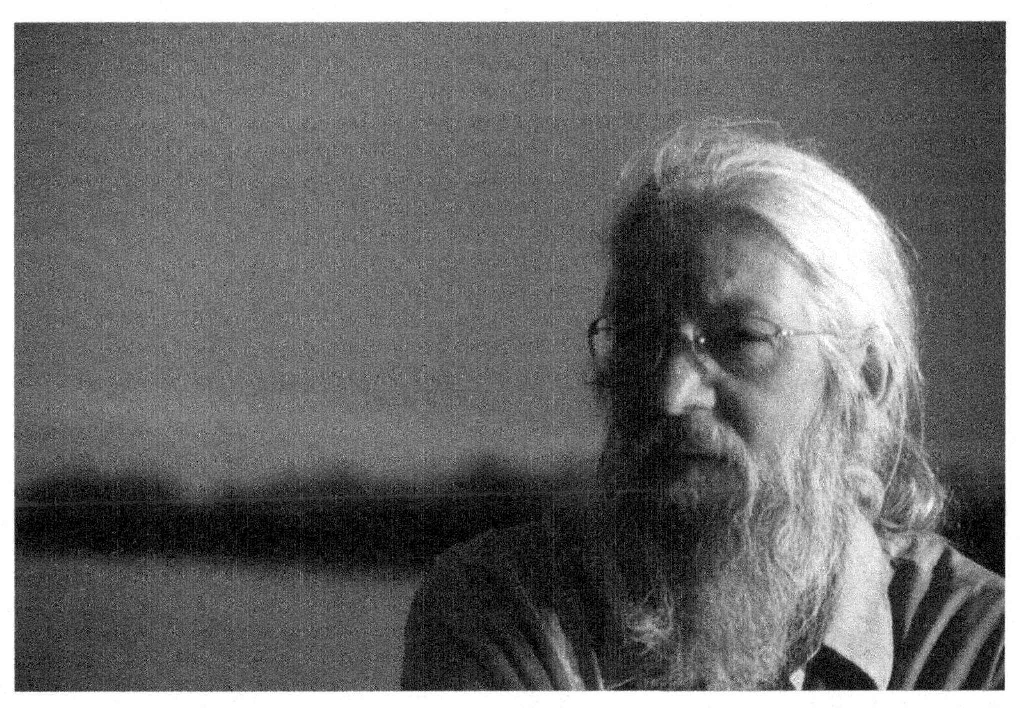

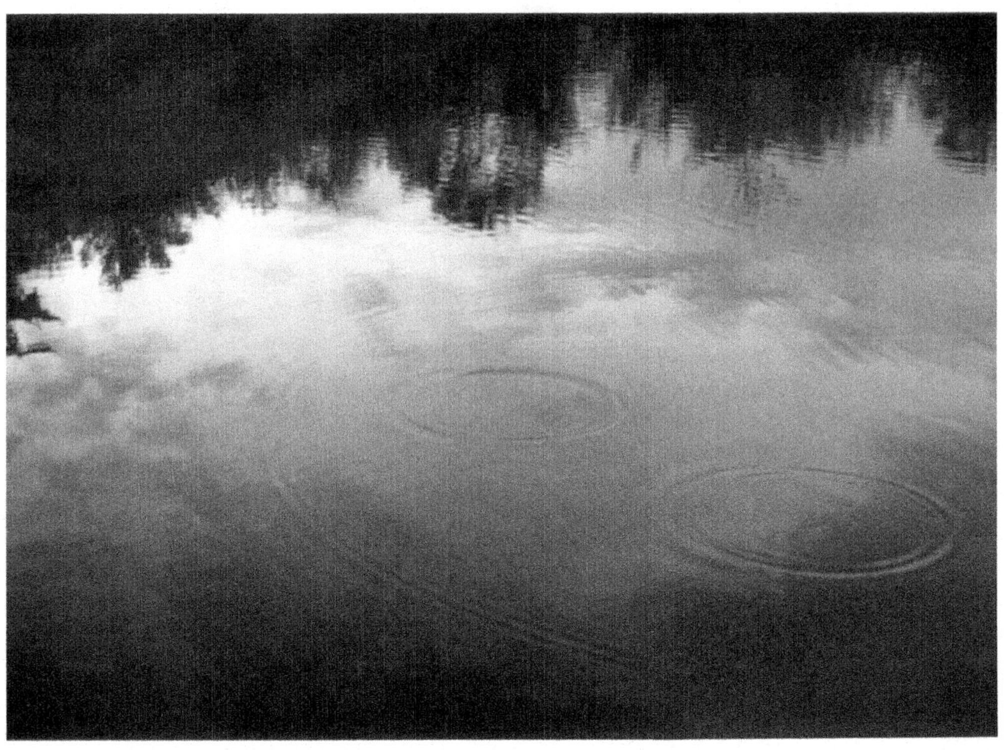

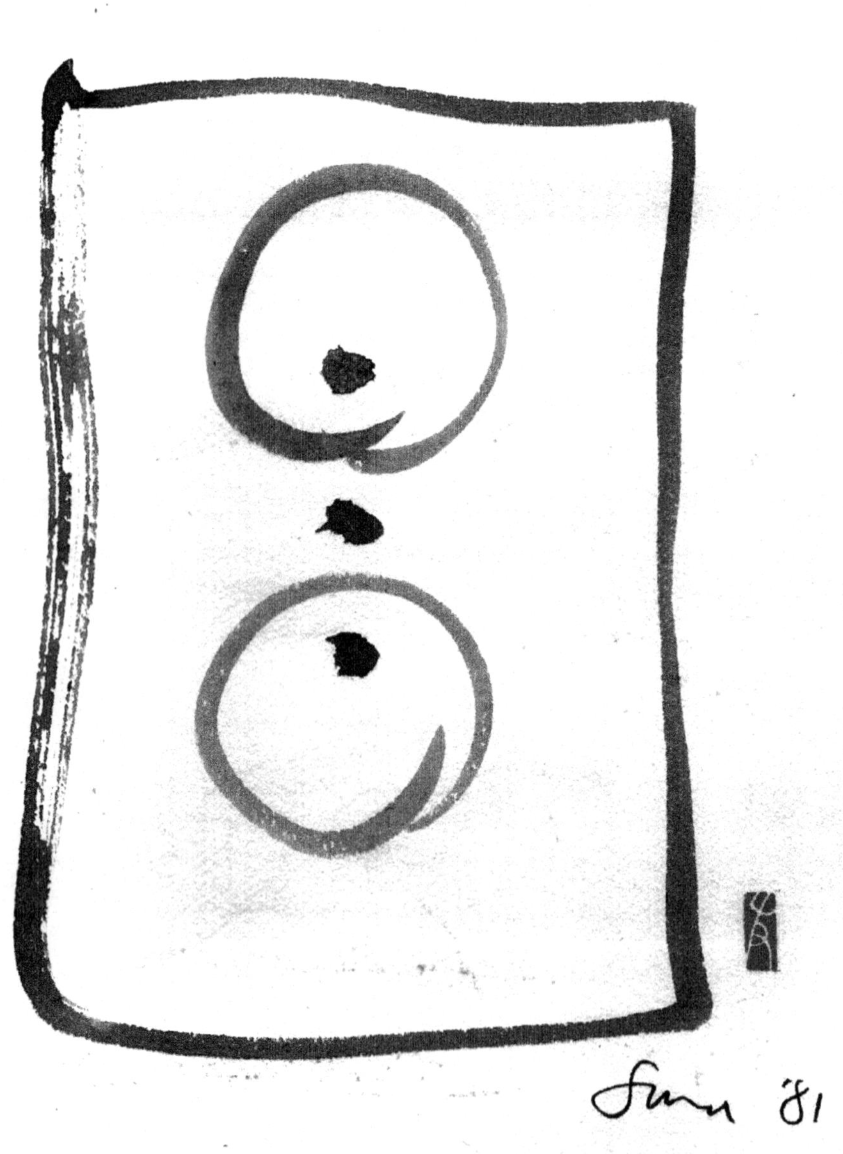

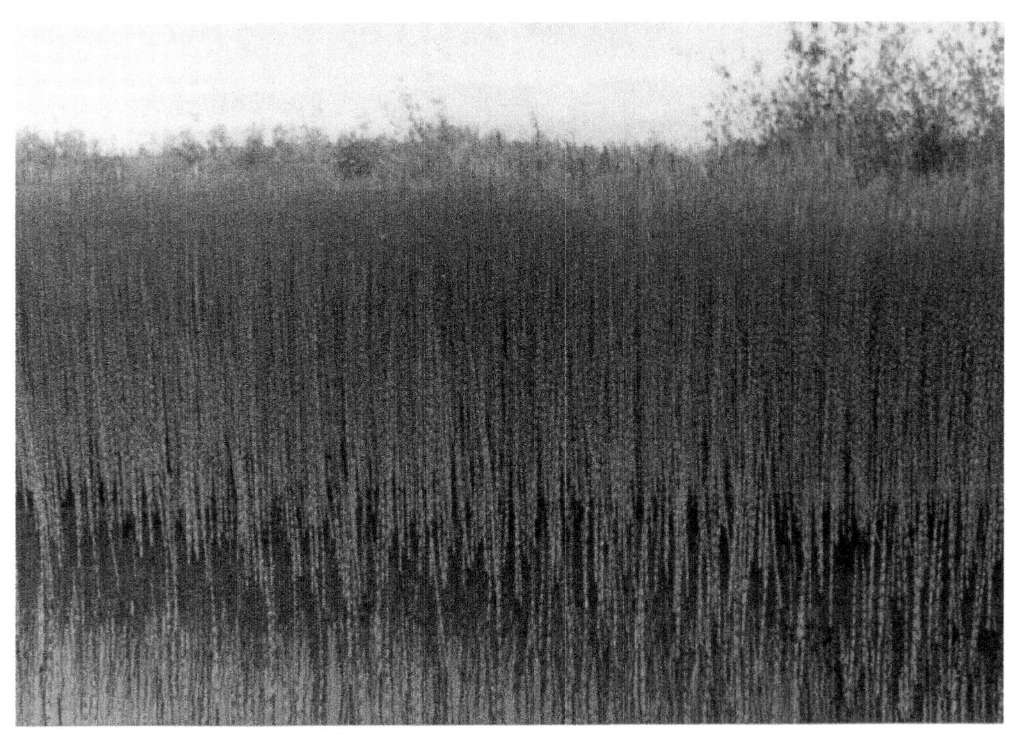

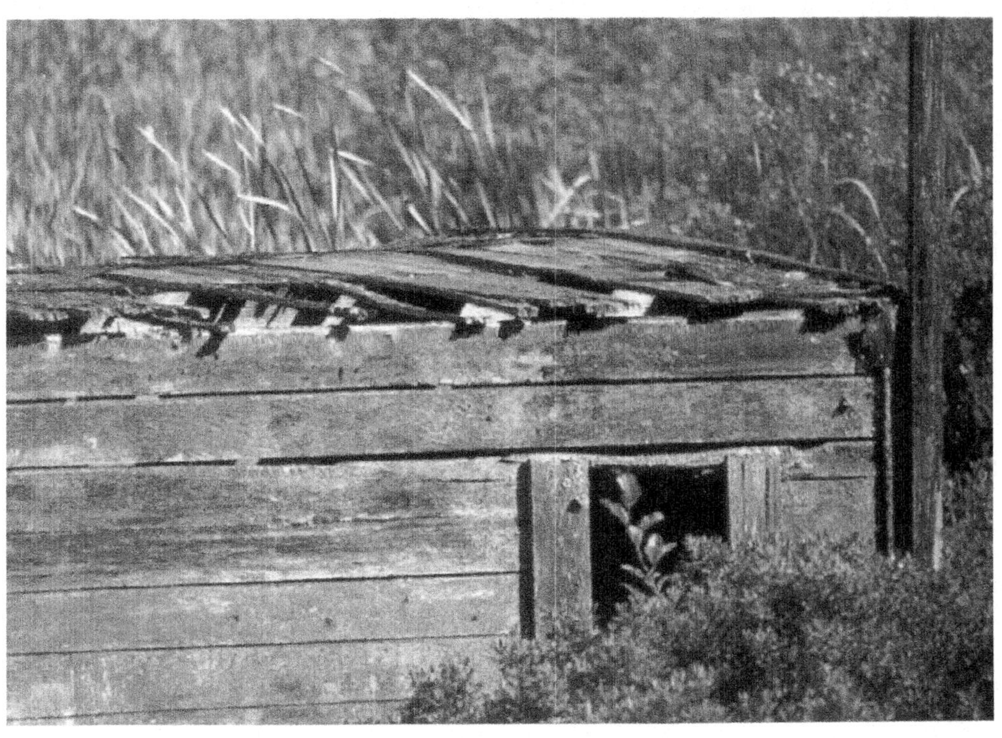

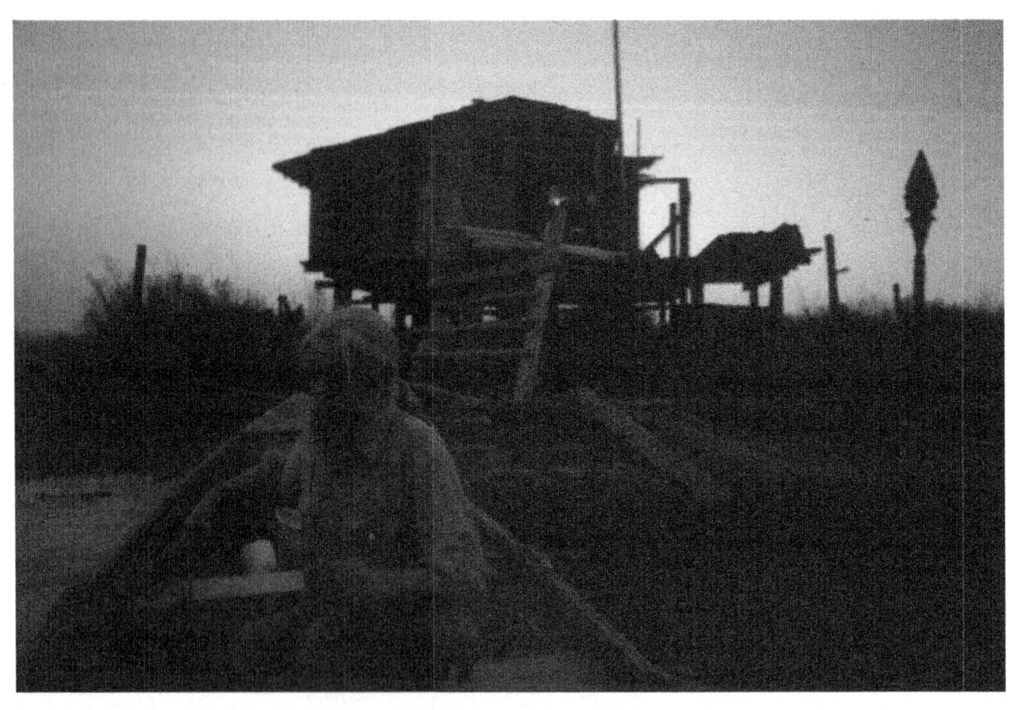

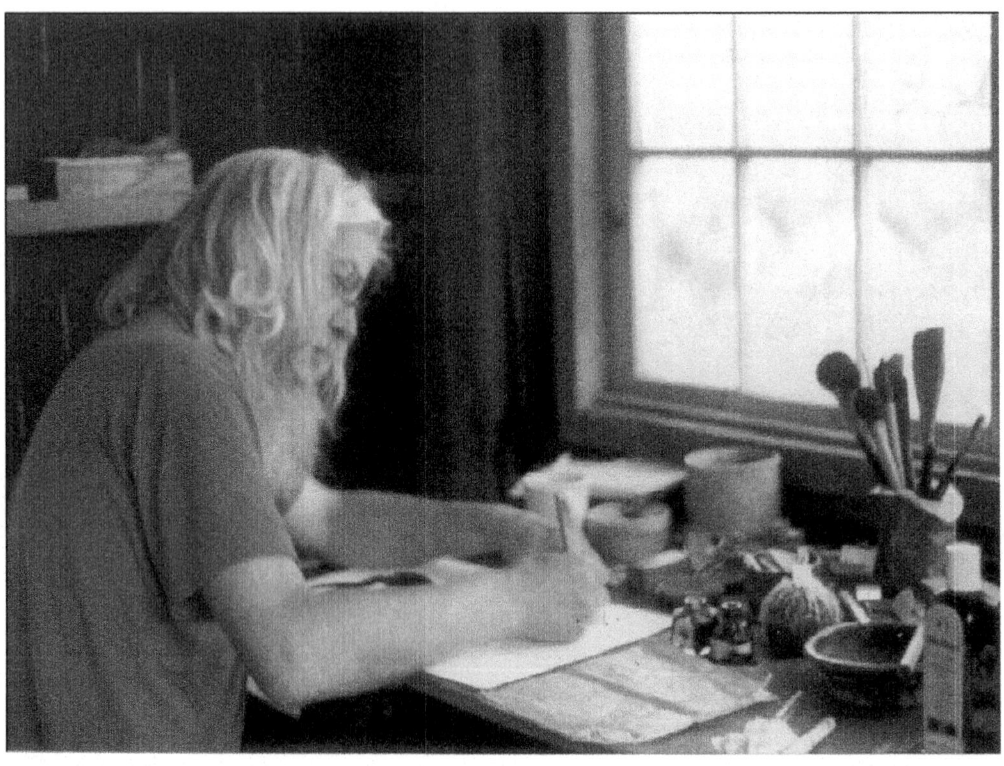

FRED OWENS: ROBERT SUND'S SOLILOQUY

Guiding a stray bee out of the house—enough work for one day!

At 8 p.m. the sun was still high in the sky, but the air felt like evening. Robert Sund came inside the Boom Shack and went over to his stand-up writing desk. He picked up a small book of his own poems and looked them over.

It is time for the ink to spill this summer evening, he thought.

If I make a dot of ink as big as a dime, I can almost see my reflection in the glossy surface. I could see the future or past lives if I was interested, or the Jersey cows back on the farm where I grew up. I can see many things. And then the black ink dries and dulls as it settles into the paper, going to a charcoal matte finish, which does not reflect, and leaves no image, but for me, I can even peer deeper into ---- into what? I see a merry old man sitting by a small river under a blossoming tree. If I look closer – ah, the old man is drinking plum wine, he shouts in a drunken glee. He stands up, strips down and jumps into the flowing river, waist-high, roaring with pleasure, scattering the ducks.

That's how I find my poems, from this ink bottle. I see the old man sitting by the river. He is as real as my own thumb, but does it make a poem? Are the words right? And is it true? More than anything a poem has to be true.

It wasn't like this when I was a school boy in Chehalis writing on Big Indian Chief tablets, that rough paper with light blue lines widely spaced for young hands to try their pens. I often smeared my long-sleeves into the ink.

My mother would scold me when I came home. Her scolding was so light it was almost a pleasure. If I smiled at her she would have to start all over again, "Robert, you made a mess with the ink. You must be more careful. I have to scrub your shirt now so it won't stain."

Then I would bow my head and wait a little, and then I could smile warmly at her, looking up. She was only a little taller than me.

I came to the farm as a bundle in a blanket, to this Swedish home with cedar rail fences and a pasture leading down to the river, full of old stumps. It was 1929. Herbert Hoover was President, and I was a baby in a blanket, and much loved. But even then somehow I knew I was a replacement for my brother Don who had died two years earlier from diphtheria. Don was buried in the church yard not too far from our farm and my mother and father never ceased to mourn. I was supposed to make them happy, and I almost did. I wished I could sing for them or do something to make them happy, but I was only a baby and my mother gave me a warm bath every day, until I grew up and ran in the fields and became a school boy.

My father, he knew how many beautiful August evenings sur round an ear of corn.
And my mother, she knew that without love of Earth there is no love of heaven.

That's how I wrote about my mother and father, with tears in my eyes. They loved me as much as they could, as much as I needed, but I felt different just the same. The sorrow never left our home, like a dampness in the corners even on the driest, hottest days of August. I chattered to myself and played with small stones in the yard, making stone diagrams of houses and forts. I took fern leaves from the bushes and made fern railroads coming up to the houses in this tiny Swedish village. I dreamed of lingonberry syrup on pancakes. In my play village the people were truly happy. I could even hear the sound of light laughter.

I worked hard enough in later years on the farm, doing chores, but it was never going to be my farm. My father knew that, he never said it would come down to me. He would not force me to be what I could never be.

I watched the Chehalis River flowing and wanted to go downstream to Grays Harbor, to the wide world and leave this farm. I knew I would never come back.

I found poetry at the University – I began to keep a small book and put words together. Then I left school and went over to the Eastern Cascades, to the Palouse, to work on dry-land farms under skies that never ended. I bucked hay in the heat and dust. I loaded wheat in the silo and almost died in an explosion. The farmers understood me – who I was and why I was there.

I came there to learn from the farmers because I thought I was special, and they taught me in the wheat field that I was only dust in the wind. They were true Buddhists. No reason, no meaning, no hope, and no chance of heaven. What a relief!

I returned to Seattle and lived in Cloud House. I married a woman because she was kind to me.

I left my wife in Seattle and moved to Shi-Shi Beach. That was my time on the wild ocean shore. It was so much bigger than the river. I sat there long enough -- it took years – but I sat and sat in a shelter under the wind until all of my poetry dissolved into nothing. Then one day a raccoon told me I was getting lazy. He stole my last handful of Cracker Jacks. I chased him out of camp before I realized how much he was disturbing me. Oh Raccoon Teacher, what were you telling me?

Telling me to leave Shi-Shi Beach and go back to town. It was time to listen to those busy town voices. So I came to LaConner and lived in a room upstairs at the Planter Hotel. I had no money. I made calligraphies on expensive paper. I sold one or two. I played pool at the tavern, I kept making poems and I refused to work.

No money for rent! Hunger! The Muse pays so poorly, but she is so lovely. She lulled me to

sleep in the early hours before dawn.

I suffered. I was lonely. I was bitter and proud. I hated the world of success spinning all around me like jets flying overhead. I got drunk. I laughed but it was forced.

I know I am worse than anyone. I am guilty. My poetry is all lies, but I never let anyone know.

Now I have this small cabin in town, courtesy of Nelson Hardware. My poems amuse the Nelson family. They let me off easy for the rent, which I haven't got anyway. Why do they trust me? I am a fraud. I owe money all over town. I clutch these papers and say this is my work and it has great value. The days are hard, but late at night, when the moon is quiet and bright, I see it all becoming true and beautiful.

JANET SAUNDERS and JIM SMITH: Robert Sund's Anecdotes, etc.

Back in the '80s, Jim chauffeured Robert (car-less at the time) down to a Washington librarians' conference south of Seattle where (Jim recalls) Robert had been asked to be the keynote speaker. After they found the place and did some meeting and greeting, Robert suddenly disappeared. Jim took a seat at the head table next to Robert's empty chair. Some more time went by and the dignitaries at the table started to wonder aloud where that poet was.

To Jim's relief, shortly thereafter, Robert strolled back in, cool as a cucumber, took his seat and followed up with an excellent talk, punctuated, no doubt, with his poetry – all of which was thoroughly enjoyed by all.

The delay? Jim knew all along what Robert would confess to later: he had just gone out to the car to have a little "smokie wokie" to calm any jitters before the speech.

In those days Robert was renting a spacious apartment in an old building on top of the hill in La Conner that had originally been the Methodist church. His landlord was Kirby Johnson, a local farmer and landowner in town. One day, Kirby knocked at Robert's door. Robert welcomed him in and they sat down with cups of hot coffee and Robert, always a fine storyteller, regaled his guest, most likely, with tales of characters around town and local gossip, etc. When Kirby got up to leave eventually, they shook hands and the landlord headed toward the door. "Oh, by the way, Robert," he said, turning around. "You're six months behind in the rent."

Jim recalls that when Robert's power was shut off in that same historic building, he would run an extension cord out the window and plug it into an outlet in the basement. Despite his starving artist life style, neither Jim nor I remember his being stressed or depressed by his often cash-strapped circumstances.

On the whole, Robert seemed pretty content with his simple life, writing and giving readings of his poems, staying often at his shack on the bucolic banks of the Skagit River when the weather allowed and raising a garden or having friends over wherever he stayed on dry land in the summer. He liked to drink beer and shoot pool at the La Conner Tavern and, as Jim used to say, as long Robert could get up each day "at the crack of noon," he was fine. He often made himself "a bowl of good mush" to get through the day.

I would say that Robert did not suffer fools gladly. I remember one instance that could fit the expression. He was hosting, I guess, a party at another friend's house in La Conner. Well, maybe he wasn't hosting, but he was answering the door and greeting guests as they came in. One fellow who was also a poet and was well known and liked around town despite his chronic inebriated state came to the house in his usual bumbly, stumbly manner. When Robert opened the door on this other poet, Robert immediately barked, "I DON'T think so, Clyde!" and closed the door on his face.

Robert was also annoyed by tourists who cruised around the Swinomish Channel in big flashy boats. He called these visitors "pukers" because they were so seldom in their boats that they'd easily get seasick and vomit over the side.

During Robert's stay with us, an opportunity arose for Robert to rise to new heights when the *Channel Town Press* announced that there was an opening on the ballot for mayor of La Conner. Robert, apparently hit with a surge of energy, creativity and excitement, set to work on a Sund for Mayor campaign. His major areas of focus, it seemed to me, were publicity and platform.

Publicity took the form of ½-inch plywood signs, about 1 ft. by 2 ft. high, skill-sawed in the shape of a house with a pleasant winding path leading to its front door. Painted green and white, with a blue sky and black lettering, the signs invited all to Vote for Sund for Mayor. Needless to say, they weren't the kind of signs you could crank out and tape to telephone poles by the dozen. I don't know that an actual dozen were ever produced. (We do have one survivor though that still is hanging in our tool shed.)

I'm fuzzier on the details of the platform, but I do remember that as the new mayor, Robert would insist on monthly pot luck dinners for the community where the participants could chat, eat, drink and discuss anything that needed discussion. Sounded like fun.

According to Jim's memories, Robert made a respectable showing, but did not win the election.

At some point in the '80s, Robert was diagnosed with diabetes. Since that meant his life was now dependent on daily insulin injection, balanced diet and generally sensible living, he was determined to cut, if not end, drinking alcohol and eat regularly, maybe even cut down on the hand-rolled cigarettes. As I remember, he was pretty successful. Of course, he wasn't able to stay out at the river shack that he loved; there were definitely no pharmacies or doctors on that bank of the Skagit. It was then that we asked him to move into a spare bedroom in our house until he got stable and on his feet again, however long that took. It turned out to be several months. Needless to say, Robert was a pleasant, interesting housemate

FRED OWENS:

There were passionate debates in LaConner among the artists and poets. There were meetings and collaborations. There were group shows of artists, and group readings of poets. There were alliances and feuds. Especially with the poets, there was a definite school...Gary Snyder's tight and spare poetry, his extensive education in Japan, and his earth-centered, regional approach—those were the guidelines of the school. The school's chief exponent was Robert Sund and its name was the Great Blue Heron Society. Sund never compromised in his dedication to being a poet. He never married (Sund married briefly in the 1960's before moving to LaConner) and he never owned property. He never took a day job. But he painted as well as wrote poetry, and he could sell his paintings for a few hundred dollars. And he might earn fifty or a hundred dollars for a reading. Nevertheless Sund was frequently broke and constantly on the make. He suffered the indignity of begging and borrowing, but if ever a friend or acquaintance suggested that a poet was not worthy of his labor, then Sund became unyielding and resolute, and was prepared and willing to declaim poetry and its value until the tavern closed. With that quality of determination and with the quality of his poetry, Sund became a regional leader.

The committee to Elect Robert Sund Mayor invites you to consider his views ....

In the fall of 1983, Robert announced in a newsletter: "My name is on the ballot this year because many people have asked me to run for Mayor and 'do something'."

CHARLIE KRAFFT:

We did a lot of drinking and pool playing in the La Conner Tavern that year. The tavern was Robert's campaign HQ. We'd sit around on rainy days dreaming up whacky things Robert could use to win hearts and votes. The two things I thought were hilarious about Robert's platform in his run for Mayor of La Conner were:

1. Getting farmers to plant their corn closer to the road so people didn't have to get out of their cars to steal it.
2. Capping the pilings along the La Conner side of the Swinomish Slough so the seagulls standing on them all day long wouldn't wear them away.

There were more "talking points" that actually made some sense.

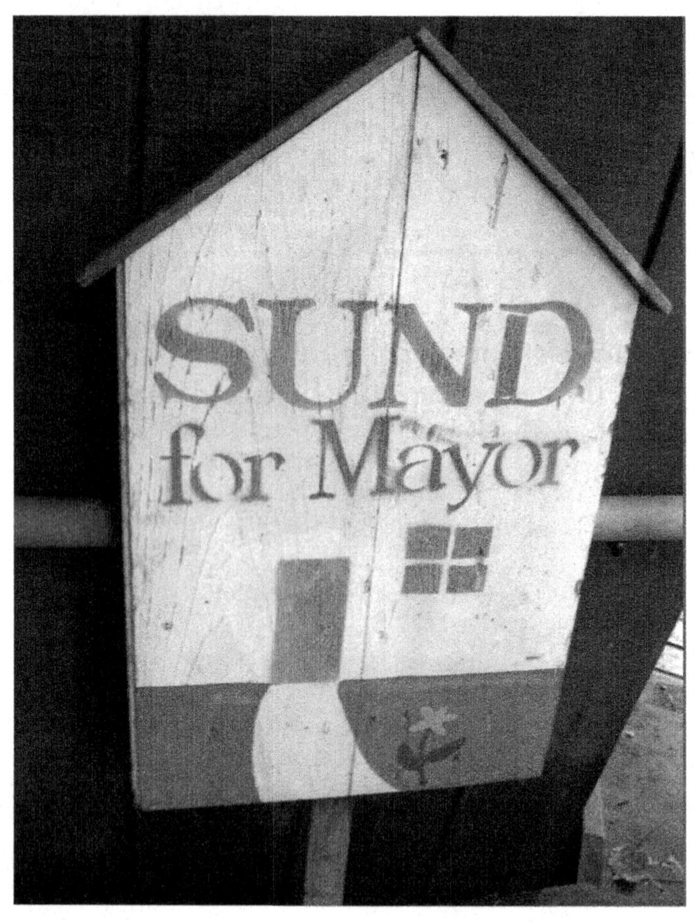

Photo courtesy of **Jim Smith & Janet Saunders.**

Sund's newsletter is supported by quotes from Emerson, Thoreau, Voltaire, Gary Snyder and Wendell Berry. He voiced his opposition to condominiums on the waterfront: "The benefits of a Condo would go to the few. The loss of waterfront would alter the spirit of the town as well as its character." He supported building a Recycling Center, and cleaning up the confused language of the town ordinances. He proposed the formation of a Citizen's Advisory Council made up of townspeople, "to oversee the activities of the Mayor and Council and the various Commissions...Every street (east, west, north, south) will select one person to be a member," with the result that "There will be more room for speaking up and taking part. More room for shared thoughts. And the more open exchange there is, the more satisfaction there will be." To bring together mayor, council and citizens, Robert offered the creation of a community center in Maple Hall, above the old Fire Hall: "It has plenty of space, with pleasant windows facing the channel, and a kitchen as well. The kitchen should be put to use. We could have a pot-luck dinner together, visit, then go on to the formal business." The hall could be further improved by: "Using a small part of the parking lot, plant trees (vine maple!) and flowers...raise the ceiling...Let the Light In." Then, "Once a congenial Center is made, the building will be a treasure-house where we entertain the kind of community events the town has seen in abundance in the past: plays, dances, classes, performances, music, meetings." Although Sund lost the election, these ideals for a center would lend vision to the creation of his Poet's House.

TIM MCNULTY: By Heart

As one of the group of gifted young poets who studied with Theodore Roethke at the University of Washington in the 1950s and 60s, Robert Sund took a different tack. Maybe it was his rural, hardscrabble origins, maybe his gregarious nature, or just plain contrariness. But Robert shunned the academic-teaching track followed by his fellow poets. Instead he kicked around close to home, fishing Southeast Alaska, working the wheat harvest in eastern Washington, washing buses in a Seattle garage. In the process, I think, he became something rare among his generation, a poet of community.

Robert once complained to me that for too many of his peers, poetry became "a concern of the upper middle classes." He rejected that premise completely, and his first book, *Bunch Grass,* gave eloquent voice to the field workers and rural landscapes of eastern Washington's wheat country. Throughout his life, Robert delighted in bringing poetry to his small-town neighbors -- farmers, fishermen, carpenters, waitresses, and backwoods hippies -- as well as to the writers, painters, and sculptors he hung out with in the city.

Robert's readiness with a poem harkened back to his mentor. Roethke challenged all his students to commit poems to memory. "Sing it" became his command regarding any poem his students mentioned in his workshops. Robert and his fellow poets spent late nights memorizing poems by heart. (He told me that James Wright set the bar impossibly high one day by reciting Yeats's masterpiece "Adam's Curse" flawlessly.) Later it was a central part of Robert's practice as a poet to have poems, his and others, ready to give poetic voice to a shared moment, no matter the occasion.

I'm lucky to count a number of poets among my friends. As a young writer, living in the wider orbit of Port Townsend, Washington, during the 70s and 80s, I benefited immensely from the flotilla of poets fetching up to Centrum Foundation's summer workshops at Fort Worden or Copper Canyon Press. There was also the lively younger circle of poets that coalesced around Empty Bowl Press, poets, as Robert would have it, "with mud on their shoes." But I never met a poet for whom the presence of poetry was as vital a part of everyday life as it was for Sund.

He could sing Swedish folk songs with the old timers in the bar at the Lighthouse in La Conner, recite Thomas Tranströmer or Rabbe Enckell for the afternoon crowd at the La Conner Tavern (I've seen pool games come to a halt while Robert held forth), or evoke Bashō or Buson, pausing at the oars while rowing back to his shack on the Skagit estuary, the moon through clouds making a path over the water.

Robert saw poetry as a necessity for everyone, across the board, and he brought poems to government hearings, peace rallies, potlucks, and all-night bonfires. He was a masterful presenter of his poetry; Robert Bly thought him the best in the country at one time. And he was grounded in an oral tradition from his Swedish-speaking days on the family farm in Elma. Robert considered his readings far more important to him than publications. His ability to bring forth a poem that would crystalize and deepen a moment was at the heart of Robert's calling. To my mind, that's the mark of a poet born to the craft.

* * *

Many instances bring that gift to mind. Most vivid among them was a winter afternoon twenty-five or thirty years ago. Robert had come to the Olympic Peninsula for a reading. The next day we were walking the shoreline from Chetzemoka Park to Point Hudson in Port Townsend. An outgoing tide lapped the beach stones, and low clouds shrouded the Sound. The beach was empty. Then figures emerged from the fog; two women stood at the water's edge facing the inlet. As we approached, we saw that they'd launched a small boat of some kind into the water. Closer, we saw a candle and some flowers on the tiny craft, and I recognized one of the two was an old friend.

Janette Force has long held a special role in the Port Townsend community. She helps facilitate ritual, be it a wedding, a coming-of-age or memorial service, or some other passage. I realized that Robert and I had inadvertently wandered into one of these moments. Janette told us her friend's father had died recently. Her friend was grieving, of course, and they were there on the beach to say goodbye. A short distance out on the water, the spirit boat they had fashioned held a prayer along with candle and flowers, and hopefully a portion of Janette's friend's sorrow. It bobbed faintly in the outgoing tide casting a small pool of light over the water.

Robert and I shared condolences and apologized for our intrusion. As I was about to turn to go, Robert asked if he could offer a poem. "Of course," they answered, and into our small circle he recited Juan Ramon Jimenez's remarkable poem, "Oceans."

> I have a feeling that my boat
> has struck, down there in the depths,
> against a great thing.
> And nothing
> happens! Nothing... Silence... Waves...
> --Nothing happens? Or has everything happened,
> and are we standing now, quietly, in the new life?

It was as if the poem looked directly into the heart of the human condition as it expressed itself that moment and gave voice to an insight we all recognized as true.

* * *

Robert's friend Kenneth Rexroth defined the role of the poet as "one who creates sacramental relationships that last always." It's a high bar for poets, especially these days, but one that is rooted in the old bardic tradition. Like Roethke, it was a role Robert took to heart.

Looking back on the encounter years later, Janette is still filled with gratitude. She said Robert's particular gift was "allowing poetry to become the language of our shared experience." And she reminded me of an additional detail about the encounter. Robert later calligraphed two copies of the poem and sent them to her, one for her friend. Decades later, she quotes from it easily. The gift passes on.

"Our fathers / carried us / a long way into the world," Robert wrote in a poem for Sam and Sally Green when Sally lost her father.

> They leave us one day, and die.
> And we carry them
> the rest of the way.

For Sund, poetry was a way to carry our grief, love, joy, friendship. Our aloneness, and the sheer exuberance of being alive and awake to the present. Poems bind us to each other and to those who came before us. Robert saw it in the old classical Chinese poets he loved -- at night with his books when he went "looking for friends in history." And he recognized it in those around him, whether they read the stuff or not.

At his best moments, Robert could "float out / on a sea / of these friendships." At his worst he foundered and shipwrecked on the nearest shore. Somehow, the deeper truths of poetry always returned for him. "A cold morning and slowly growing light," he ended his poem for Sally. "The birds start up / one by one."

SAM AND SALLY GREEN: Memories of Robert Sund

I met Robert for the first time back in the mid-'80s. The very fine poet Tim McNulty introduced me. Robert had come over to Anacortes where Tim and I were both working as poets-in-the-schools to have dinner with us at a Mexican restaurant near the post office. I'd heard Robert read his poems at Centrum, had read *Bunch Grass* with great pleasure, but, though we had many friends in common, we hadn't met.

He brought along four or five new poems to read to Tim and me as we ate. He was gracious, and I could easily see the man behind the poems. He had a working class background that appealed to me, who had been born into a family of loggers and commercial fishers. He also had a sound academic background without any trace of the pedant. It was a good meal.

I remember attending his 60th birthday party somewhere in La Conner. Wherever it was had an upstairs that friends of Robert had reserved for the occasion. It was crowded with well-wishers. Robert was happy, and kept clasping his hands together and bowing to friends who offered tribute after tribute. I recited a Yeats poem, I remember, as a gift. Robert smiled, put his hands together, and bowed very low.

Sally and I only published a few of Robert's poems, one in *Hands Joining,* a collection of poems done in each poet's particular calligraphic style, and then in *Eleven Skagit Poets,* a letterpressed anthology of work by poets living in the Skagit Valley. Robert admired Sally's expertise at the press and her facility with design, something about which he had strong opinions.

Not long after publication of *Eleven Skagit Poets,* a reading was arranged in Rockport that included Jean Haight (Hallingstad), Clifford Burke, Robert and me. I was helping to coach the middle school wrestling team for Anacortes then, and I was in Burlington that day for a match, so Clifford and the others stopped to pick me up and we headed off to Rockport in two cars. We hit snow, of course, and it turned treacherous. We stopped both cars to get out and talk things over, but we voted to keep going. Finally got to town all right, though it was slow going. The reading was in a restaurant/tavern. The restaurant part was separated only by a sort of interior half-wall, or fence, so that families could legally share the space with the tavern group. We had dinner (spaghetti) and then read our poems, one after the other, to a small, but very enthusiastic audience. Robert wanted to go last in the line-up. By the time it was his turn, though, some of the guys at the tavern bar had gotten a little rowdy, and they began heckling Robert, who made the mistake of trying to engage them, win them over to our side. It didn't work, and he was very frustrated by the time he sat down, not—I think—even finishing all the poems he had in mind. He couldn't talk about anything else on the long drive back. I was just happy to have read early on, getting away pretty much unmarked. Robert, though, was used to being able to address such crowds and win them over. He brooded about it, I can see now, trying to figure out what he might have done, already preparing in his head what to try on the next such occasion, while I was more inclined to figure out how to *avoid* another occasion like that.

Over the years we occasionally encountered Robert in La Conner or, after his move, at his snug little house in Anacortes, which he likened to living in the discipline of a boat's space. Occasionally we received in the mail a wind-card or a calligraphed sheet with a poem on it in Robert's distinctive calligraphy. We exchanged letters, as well. After Sally's father died, Robert sent Sally a beautiful poem he'd written for her and then scribed out on a large sheet of paper. It was a typically generous thing for Robert to do, and it meant a great deal to Sally.

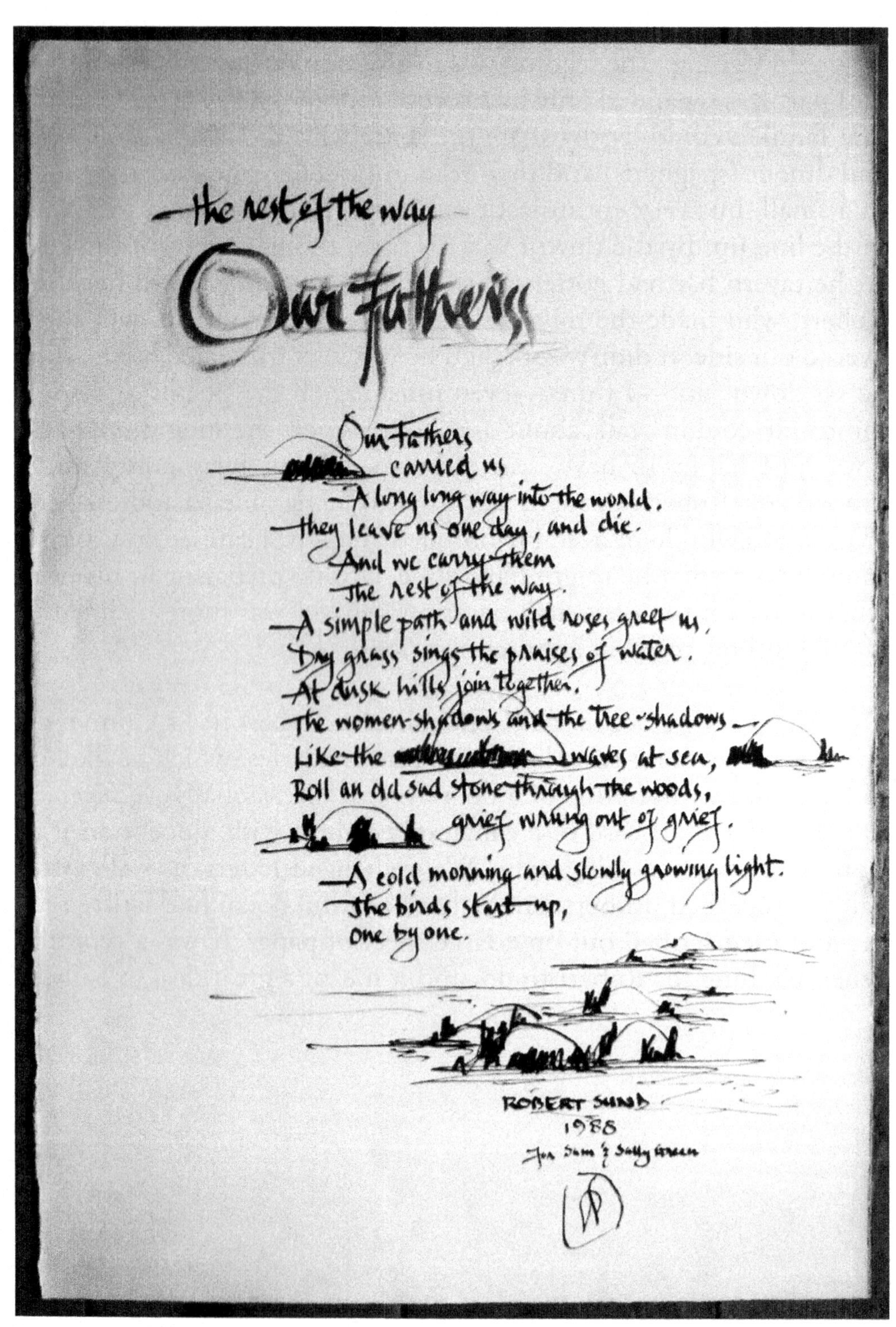

Courtesy of **Sam and Sally Green.**

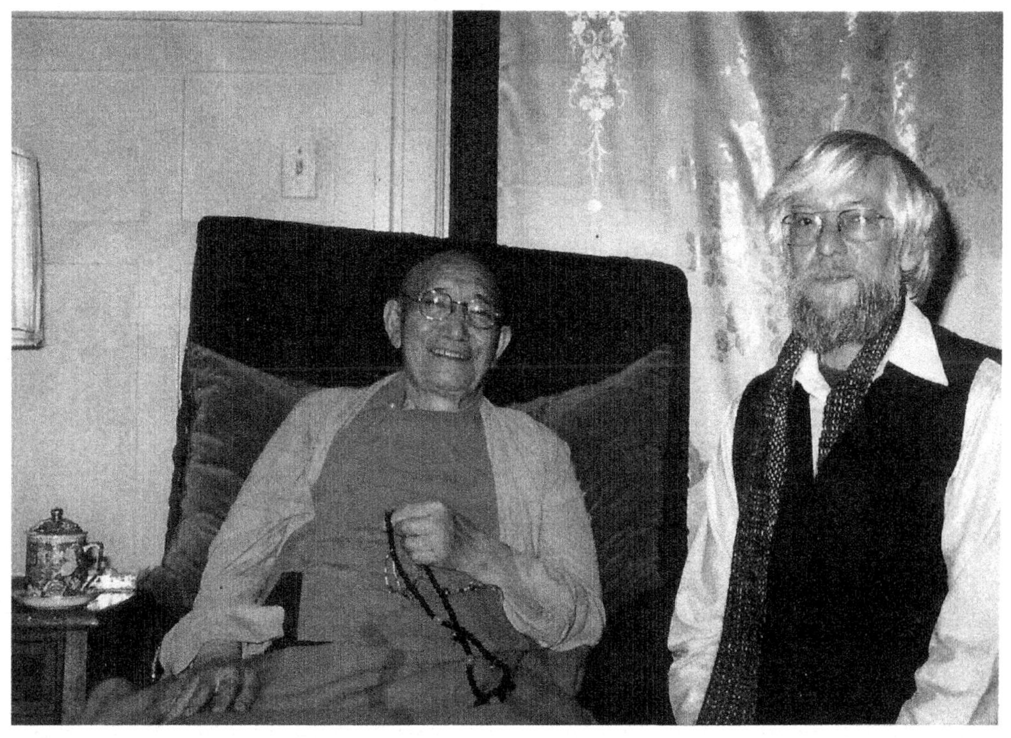

Photograph taken at the Tibetan Center residence in Seattle on January 20, 1986, at a send-off party for Deshung Rinpoche, who was leaving for the newly built monastery of his lineage in Nepal.

ROBERT SUND: In the early 1970s in Seattle, Deshung Rinpoche gave me my Tibetan name: Nyawang Tön Yö. Ever after I have tried to honor his being, his generous spirit and his kindness to me. Before he left Seattle I gave Rinpoche some of my poems at his house. He said, "We think this is the highest form of poetry in Tibet."

The Fishtown Woods comprised 66 acres of old growth mixed fir, spruce, hemlock and big-leaf maples between Dodge Valley and the artist's community of Fishtown. Wildlife was prolific, and the undisturbed beauty of the woods was inspiration to many of the artists who lived in Fishtown. After more than a year of protests, the woods were ultimately clear-cut, and many of the Fishtown "shacks" were torn down by the landowner. Robert Sund's letter, dated December 22, 1987, was written before the eventual clear-cutting and destruction of Fishtown in 1988.

Robert Sund
Box 92
La Conner,
Washington
98257

Mr. Rick Cooper
Asst. Regional Mgr.
Wash. Dept. of Natural Resources
919 North TOWNSHIP
Sedro Woolley,
Washington 98284

December 22 1987

Dear Mr. Cooper –

I would like to see a sensible solution to the "Fishtown" woods crisis. It is fairly clear to most people in the vicinity of Dodge Valley that this particular logging venture is mistaken and misplaced endeavor.

Those of us who have had long association with this forest know the kinds of creatures who depend on its being left as it is, untouched.

We can all leave this woods alone for deer and fox and coyote, for all that live in burrows at the foot of trees for those birds feeding on huckleberries, and those higher up crying to the heavens

From high windy branches, the heron,
the eagle the owl.
And down in the tidal marsh so near,
where the river gives itself slowly to
the bay and the islands.
Thousands of geese and swans and ducks,
numberless small birds scattering songs like seed over the estuary
and thousands of fish passing by on
their way upriver to home....

The woods, the River, the Bay; the whole
great Estuary of the Skagit – it's a
great wide table where many creatures
live and eat, and gather to sing
their songs. It needs to be left as
it is.
A way can be found.
Let's stop the logging now and work together
on a solution that will be considerate
and just.
This part of the valley should be left.

Hasn't the Skagit River been declared a "wild & scenic" river?

When are we going to stand by our words? The time has come for us as a people living here to be a part of this jewel of life, and speak for the river and the valley — now, before it slips away once and for all.

Just Speak!

CHRISTINE WARDENBURG-SKINNER:

In 1987, when I was then affiliated with the Burlington Little School as its Director, I asked Robert if he would co-teach a children's art/ poetry camp during the summer. He agreed, and we did this for four years, offering four, one-week sessions each summer. The last summer, in 1990, I had applied for, and received, one of the first Artist Trust Gap Grants, using those funds to offer scholarships to children who could not afford to pay for camp. That session was huge and held at Edison Elementary here in Edison, with four instructors. Robert and I had something of a falling out after that year and I continued on (to this very summer) offering Patterns in Nature (the name Robert and I chose) for the 29th summer.

Robert designed a beautiful flyer for our camp, and I recently unearthed the original from myriad piles of artwork in my studio. It is a bit tattered, but mostly intact, and I would be more than happy to share that with you.

Robert was a marvelous model and teacher. It was wonderful for the children, aged 5-12, to see this white-haired poet cavorting up mountain sides, at the beach, in the fields, holding forth with poetry, song, and working side-by-side with the kids making art.

Our sessions included daily field trips, book-making, artworks using a variety of art mediums (clay, batik on cloth, water color, chalk pastels and charcoal) to represent the many locations we visited. We were offered a van from a local car dealer which we picked up on Monday morning and returned on Friday afternoon, always washed and vacuumed by us. We planned our curriculum together and often asked guests to share the week, such as a local geologist or botanists, to better explain the flora and landscape to the children. The sessions always ended with an art exhibition of the children's work for parents and families on Friday afternoon, a schedule that continues to this day.

To watch Robert holding forth as a poet, reciting and sharing, follow his creation of beloved mandalas, always creating his own wonderful art, was to offer a unique example to young children where age does not matter, and allowed a kind of wonderment for their young eyes.

THE BURLINGTON LITTLE SCHOOL

SUMMER SESSION

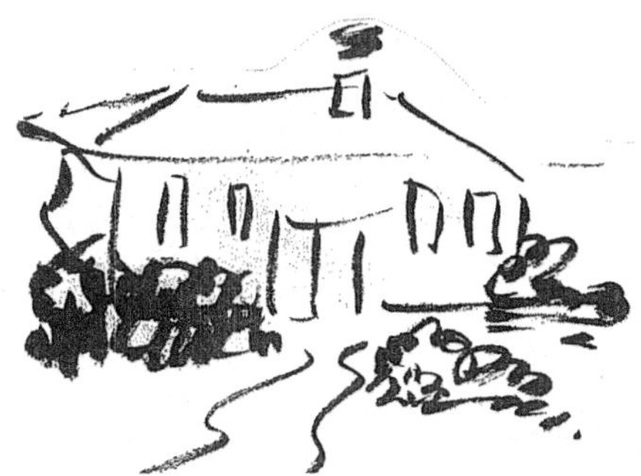

Any time of year is a good time to observe patterns in nature, but summer with its special enchantments lies just ahead and it brings us more fully into the picture:– we not o[nly] observe, we participate. The weather stimulates us a[s] ... as the sun opens a patch of clover in a grassy field.

So we'll go to the meadows – by lakes, by streams, by ... We'll learn about roots and stems, flowers and weeds, fish and birds. We'll get to know creatures living from sea level on up into the mountains.

Each of the four one-week sessions will focus on special topics and particular places. Field trips and classroom study will be brought together in the Book-Making Project, a gathering and centering device through each session. All sessions will include poetry and music – and drawing, with special emphasis on patterns and relationships in nature.

WEEK 1: July 6–10th

LAKES AND PONDS. Field trips to Fragrance Lake and Chuckanut fossil sites. Marsh ponds in Cascade foothills. SPEAKER:– Naturalist/Botanist – Tree and plant identification. SPECIAL CRAFT: grass painting, flower pressing. HALF-DAY TRIP: – Padilla Bay.

WEEK 2: July 13–17th

MOUNTAIN MEADOWS. Mt. Baker high meadows, gathering of plant specimens for Book. Stories and legends. SPEAKER:– National Forest Park Ranger. SPECIAL CRAFT:– Batik based on mountain experience. 1/2 DAY TRIP:– Mt. Erie and the eagle sculpture.

WEEK 3:– July 20–24th

SALTWATER BEACHES: Field trip to Padilla Bay, Breazeale Interpretive Center – the Estuary & upland woods. Whidbey Island beach at Ebey's Landing. SPEAKER:– Marine Biologist. SPECIAL CRAFT:– weaving, incorporating materials gathered from trips. 1/2 DAY TRIP:– Wooden boat builder, Anacortes.

WEEK 4: July 27–31st

FRESHWATER TIDAL MARSH. Field trips to Fir Island Wildfowl Preserve, and Rosario Head beach. SPEAKER:– Waterfowl expert, wood carver. SPECIAL CRAFT: pottery and brush-painting. 1/2 DAY TRIP:– visit to potter's studio.

The Staff:-

CHRISTINE WARDENBURG teaches and directs the Burlington Little School. She is a certified K-8 teacher, holds a BFA in fine art and an M.A. in Art Education. She has worked as a studio potter and has taught children's art classes in clay, drawing, sculpture and batik. Ms. Wardenburg is a certified life-guard and CPR.
ROBERT SUND, poet and painter, is the author of two books of poems: BUNCH GRASS (U. of W. Press), and ISH RIVER (North Point, San Francisco) which won the Washington State Governor's Award in 1984. He was the first poet-in-residence in the Seattle Schools and has taught here in the valley through the Artists-in-the-schools program. Music and calligraphy are related interests. He has written two books for children (as yet unpublished): WHERE THE ANIMALS WEAR SHOES, and THE GREAT CORN MAIDEN'S FULL MOON PARTY.

TWO ASSISTANTS will accompany the Staff at all times. STUDENTS provide the own lunches and snacks. Each student should bring a backpack, sun hat, swim suit, and wear clothing and shoes appropriate for all outings.

CLASSES will be limited to sixteen students. The minimum age will be eight, with exceptions by special arrangement. HOURS: Monday through Friday, 9 A.M.-3 P.M.
Each Session:- $65.00 plus a $5.00 materials fee.
Please return the Registration form below. Phone: 755-9595.

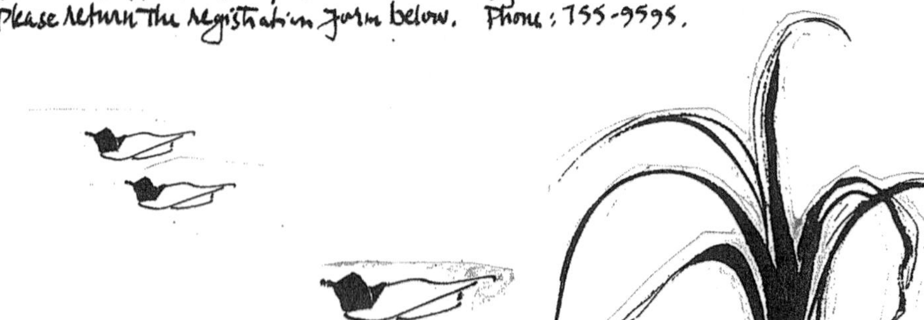

REGISTRATION

Child's Name: ____________________ Age: ________
Parent's Name: ____________________
Address: ____________________
____

Home Phone: ____________ Work Phone: ____________
Emergency Name: ____________ Phone: ____________
CHECK BOX(ES) TO INDICATE
WHICH SESSION YOU WISH TO RESERVE: WEEK 1 ☐ WEEK 2 ☐
WEEK 3 ☐ WEEK 4 ☐

BRAD KILLION:

Robert and I became very good friends during the last 13 years of his legendary life. Playing music together was one of our favorite pastimes (I play guitar). We performed live on a handful of occasions, sometimes interspersed with his poetry readings. A few recordings exist, though of course I wish there were more. I have a music book of songs we compiled along the way. I arranged some pretty elaborate pieces, many of which he absorbed with enthusiasm (many recopied in his stylish, calligraphic handwriting). Keeping rhythm was his biggest challenge, but he improved more and more as time went on.

Yes, the autoharp still exists (actually, there are 2 but only the new one is really playable at this time). Once in a while we take it out and let it ring. Robert was a phenomenal individual. I miss him dearly, often.

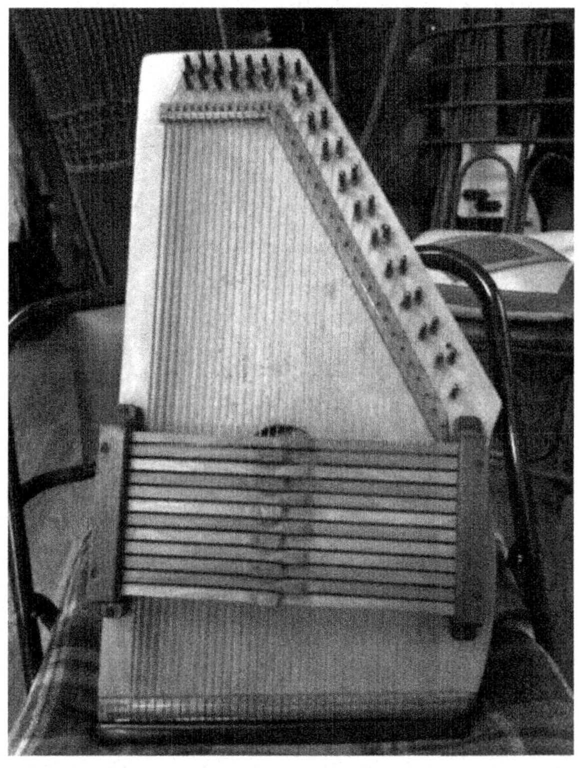

Robert Sund's autoharp today, photo courtesy of **Brad Killion.**

BARB HATHAWAY:

I first met Robert in 1989 in a community education class at Skagit Community College. Over the years I would stop by and visit Robert and have a cup of tea after work or on a weekend. He would read me a new poem, sing me a song or play me some music he was working on. Robert had a nickname for himself, Humphrey Klinker. I worked in Mount Vernon and he would call me up at work every couple of weeks and give me a shopping list for groceries he needed for dinner. He would say "Hi Barb, this is Humphrey Klinker calling and could you please stop at the co-op on your way home and get me some groceries?" The thing to note is that he only referred to himself as Humphrey Klinker when he was feeling lonely or insignificant, and that usually he wanted some company at dinner.

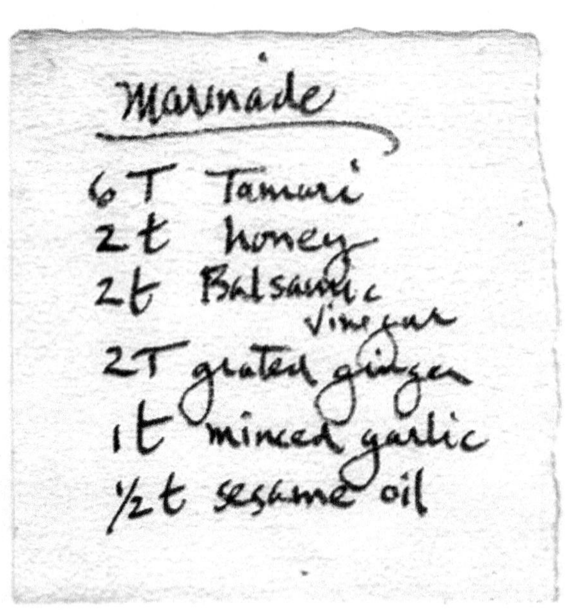
Marinade

6T Tamari
2t honey
2t Balsamic vinegar
2T grated ginger
1t minced garlic
½t sesame oil

GEORGIA JOHNSON: Robert Sund

My friendship with Robert revolved around my ability to make a pretty good loaf of wheat bread and my Danish pastries, particularly a strawberry and cream cheese Danish. I never had the courage to ask him for any special mentoring, but we did spend a few hours poring over poems by Galway Kinnell, Gary Snyder, and others, listening to the sounds, the line breaks, the movement.

Of course I had the opportunity to hear and see him deliver, I'd never describe it as reciting or reading, his work in public. This was in the long bardic tradition. Robert could move you, sometimes to the point of cracking ribs, he could get into your heart with his words.

In *Bunch Grass* he writes in #7
"Rule out everything arbitrary, money, happiness, the future."
I had to look up and ponder the word "arbitrary".
"Capricious, un-democratic, tyrannical".
This reminds me of what I think was some of his philosophy, that he knew to be moved by spirit rather than economy or culture, that spirit came first and those things came after. Clearly he rejected our culture of "things". And yet his care for things of his domain is legendary.

Robert's poverty. Many friends were awed by his ability to live without a paycheck, without responsibilities. In my mind he didn't take on responsibilities he couldn't handle, wouldn't forget. He was responsible for his simply crafted life. He had debts with people, neighbors, not institutions. He traded in words and beauty. He might convince you to drive him anywhere, and the payoff was a grand story, a song, and wind letters later.

He was known for his way of making a beautiful living space out a pile of boards or driftwood. Everything useful. Making things that serve. Read *Shack Medicine.*

Robert made maps. "The Hall of Light" is a map towards spirit, a song about a pen, my favorite to read out loud.

JOAN CROSS:

I owned a parking lot in La Conner on which I wanted to paint a labyrinth for early morning walkers and have some thoughtful poetry scattered around the curving lines. When I asked Robert if he would allow me to use some of his short insight poems, I didn't know how particular he was about the surface on which his poetry was printed. He would agonize over which rice paper to use, what font would be best for a certain poem, how to space the words and lines. He was so precise in those details it almost paralyzed him from publishing. So his response to my request was: "And you want to paint it where?...on black top? I don't think my poems are up to that!"

A Painting can be a place we give feeling to: over a time it's a place where we leave our thoughts with it (like something placed in a nook) – we come back and find nourishment in it: – We are involved in the ritual of seeing — the painting looks back. its silence is what gives a home to all we bring to it. A treasurehouse, and, in a way, mysteriously empty.

Not all paintings are like this. Not all paintings are so useful!

Robert Genn
July 1988

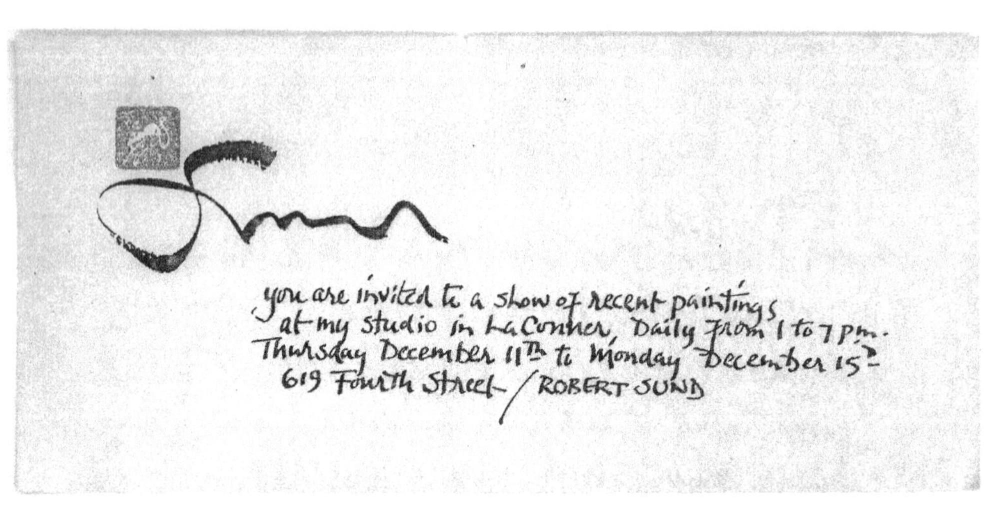
you are invited to a show of recent paintings
at my studio in LaConner, Daily from 1 to 7 p.m.
Thursday December 11th to Monday December 15th
619 Fourth Street / ROBERT SUND

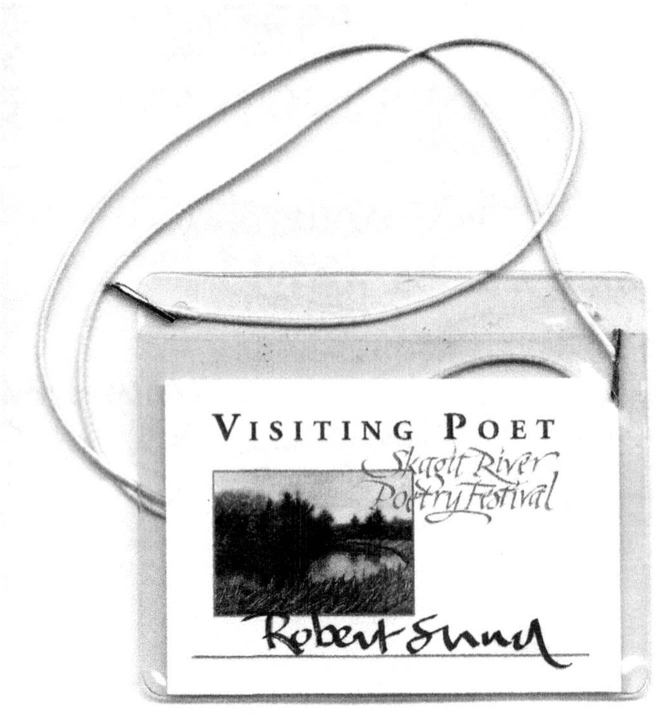

ROBERT SUND: Previously Unpublished Excerpts from the "Taos Manuscript" (April 3-May 8, 1991)

For companionship reading I have two new books from North Point Press, cloth bound: *The Practice of the Wild,* signed by Snyder on the night of the Berkeley reading at a festive celebration afterwards at Black Oak Books, & Wendell Berry's signed *What Are People For?* So those, plus Bankei, and Berry's *Collected Poems* have kept me company.

*

It's funny how the archaic routines fit so well wherever you are. By the time I'm up, Arthur and Ginny are at the Apple Tree Restaurant and Margaret is off to Taos Valley School, 4th grade. There is only Osa, the dog, and me. Put on the coffee, put raisins in the mushwater to plump, roll some Three Castles, wash face, pour coffee, and go out on the porch and sit, and read some Berry poems interspersed with trips back to the kitchen, three slow cups. Then put the co-op oats in with the raisins.

*

Outside now on the warmest sunny days the choir practice begins in the new-leafed-out cottonwoods and lilacs. Some of these will maybe be up in the Skagit before me. The goldfinches are well hidden in the green-yellow cottonwood foliage. It's not the tree we have up home. It's branched out more like a silver maple, and the leaves are smaller, with clusters of small round pods (about the size of a lentil, but a glowing light-green) — these fly in the gusty winds and fall everywhere, some far from the trees they arrived in.

The trillers are red-wing blackbirds. The exotic is the magpie. A good sized bird, wearing the glossy blue-black, with a white vest underwing — they swoop through the trees, kind of looping and floating. The song is not much, more of a slightly elongated declaration. But very exotic. I think the long tail feathers must give it its distinct flight.

*

This is a vast mountain high-desert plateau. The distances are clear and absorbing. The eye alone finds much to wonder at, seeing how the earth was made and then changed and made again, according to the slow old motions that every ten thousand years leaves another deep layer unclothed and open to the sun and the wind, the snow and ice. The sage, the fragrant piñon arroyos, river canyons cut deep in the grassy plateaus — a sudden drop-off to the river, the sloping fields of rock-fall. Some of the rocks making their way to the river, one more oblivion to go and they'll be there, where the country of stone meets the country of water, and the choir is fully aubible.

*

The mind rolls along.
It's lucky to
catch a few meaningful
essences.

There is no such thing as
a small rain and a big bucket.
It's always
the other way around.

*

A gift emerges

It comes like an inward light
that flows into a person
so the body fills up
and the person
and the body become an
invisible cup.

A grey cup if the weather is grey.
A blue cup if the sky is blue.

Light inside,
light outside.

Into its clarity
anything might fall.

In its presence
the sky
finds itself at home.

There is room for stars that
have fallen,
and
for
long praises,
for lost prayers to be
gathered,
and sent back into the world.

*

I have only one theme now.

Find the right way to be with
the beauty of things.
Revere it
increasingly.

"Point them directly to nature,"
said Arthur Greeno today,
quoting Bodhidharma
from long ago.

What can I say
to set things
right?

TIM MCNULTY:

In his later years, Robert Sund turned more and more to the work of the Japanese haiku masters. It was Robert's practice to stay up nights with his calligraphy pen and a pot of green tea and rework translations of Issa, Buson, Bashō and others. Robert didn't read Japanese, but worked from a range of scholarly translations in English as well as transliterations of the Japanese. He called the process "bringing friends over," adapting the poems into a more American idiom.

ERICA PICKETT:

I once asked him about that because his second language was Swedish. The family which adopted him spoke Swedish at home and his accent was good because of that. No, he explained, he doesn't speak any of the Asian languages. What he did was to alter the rather deplorable translations which existed in order to make them poetic. And then he would check with some of his Japanese-speaking friends who told him that he had indeed captured the essence of the original in his "translations." It seemed to work and I never have heard any Japanese folks complain about Robert's version of these ancient poems. Ingenious.

TIM MCNULTY:

The "windletters" are longish strips of heavy art stock on which Sund calligraphed short poems and translations, black on white, usually with a small red Chinese seal. He'd punch holes in the ends, tie feathers or beads or bells onto them, and hang them vertically. They'd blow lightly with any stirring of the air. His original idea was to sell them, but he ended up giving most of them away.

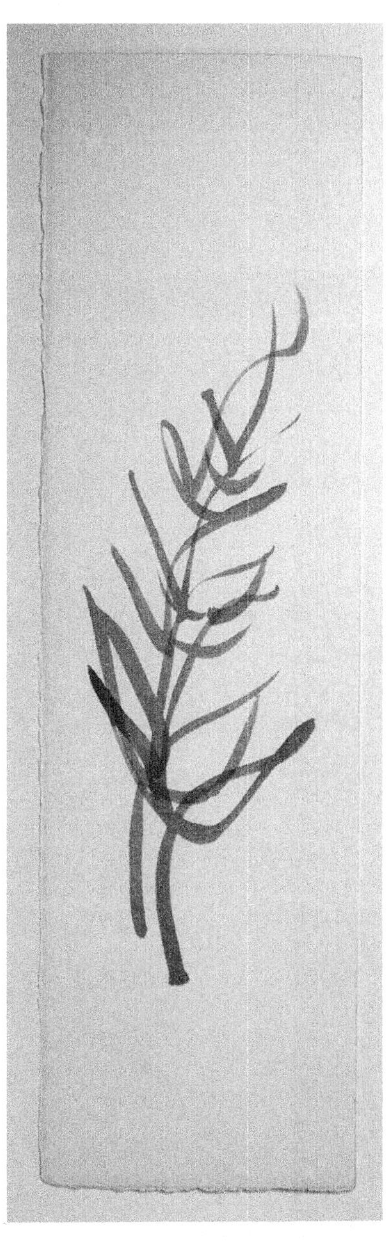

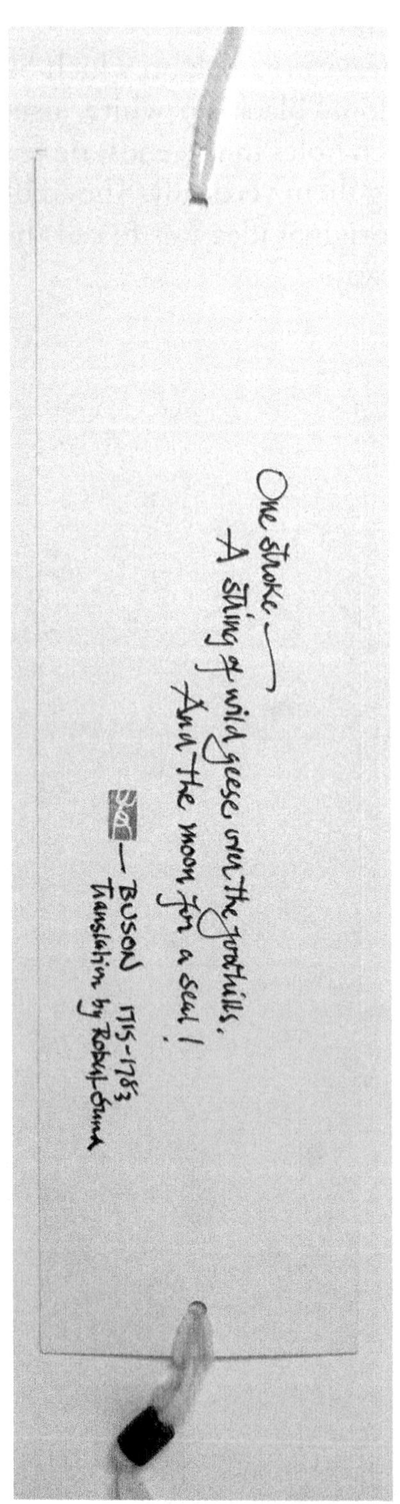
One stroke —
A string of wild geese over the foothills,
And the moon for a seal!
— BUSON 1715-1783

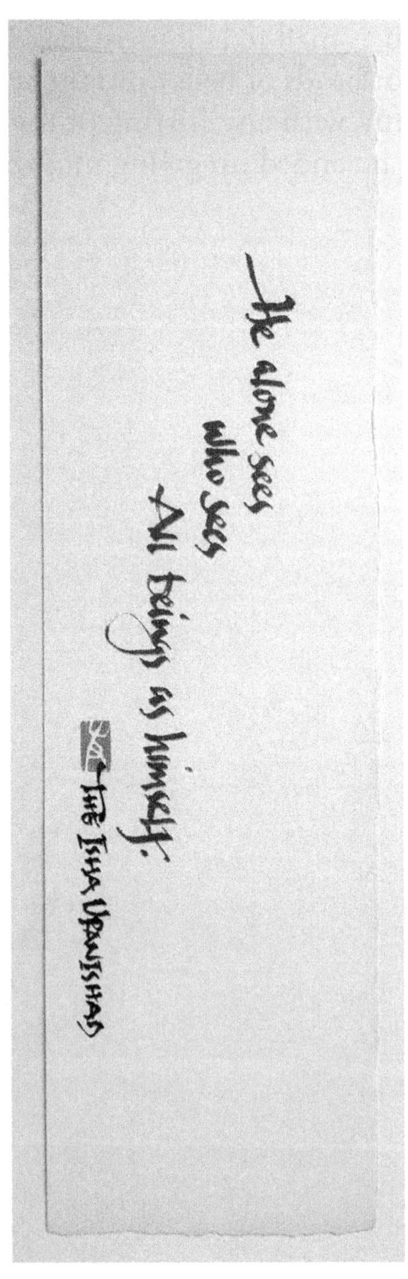
He alone sees
who sees
All beings as himself.
— THE ISHA UPANISHADS

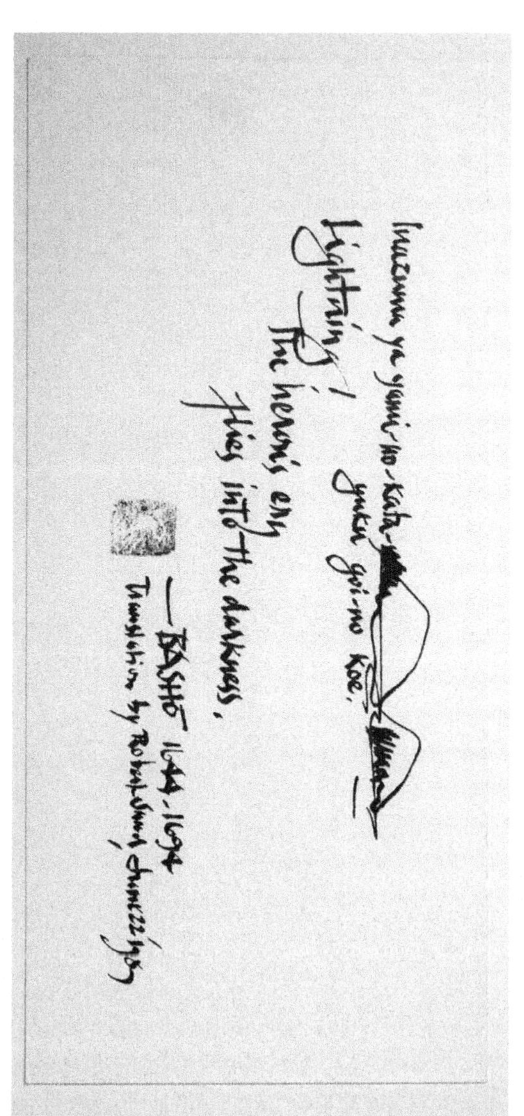

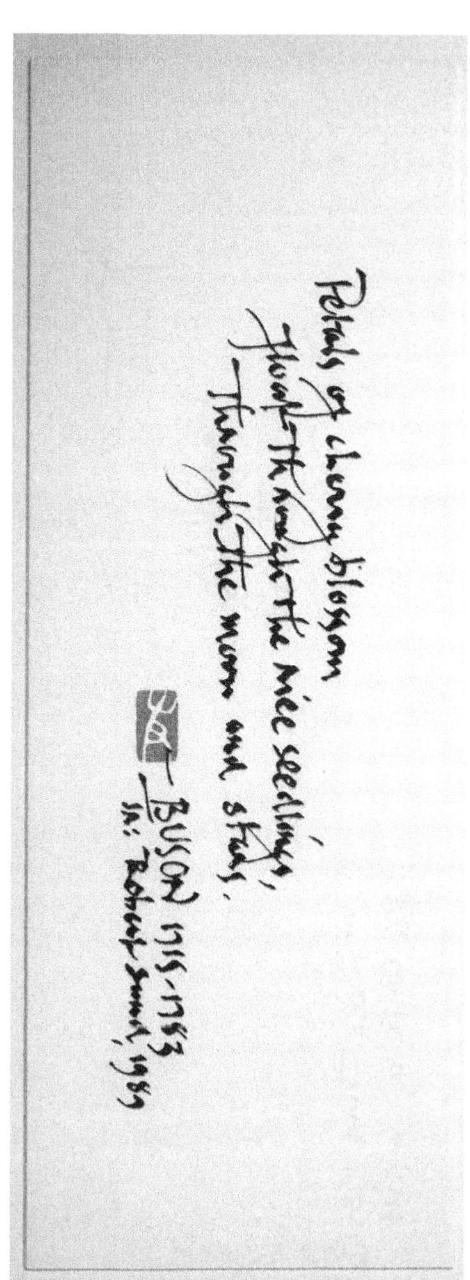

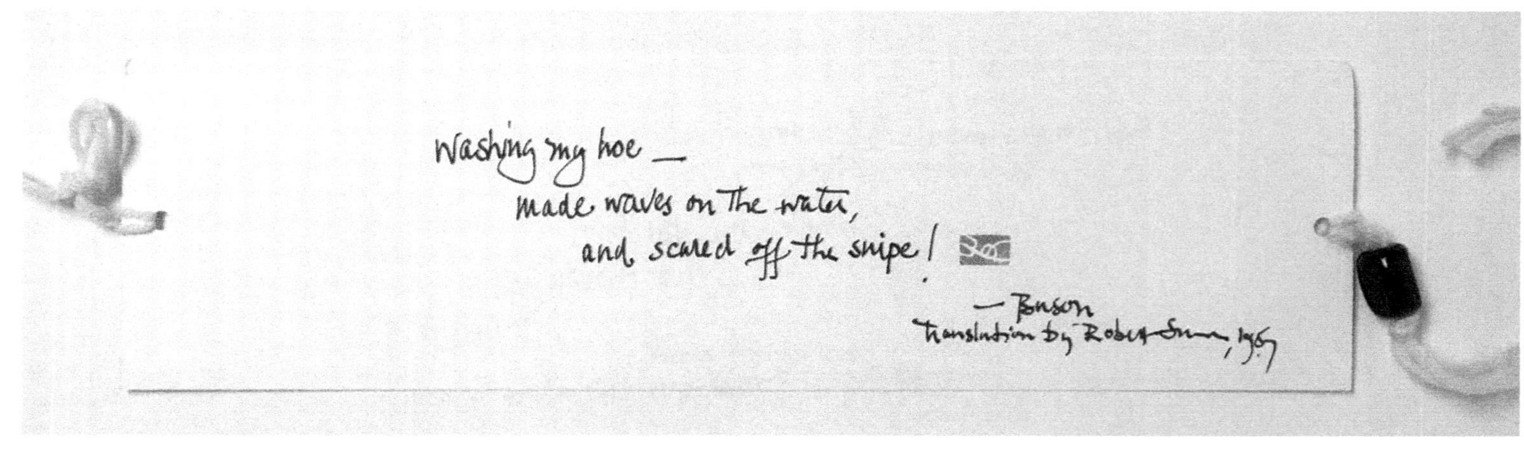

Poetry:
How white
The white camelia!

— Robert Sund, 1987
(after Onitsura, 1660-1738)

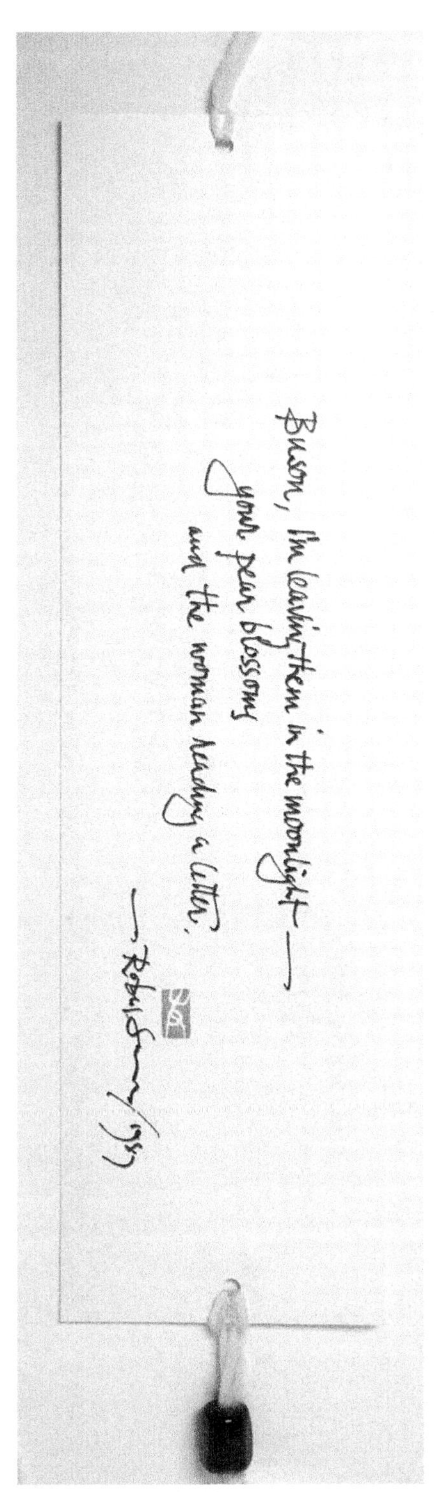
Buson, I'm leaving them in the moonlight —
your pear blossoms
and the woman reading a letter.

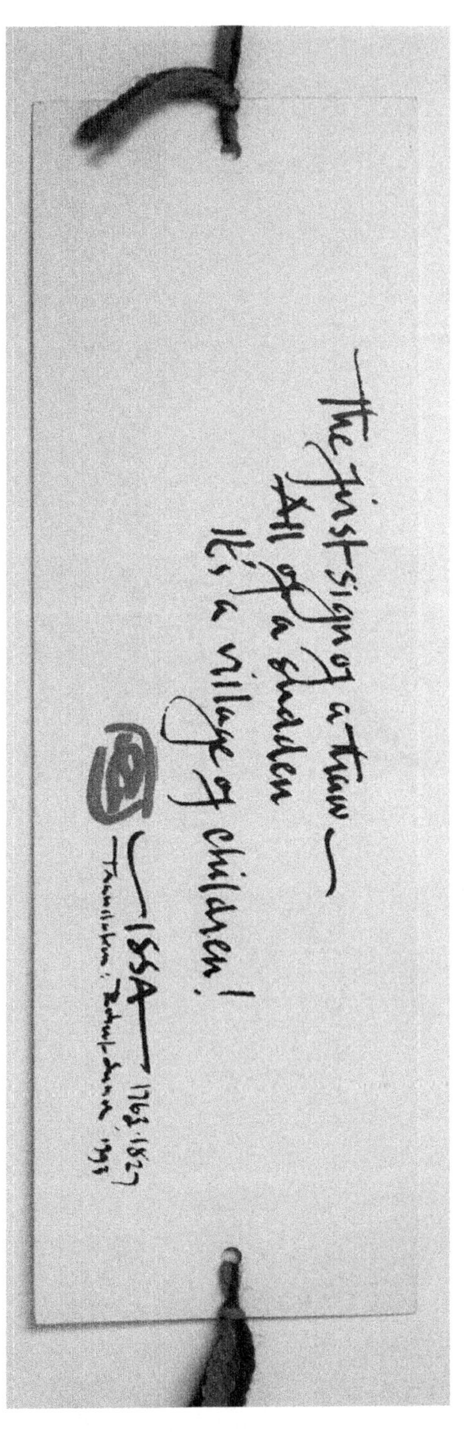
The first sign of a thaw —
All of a sudden
It's a village of children!
— ISSA —
1763-1827

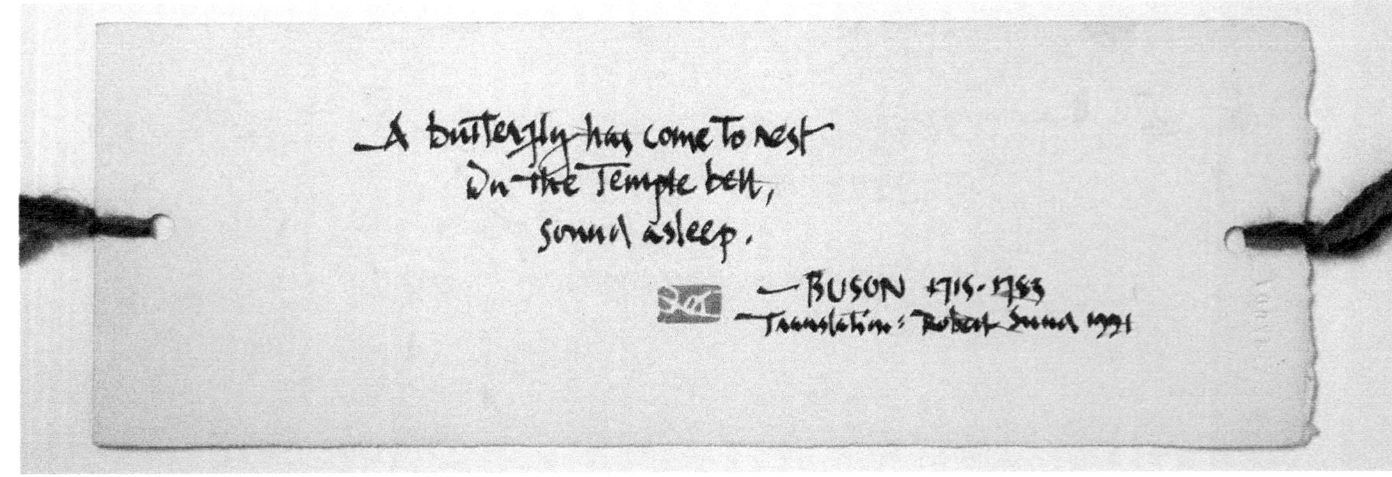
A butterfly has come to rest
On the temple bell,
sound asleep.
— BUSON 1716-1783
Translation: Robert Sund 1991

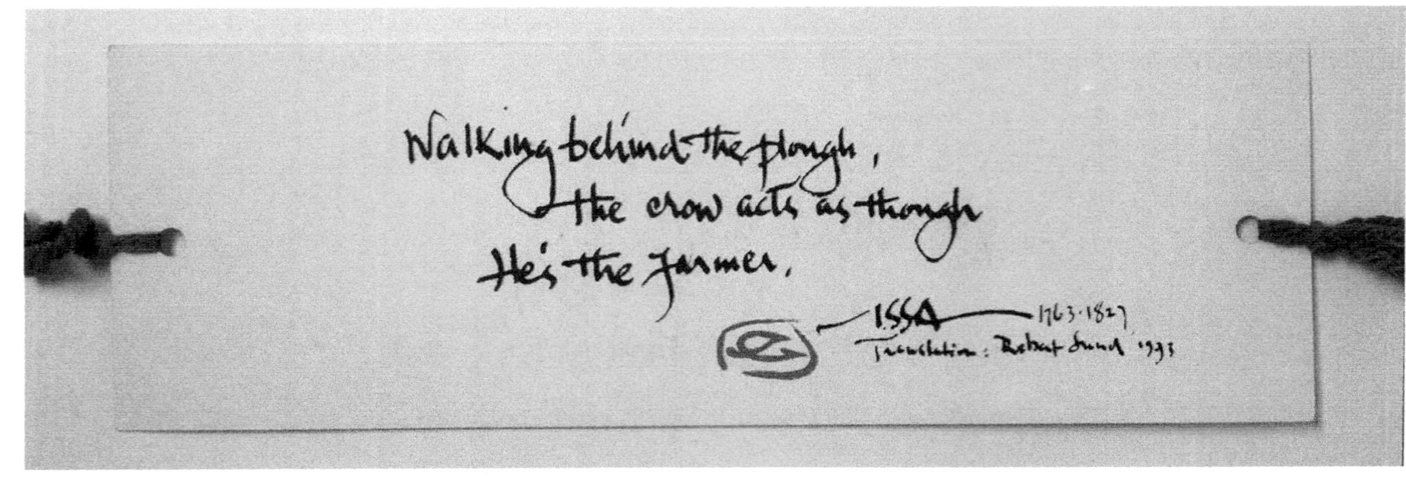
Walking behind the plough,
the crow acts as though
he's the farmer.
— ISSA 1763-1827
Translation: Robert Sund 1993

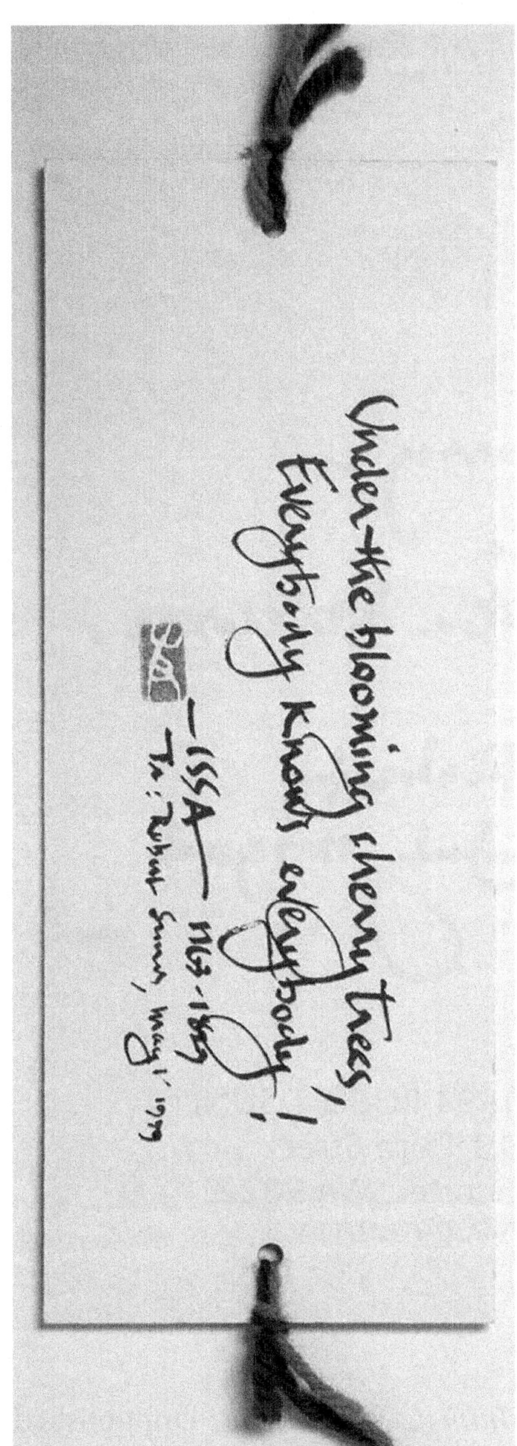
Under the blooming cherry trees,
Everybody knows everybody!
—ISSA—

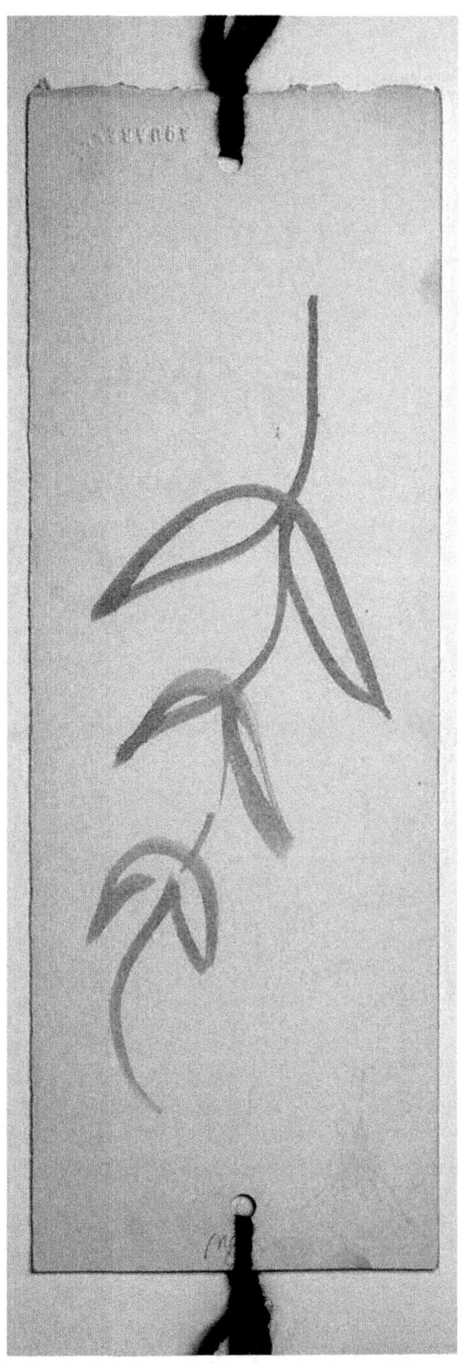

WHERE
the ANIMALS
WEAR SHOES

poems for children

by ROBERT SUND

For Bob & Mary —
Among the
other blossoms.

— Robert,
July 12 1994

1013 Third Street
Anacortes, WA 98221
(206) 299-8011

ROBERT SUND: *Where the Animals Wear Shoes.* Unpublished manuscript, 10 poems for children: Turtle, Pig, Turkey, Walrus, Lark, Cow, Hippopotamus, Elephant and Hen, Giraffe, Shoes.

WALRUS

The Walrus in the rocking chair
        Has a most melancholy air.

He tried to find slippers
For all four of his flippers

        But only found one pair!

SHOES

Next to feet,
What a shoe likes most
Is just another shoe.

I'll tell you how I know:
Wherever you see them go,
Whatever the weather,
They're always together.

        Down the street
                Or up the stairs,
        You always see them
                Walk in pairs!

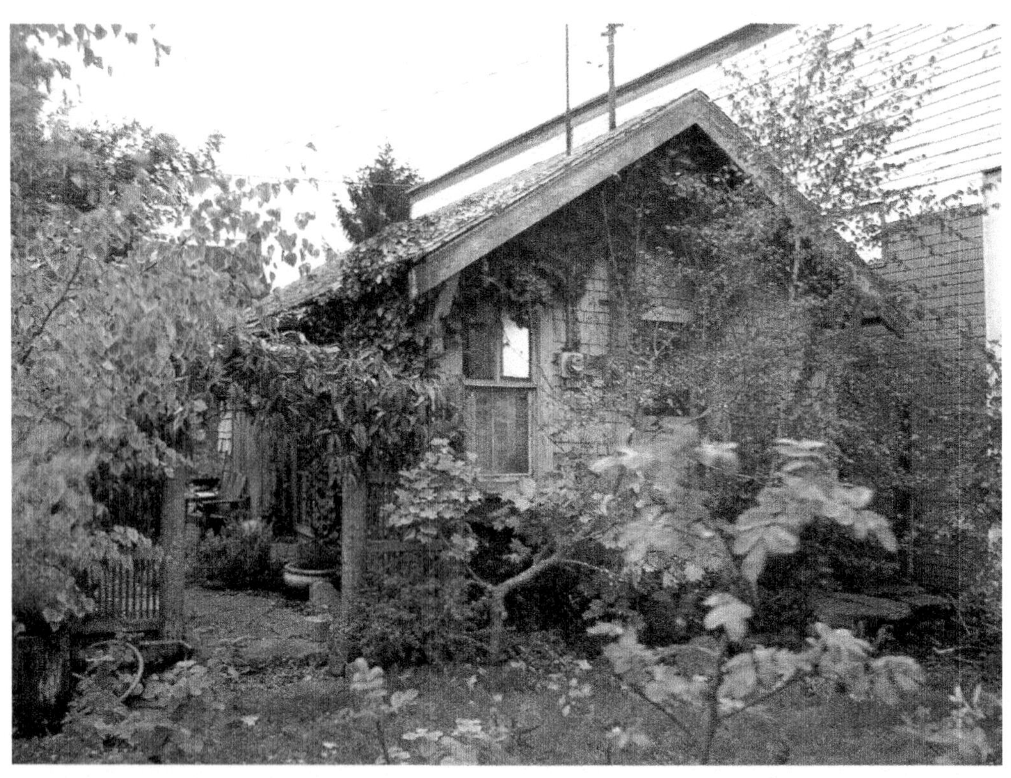

Robert's final house in Anacortes, surrounded by garden. The building to the right is Flounder Bay Boat Lumber. Photo by **Chuck Easton.**

ERICA PICKETT:

I had met Robert through my friend Ron Moe back in about 1965. Ron worked at KRAB radio and Robert had a poetry show on the air. And I think Ron may have spent some time at Fishtown with Robert. Anyway, my husband Bob and I moved to Anacortes in 1971, back when the billboard went up in Seattle saying "Will the last person leaving please turn out the lights." We found work refinishing boats here. Robert and Charlie Krafft showed up at our house out at Lake Campbell one day with a beautiful broadside they had collaborated on. It became faded and fly-specked on my wall. Then we lost track of Robert for most of the years he lived out at Fishtown and LaConner.

Our business became Flounder Bay Boat Lumber at the corner of Third and O Avenue in Anacortes. As it had grown we had been able to buy up the adjacent lots, one of which had a little shack on it. It was in really tough shape, but it was rented out when we purchased the property and the tenant remained there until her death. Then one of our employees rented it for a while and left it somewhat the worse for wear. We decided not to try to rent it again because we didn't have the time and energy to invest.

So here comes Robert one day in about 1994 and he is without a place to live. He asked about the shack and we offered it up "as is, where is." Brad Killion and Andy McConnell, now both members of the Poet's House board, helped quite a bit to shore up the floor in the bathroom and make other repairs to render the place more livable. After about a year we did charge Robert $85/month which covered the water bill and the taxes on the lot. That was his last home and he kept the most beautiful garden there. My husband Bob always teased him that his house was going to wind up on the cover of "Shack Beautiful."

I was trying to think of a story which might be good to include but I am not sure I really have one.

Once I was out in a speed boat on Lake Union with Robert and some of his friends. He was drinking a beer and, when it was finished, he lobbed the empty bottle into the lake with abandon and a big laugh. A few seconds went by and he became deeply repentant and we had to turn around and collect the floating bottle. That was Robert: an enchanting mixture of joyous impulse and conservative duty to the earth and to his friends. He was always very generous with his work. Tim McNulty remarked that Robert would immediately begin handing out copies of his latest work to all his friends as soon as it left the printer. Tim said, "What a business plan!"

Robert's dream for the Trust board he created was that we would somehow create a house designed in the tradition of the water tower from his grandfather's farm. He drew it for our logo and I attach it for you.

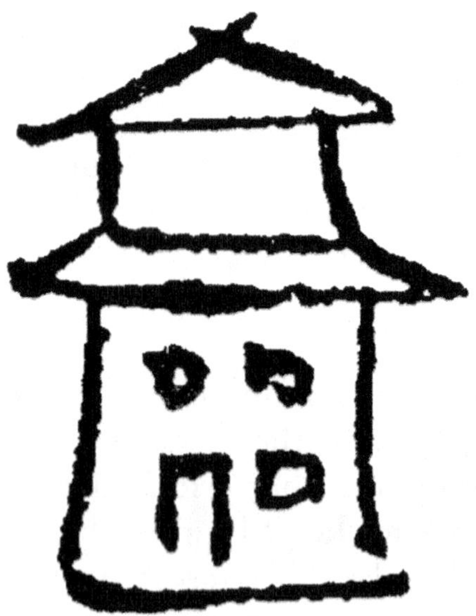

The Poet's House would be the residence of a poet, a potter and a calligrapher. They would inspire each other and would teach in the schools. It is a remarkable dream and one which would be entirely practical if Robert were alive to be the poet and genial host. The Trust board, some of whom had rented to artists over the years, decided that our first task would be to make sure that Robert's poems were not lost and that is why the series of books has occupied us.

Robert was a perfectionist and this caused problems for printers and publishers. A friend of his once offered to underwrite the printing of a chapbook for him and Robert very excitedly decided that it would be printed on bamboo paper. He lined up another friend who was going to China to find just the perfect paper. She returned with a handful of samples and the perfect paper was ordered. So all of this took many months, if not years. Then when Robert received the proof of the little book he took one look and said, "It's not right." And that was the end of that particular chapbook.

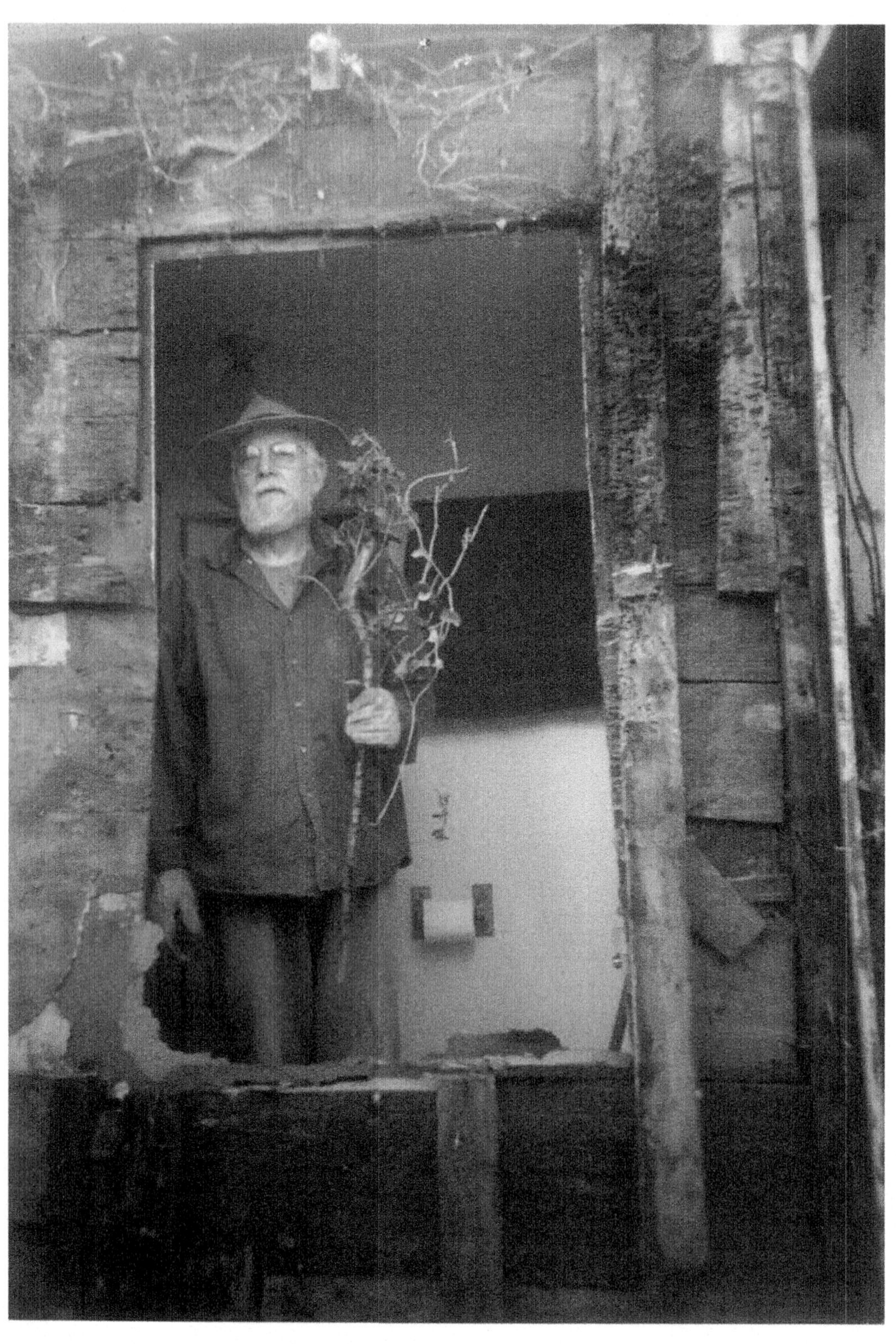

Photo by **Andy McConnell.**

ANDY MCCONNELL:

The photo was taken outside Robert's bathroom at his little house in the Flounder Bay Boatyard (note the TP low on the wall behind him). He called to say he had to move. He had been pulling the ivy off the house and the wall disintegrated into a heap. The house was doomed.

I grabbed some tools and drove up from Seattle to see just how bad things were. When I arrived, I found the remains of the wall: a spongework of rotten, scabbed together 2"x4"s, equally rotten sheathing and the sink more balanced only on the memory of where it belonged. It was a mess, but I assured him that we could fix it once we removed the bad material.

The photo was taken midway through that process. Robert was standing in front of where his sink had been, the ivy in his hand like a sad toothbrush. He said something like, "I think I've found the culprit!" At that point, we were having a pretty good time.

But putting the wall back together was mild pandemonium. His 2"x4" cache turning out to be about nine 3' stubs of 2"X You-name-it that actually belonged to Brad Killion. Anacortes on a Sunday night. Not a 2"x4" for sale anywhere.

All worked out in the end (as things were apt to with Robert) when about at 9:30 his landlord, Bob Pickett walked by and told us to help ourselves to a bunk of salvaged lumber sitting in the boatyard. The tight knot cedar smelled like gold to me at that point.

Robert had a gift with removing the unimportant and replacing it with something fortuitous and beautiful. In retrospect, any distress he felt going into the project was an unnecessary step. I guess he was a lot like any of us in failing to see how his unique strengths could get him through the worst of times.

Even in the end, lying on his deathbed, Robert was surrounded, around the clock, by a steady stream of friends, some coming from overseas to sit with him one more time. I have yet to meet another person for whom that's the case.

MARY HEDLIN:

One of the things that Robert said in one of his poems that has helped me so much and gives me a lot of hope when sometimes things have been a little rough is the line: the little bird that is going to heal me is hopping around in the bushes.

TIM MCNULTY:

I couldn't believe the parade of people that came to the hospital in Robert's final weeks. Here were hundreds of people coming through and wanting to sit up all night and hold his hand.

ERICA PICKETT:

When he was enjoying his last days in the care center, one of the staff approached and asked who he was. I replied that Robert was a poet and the staffer said, "My gosh, I thought he was a rock star. I think we have had 200 people through here to visit him."

ANN SPIERS:

Hans Nelson told me that Robert had requested people come visit him during his last days in the hospital. I visited, and he surprised me with this request.

You Say, "Remember Me."

for Robert Sund

You ask for a kiss,
lips to lips,
and I ask for a second kiss,
and as our lips press again,
I think of white iris,
its golden throat warming,
breathing fragrance,
and you turn away
to grieve for yourself,
perhaps not for the dying
but the leaving so soon
while fall frogs carouse,
and vine maples redden
their seed wings for flight
over the river always running
into the ocean pressing and pulling
as your graceful hands, now wind,
now rain, lift to dance
with each phrase,
teaching us how
again to say your poems.

FINN WILCOX: Not Letting Go

As much as I'd like to think of it as a connection to the universal, or a linkage to what we think of as mystery in its fullest form, really what it was, was my wife Pat's and my turn to sit with Robert while others had a chance to take a break. So there we were, holding his hand, rubbing lightly his pale, pale face, telling him in the kindest way possible it was ok to let go. It was clear time had come to an end for our old friend and we wanted nothing more than to be a soft buffer to whatever came next.

Robert had no interest in giving it up. Not that he was afraid of death, though he hit the brakes hard and cranked the wheel hoping to miss that hooded fucker standing smack in the middle of the road. No, it wasn't death, it was life and dirt and love and friends and railing at the stupidity of world leaders he wasn't easy letting go of.

In the morning, when it had all come to an end, Pat and I went to the café where Robert often had his breakfast. A quiet sadness hung over the whole of Anacortes, and our waitress burst into tears when she handed us our bill. I'm not a huggy kind of guy but I took her hand and smiled into her eyes. We both knew the world hadn't changed, but our world had.

In line at the ferry that would take us home to Port Townsend, in a strange but warm blanket of grief, Pat told me a story about Robert. When she lived in the miner's cabin down the beach from him on Shi Shi Beach, she would visit him for tea in the mornings. She was struck by the beauty of his chosen form of poverty. Not the poverty of want or of cities that tear down the soul. But a poverty of stuff, a letting loose of all that's not needed, and what was needed had been distilled into a simple, profound elegance. A clay teapot. A river polished stone. A cedar plank door that held off the sea's relentless blow. When she finally moved back to town, she went through the cupboards in her house and threw away every plastic plate, bowl and cup she could find.

A couple months later I was sitting at our local tavern having a beer when a woman I'd never met came up to me and asked if I was Finn. She said she had been friends with Robert and heard I'd been with him when he died. We talked for a few minutes and when she got up to leave she put her hand on my back and said, "What a gift it was for you to have been there with him at the end."

I know full well what she meant and I know she was just being sweet, but it somehow hit me wrong. As she walked out the door I thought to myself, "Yeah, it was a gift alright, one I'd gladly return for one more hour at this bar with Robert by my side. A no money back return."

Hell, I'd even throw in a set of plastic plates.

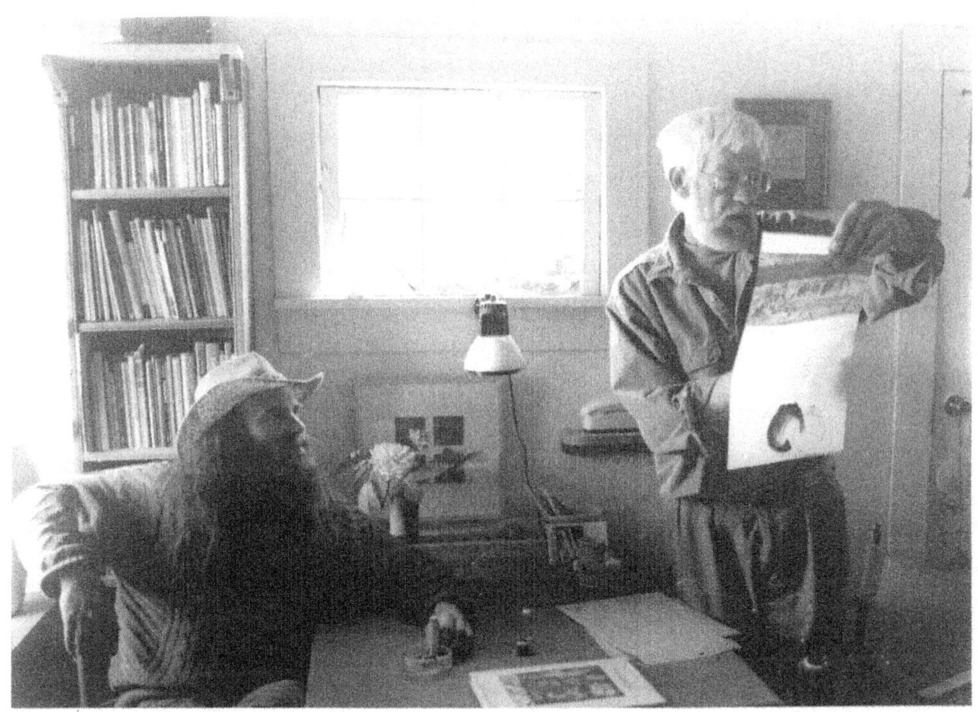

Finn Wilcox and Robert Sund, Anacortis, 1994 Steven R. Johnson

ROBERT SUND:

AUTUMN EQUINOX

Full moon sky.
When I die, peaceful, let it be
peaceful.
I hope I go like these waves
          breaking on Shi Shi,
wave rising out of the dark sea
turning suddenly white,
vanishing.
Wave after wave turning suddenly white.

May the song that comes of my dying
soothe the night birds;
may I wake myself, life after life,
in no less holy a place than this.

In the place between waves, especially,
Shi Shi, carry me
deeper into your silences.
Take me down
to the pure speech of whales,
down through swimming seals
          and schools of salmon.
Take me far.

When the first streams
          of swirled sand sweep over
          the white shell
          that is still falling
          through the dark sea,
take me with you.
Kneel down among the sea lice;
be there when I give my songs to the
          smooth round stones.

Be with me in the world of flying birds,
the gulls
and the ravens,
the songbirds among the driftwood.
Be with me on nights like this—
I can hear the earth crying for a voice!—
Be with me when I sit looking out at the sea
and don't know what to do,
some days helpless, some days
like a lion rising.
While I go between these waves of
day and night,
make the bottoms of my feet
tough as hide, and
keep my back strong.

SAM & SALLY GREEN:

On August 20 of 2001, Sally and I began the discipline of writing a poem a day for a year. We had two unbreakable rules: each poem had to be small enough to be handwritten on a postcard; and we had to mail the postcard off to a friend the next available mail day. We managed to keep this up for 365 days. Here are our poems for the day Robert died. Both of us have since published many of those in magazines and books, though these two have not made it into print before this.

Saturday, Sept. 29

Clear, then scattered clouds.

I go walking in the light
of pre-dawn stars so bright
the flashlight stays in my jacket
pocket. Another old poet has gone
into silence. At the edge of a neighbor's
pond, though I move with care,
a single mallard removes himself
from the water & vanishes
into the ambiguous dark.

Samuel Green

September 29, Saturday

Light clouds.

In the woodshed, catch a slight
twitch on a mound of sawdust,
a golden-brown moth, large wings
angled back like a fighter plane's, tilting
up, down, up, until a sow bug, gray
as a mechanic's coveralls, crawls
from underneath and bumps it
just enough to catch the wind,
so it becomes what it was
all along: a simple maple pod
spinning off to do its job
somewhere else.

Sally Green

GLENN (CHIP) HUGHES:

I wrote this poem after Robert's death, during the period that Tim McNulty and I were gathering and putting away in archives the contents of Robert's last dwelling, in Anacortes.

In Robert Sund's Shack

On the desk by the east window
calligraphy practiced
on a piece of white card stock
repeats: "Cherry blossoms."

Under the west window
a small bowl of cherries
has been placed on the table
for tomorrow.

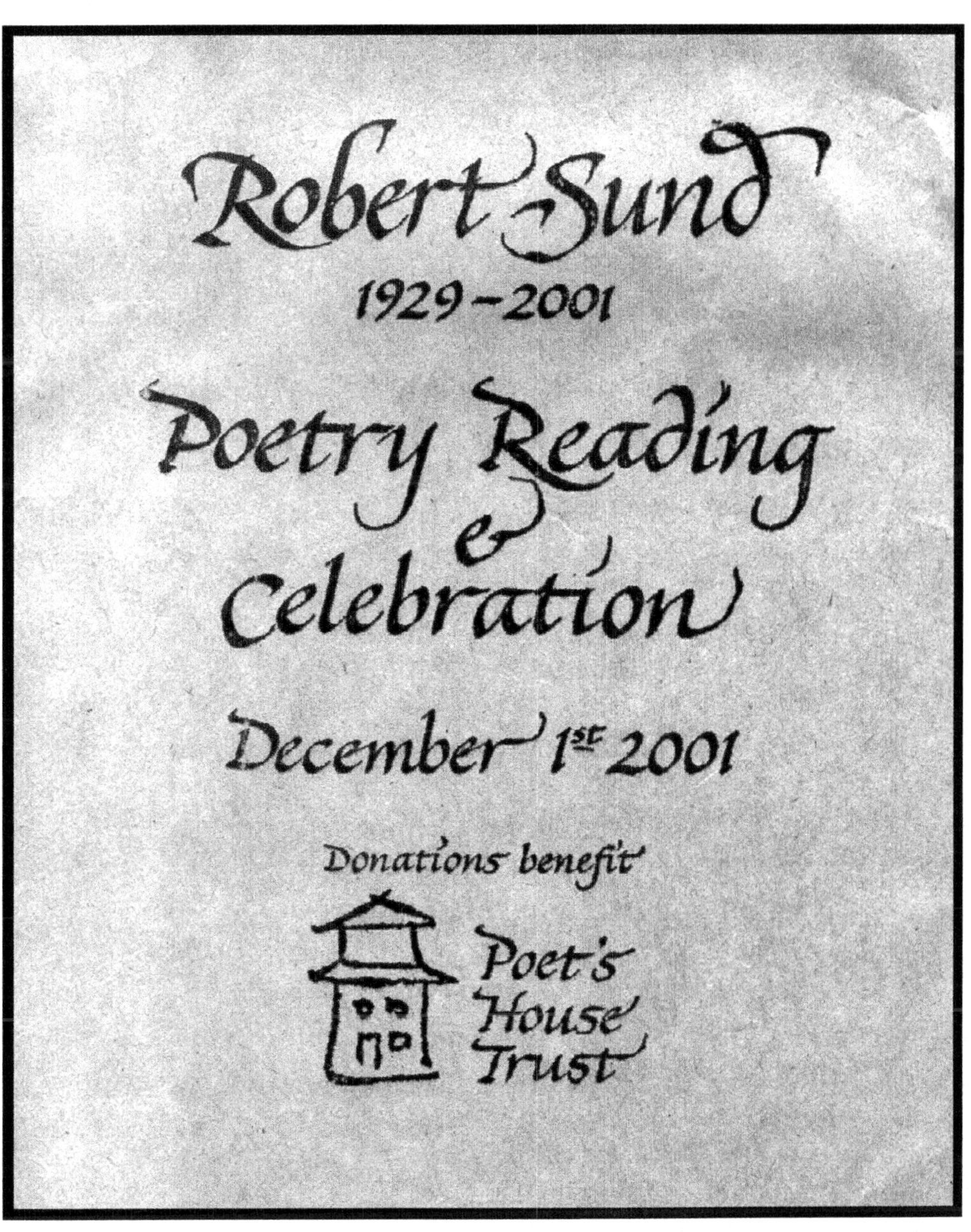
Robert Sund
1929–2001
Poetry Reading
&
Celebration
December 1st 2001
Donations benefit
Poet's
House
Trust

FATHER PAT TWOHY:
Invocation

We look to you
kindness, generosity, nobility
beyond our imagining
We look to you
kindness, generosity, nobility
beyond our imagining
We look to you this night
and we ask you to be with us
to bless our words tonight
to bless all the songs brought out
with your living spirit
We ask a great blessing going out
to all the dear ones here
to all the families here
to all living beings all around
we ask blessing this night
Most of all we thank you
We thank you for this man
We thank you that he was willing to search
all of his life
We thank you that he was willing to search
all of his life
He found it, becoming one with it
and because of that
a great kindness has come into our world
May it always be like this
may it always be like this together
in this wonderful kinship
this wonderful friendship
May it always be like this
in honor of our beloved one
May it always be just like this
the warmth of his presence
his great goodness
alive among us

PAUL HUNTER:

As Migratory Birds

It is enough you are here now.
Don't think of the rising,
the commotion that
moving through you
will lift off. The kinship
all at once in one body
waving its goodbyes.

You are here now as if
at rest among us
settling for the night, for
the shelter of a shoreline,
food and others of your kind.
This should be enough.

In memory of Robert Sund

CHUCK EASTON with AUTUMN SCOTT:

I graduated from Mt. Vernon High School in 1965 and dropped out of the University of Washington after one year (spent my time reading novels all night in the Eigerwand Coffehouse). After a break I enrolled at Skagit Valley College. This was during the Vietnam War and there was a military draft- I ended up being drafted the next year (amazingly enough I spent my year overseas in Korea, not Vietnam, but that's another story.)

During my time at Skagit, I heard Robert Sund read for the first time. He had written the *Bunch Grass* poems, but I don't think they were in book form yet. I remember that he had a number of copies of *Cascades, Magazine of Pacific Northwest Bell* with a few of the *Bunch Grass* poems in it, along with photographs of combines. Too bad I didn't save a copy—he was handing some of them out to people. Robert was in what I have heard him refer to as his W. B. Yeats period—wool vests, round wire-rimmed glasses, store-bought haircut, and dress pants. I'd already developed an interest in literature and poetry in high school; Japanese Haiku was, and remains, a favorite. Both Robert and I loved the work of the poet, Issa. Robert's poems at that point really resonated with me, not the least because I'd driven tractors in the Skagit Valley pea harvest in the summers during high school. I believe I attended another reading or two of Robert's around the Skagit Valley during this time.

After getting out of the Army I went to music school in Boston where I met both Tim McNulty and Michael Daley, both now well-respected voices in Northwest poetry. Tim was one of the main people responsible for getting out Robert's collected works—*Poems from Ish River Country*—he worked tirelessly on this. It proved to be an impossible task until after Robert's death—to say Robert could be difficult to work with is an understatement. I shared a love of Gary Snyder's poetry with Tim as well as a passion for mountain climbing, which we pursued together when we both ended up in the NW.

I think the first time I actually met Robert was at the Wing Luke Gallery in Seattle in 1976, where the calligraphy master, Yamanouchi, was demonstrating his prodigious brush technique. Robert may have studied with Yamanouchi, I'm not sure, but he was definitely interested in brushwork for his own paintings and calligraphy.

In 1977, I hiked with Tim, Robert, Steve Johnson, and Jerry Gorsline out to Shi Shi Beach on the Washington coast for a Blue Moon in June celebration. Autumn Scott was living in the A-frame cabin which Robert had built a few years earlier. Showing the rather unpleasant side of his personality (to which many can attest), he was extremely rude and crashed around throwing her stuff out the door. It worked out better for me—Autumn and I are now married and have been together since that time. After enough time had passed they became quite good friends, but it was an inauspicious beginning.

Autumn and I were both present when Robert appeared at the Centrum Writers' Conference in Pt. Townsend reading his Shi Shi poems later that summer—Gary Snyder and Phil Whalen were also there that week. Robert was on his game that day—gave a great reading that has been finally released on CD in 2015.

I had been in Seattle playing music and living just up the street (crawling distance) from the Blue Moon. Greg Hill, Ken Pottle, Norm Gustavson and Erik Ambjor were also living there, and got to know Robert as well. A few months later, Autumn moved in, too. Erik's photographs are on the covers of *Notes from Disappearing Lake.* Erik, along with Jeff Langlow, was also the driving force behind the expansion of the shack on Shit Creek—they went up for a week and helped Robert build the add-on. All of us, including Tim McNulty and Jeff Langlow, made a number of trips to the shack on the river to spend a few days. During one of these, rowing back from the bar in La Conner, we named the "Grotto of the three inebriates." Or was it the "Grotto of the five inebriates?"

Robert spent the fall and early winter of 1978 in Seattle crashing on our front room couch—he named the place Cloud House. Mary Randlett's photograph in *Poems from Ish River Country* was taken in the dining room. We spent many a night closing down the Blue Moon. The next morning I would make coffee and exclaim that I might never drink again. Not knowing anything about alcoholism at that time, I couldn't believe Robert would have a beer for breakfast after these nights. His mood improved markedly a few years later when he stopped drinking.

Autumn and I left for Boston in early January, 1979, as I wanted to finish up music school before the GI bill ran out. Robert proceeded to move into our little basement room, a classic Robert move.

We returned to the Northwest a couple of years later and continued to see Robert occasionally. A memorable event was his 60th birthday party at the Garden Club in La Conner, a festive fall evening with poetry, music, a candlelit meal, and friends from Ish River country and beyond. In his final years, Robert moved to a tiny house in the yard at the Flounder Bay Boat Lumber Co. in Anacortes. We visited this home and admired the elegant little courtyard garden he had created around the patio, the stone paths and the handcrafted arbor, draped with an evergreen clematis. This is where he wrote the Garden Poems. I saw him for the last time with Tim when he was in the hospital in Anacortes.

I don't think it's necessary for poetry to have a regional flavor, but Robert's and Tim's references to the natural world give it a deep resonance with place. I always say that if you live in the Northwest, you should have a wool hat, a raincoat and a copy of *Poems from Ish River Country.*

BOB ROSE:

Rain in the Chuckanuts

for Robert Sund's 60th birthday
Garden Club. La Conner

Robert, I can't say
I know the Skagit—
never lived
by its banks
but tonight I'm happy
rain pelts the windshield
one wiper lame
between my legs
a bottle of burgundy.
I'm going home
to the Skagit, coming
down from the Chuckanuts
(how the lights have grown
and sprawled over the years).

I still don't know the Skagit
its courses and eddies
barely know
the mountain
of my mind

Driving across the valley
home to Mount Erie,
to salal crevices
bluffs spotted
with ancient burned fir
and Whistle Lake
just over the ridge

Going home
to Mount Erie
going home
to my mind

Visiting Robert's Shack at Shit Creek
A May expedition with North Cascades Institute

Blake's Landing Launch

Rain drops like fish shows
Sticks whirl
in Skagit snow-melt

Entering Shit Creek
blue bright larkspur
rain blackened cliff
flash of white saxifrage

Rusted boom chains
hang from Robert's shack post
links thin as horsehair
drip rain on granite slab and bud pot

Silver smolts flash
cat-tail fluff torches

Good Medicine in Robert's shack
(for Alan Moe's kindness to strangers)

Blessed hot tea
Fishtown poems read by old friends
more friends than ever!
scuffing the rugs

Sullivan Slough

Single butterfly bush
dances in the wind

Old broken windshield truck
swimming willows, scuttling clouds
cedar stumps host alder shoots

All the old river shacks
slowly settle
into Skagit silt

Shifting channels
moving clouds
a break from the rain
tide dropping, grass roots
revealed

5/20/2012

BILL YAKE:

For Robert Sund
- in memoriam

I.
Shack walls must leak a little storm.
        Breathe. Inside, candles
        flick and waver.

Wind on snares - all night so
cliffs and shore cobble make
        a *Shi-Shi Beach*
        & silver boxcar sound.

II.
Where do we go

- characters, shack dwellers, dancers -

        after the band folds
& all the books are shelved?

III.
Shaking off the night
rain, the living
        are joined

        by death - the dead
        lie
        elbow to elbow & low like the sea.

IV.
A skiff
your poems
        remain.

MICHAEL DALEY:

When T. McNulty discovered RS's Shack Notebook for March '81

The poet Robert Sund
        looks out from his shack
                in time to see
old friend Clyde dock the rowing dory
        and plunge
                to his knees
in low tide
        hoisting aloft
                a trophy bottle of Sake.
A mound with trillium trumpets
        above the mud.

Think of Tu Fu and Li Po
            who in by now rare incarnations
question is what they invite poetry.

Here we are, Clyde says,
        at the beginning of style

On a column of trochees
        the archivist scrolled
                to an *"Imagined Marriage"*
no one had seen,
        none been told:
                Trillium Lilly
and—*Lilly/ Lilly/ Lilly/ Lilly*
        –more,
                a field all down one page.

Alone by kerosene flicker
solitaries put Fish Town on the map
with calligraphed lists to loves
        unreciprocated
    while the romance of citizens
        barreled along at Pike Place heedless
of Lilly's accordion wheeze and moan
        in sunshine cold
                in gold oblivion streets.

BO MILLER: This is a poem Robert wrote for Dana Richardson's wake back in '84. Dana was a charismatic young hippie who was a close friend of Hans and Eric Nelson and was a true resident of Seattle. He had the polished and astonishing stories of a 60 year old man who had missed very little.

Prayer for Dana Richardson

Dana, how suddenly
you are gone,
the little boat of your being
pulled up on the shore of this life a while
got swept back out to sea
far far out where we
cannot see you
and the changes coming to you —
that sea where one life goes
and the new one begins.

Go far, go well, go where
every trace fades away —
Go far and far
where the new great morning
will wrap your soul
in a mother-father embrace
and bring you again to the
shore of life.

your friends stand
on the old shore
among sand and rocks
in sight of mountains and clouds.
gathered by a little fire
we keep your laughter
your stories
your embraces
your enthusiasm, alive
among us.

God bless you, Dana,
Bless you far far out at sea,
in the wide wide spaces,
Bless you as your eyes open
on a new life,
where love will surely
find you again
and bring you home.

Robert Aitken
Woodacre
March 14, 1984

PAT TWOHY:

For me Robert was the essence of being a poet. Poor, lousy health, no place to lay his head, totally idealistic and dedicated to the word. "It takes 1000 erasures to find one true word." I always enjoyed his company. We used to sit together and bum hors d'oeuvres at a local restaurant. I knew that he mostly lived on air and spirit. He had an immense love of the written word and loved to read and share it. He was also eager to share the work of other poets he admired. When he died a great deal of love moved into the unseen world but it is no less real and nourishing for me. His self-effacing wit and steady humor even in the hardest of times was and continues to be a joy for me. I cannot be as dedicated to the word as Robert was and is. But I would like to emulate him in some small way in my own efforts to find the right words for the Mystery that enlivened and captivated both of us.

ROBERT BLY:

LUNCH TIME

For Robert Sund

Do you remember those noons in threshing time
When the women put out the food outdoors?
They had large, blowing dresses.
One of the men tried to comb his hair.

It was the Depression. A few fathers had told
Their sons when they were ten to hit the road.
To come back into the family, you'll need more
Than a pair of socks and a room in the barn.

Some forgiveness came with those lights,
Blown dresses and an extra piece of pie.
The good things that happened had to do
With so much hard work and a fondness for men.

GARY SNYDER:

Bunch-grass
(a broad term used for many perennial native grasses of the far west)
When I first saw that title I knew right then that west coast literary culture had taken a significant new turn. I wasn't disappointed. It still is my favorite Robert Sund book. That led me to look him up and meet and talk during some of my earliest Seattle visits after returning from Japan in 1968. We met again one summer at Fort Worden in Port Townsend for the week-long literary conference organized there by Jim Heynen and Mary Jo Bangs. He arrived with a party of friends, all just in from Shi-Shi Beach. They took over the stage, sat on the floor, played music, talked through big kelp tubes, and Robert sang and recited poems. & again during his stay in northern California (where the North Point Press book *Ish River* was published) we shared a few cups of sake. A unique amazing man who made his own way and walked his own path. I admired him all those years—mostly from afar.

WENDELL BERRY:

I have admired Robert Sund's poems for a long time, but I met him only briefly and only once. He was in the audience at a reading I gave in a bookstore in Bellingham (I'm fairly certain), to my great and lasting, pleasure. We exchanged a few letters. But I have no personal memory of him to offer you. I wish I did. Sincerely, Wendell Berry.

GINNY GREENO:

Robert was an amazing whistler. He could imitate many bird songs and enjoyed conversing with them. Wonder if there are any recordings.

BRAD KILLION:

Robert and I played music for about ten years. We would start with this song called "The Tuning Song." And this is how he remembered it—he had to give it a little mnemonic device—so what he decided after a very short period of time, was that he would call it this: Every American Dog Gets Bones Equally.

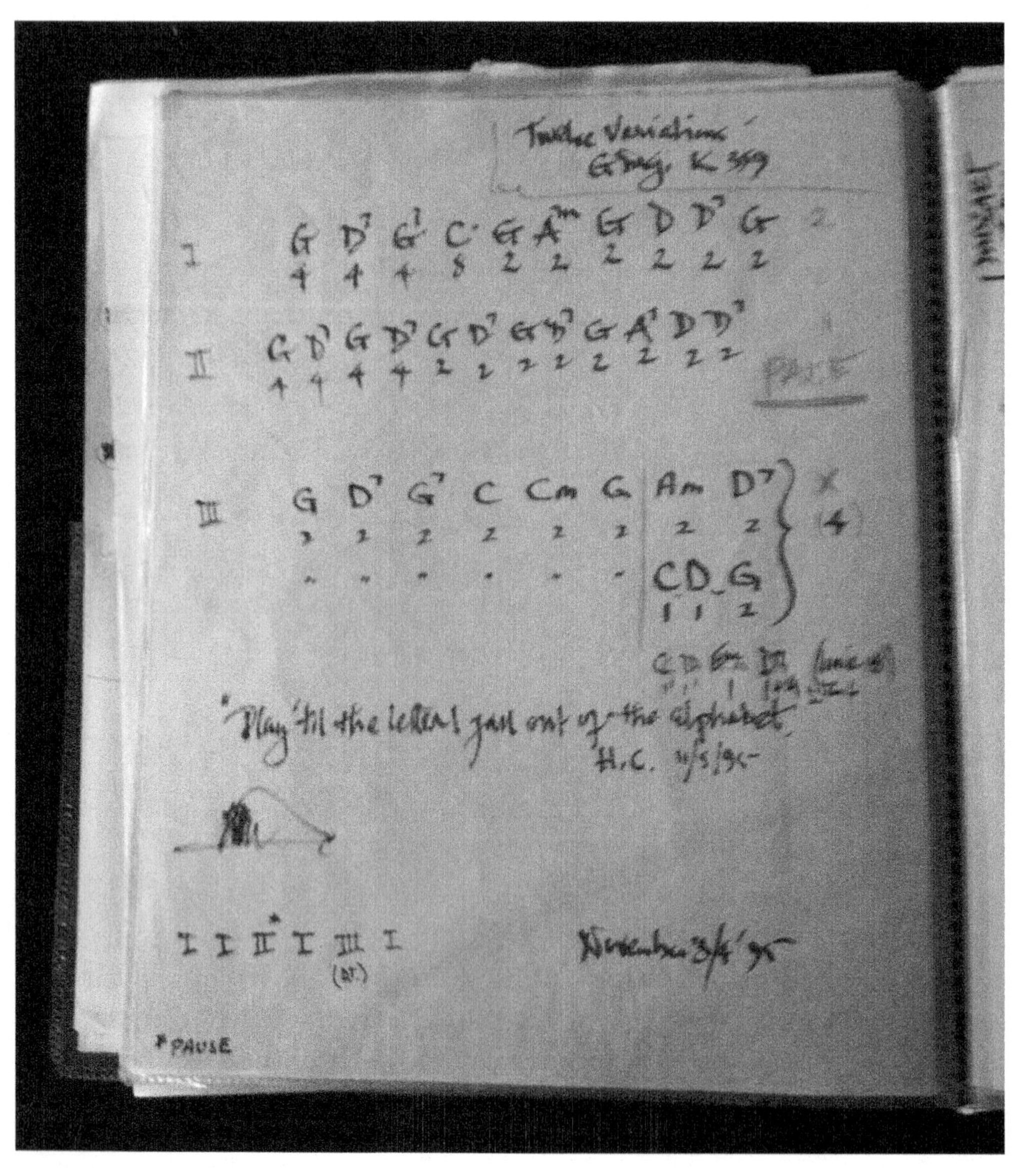

Robert Sund's Mozart sheet music, courtesy of **Brad Killion.**
"Play 'til the letters fall out of the alphabet."

BONI KILLION: Robert Sund

You never left Robert Sund's home without a gift, a wind letter inked with date and poem, a fresh zucchini plucked from the garden, or the sound of his autoharp lingering in your mind, and of course laughter... There was always laughter.

Although I had read Robert's poetry years before, I met Robert on my first date with my husband Brad, who took me to Robert's apartment after dinner at the LaConner Tavern. I think Brad, who had recently moved back to the area after teaching in Alabama, was secretly hoping to see Robert there. We walked up the hill to his then ground-floor abode in the big blue apartment building. Although it had been years since Brad had seen Robert, we were graciously welcomed, and Robert commenced to make us tea. Upon mentioning his autoharp, Robert brought out a rather forlorn looking instrument and Brad and Robert delved into the intricacies of how they might repair and salvage the piece, while I sipped tea and drank in the surroundings. Old, well-read books stood like protective friends around the walls, ink bottles precisely lined up on a small wooden shelf, Japanese handmade paper spread across a work table, and the smell of patchouli oil, chamomile tea and sweet dust lingered.

Later the talk segued into fall gardens, and Robert said he was struggling with trying to nurture a few plants he had sown on the east side of the apartment. It was a beautiful, unseasonably warm night under a full moon when we walked around to the garden he had scratched out of a flat spot on a rocky knoll. Robert carried a small teacup of water, and under bright fall sky he methodically doused each of his three struggling plants with an evening sip. It was be the beginning of several gardens and a friendship that grew out of nurturing the earth. Although I had spent more years as a home gardener than Robert, it was Robert who gave me a deeper perspective on being a steward to the earth. I had never gardened after dark until I met Robert, who would take to his Anacortes garden in the blackness of night, a flashlight and bucket in hand. He scooped up the pesky slugs and snails and carried them across the street to the vacant lot where they would find a new home. Albeit temporary, as they often found their way back, it became a nightly vigil and his pest control was always sans slug bait.

He taught me a lot and we shared our woes and successes and our plant starts. This often led to bemused success. When I shared my vegetable starts with him, we both ended up with so many zucchini's our friends were hiding from us when they saw us coming with arms full of squash. One day when I was ravaging in my garden yanking weeds out with a vengeance, I was halted by Robert standing at my gate, saying, "It's supposed to be fun, Boni." He taught me to stop and savor the beauty of our hard work. Another time when we tried to grow blue Himalayan poppies we found ourselves unsuccessful because neither of us could pinch off the first magnificent bloom which would ensure their return. We were both so mesmerized by the enchanting blue color. Robert's gardens were a huge reflection of his life, because he loved the beauty in the world and tried to create that beauty in every place he lived. He wrote in his garden poems, "Sun Shining through Cabbage Leaf,"

> I have two maxims:
> "One zucchini is enough for any garden,"
> "Plant for beauty first."

Perhaps it is the acute observers of life who make the most gifted poets. If that's the case, Robert was a master at catching something in nature, in art, in music or even a simple phrase, and turning it into something poetic or profound. One night when we were talking about pottery, and I was sharing a story of my misfortune at trying to throw a pot on a pottery wheel. I said, "I never got the hang of getting the clay on the middle of the wheel because you have to be off a little to find the center." With this, Robert let out a great laugh, went back to his art table and made me a wind letter that said, *"To find your center, you have to be off a little."* It became my mantra.

From the first meeting with Robert until he passed in 2001, Robert filled our home with love, laughter and at times mayhem, because that's what friends do. They mix it up to make it interesting. But the best of times were the simple nights where Brad and Robert would play music in the kitchen after a dinner.

Before they met, Robert played primarily folk music. Robert's sense of rhythm was, well, let's say peculiar. Brad encouraged him to focus more on timing so they could broaden their musical horizons. It took a while, but eventually he improved dramatically. Robert told me that on more than one occasion, he would wake up in bed in the middle of the night counting out loud, "one, two, three, four… one, two, three, four…" Along the way, Brad transposed various styles of music for the autoharp, from Mozart to Thelonious Monk to Mark Knopfler to The Beatles, as well as a host of original tunes which Robert loved entitling. Examples include, "The Hides of White Horses Shedding Rain," "Swiss Almond Vanilla," "A Few Red Radishes," "Estuary in E flat," "Getting Out of Bucharest," and "Beethoven's Slalom."

He learned to play many of these songs with aplomb, quite a few without the sheet music. Robert and Brad would play for hours at a time. They performed here and there. Robert even traded a music performance at Hedlin's Greenhouse for garden starts. They often played in the middle of his poetry readings, and dinner and music at our house became a regular event. I was the cook, they were the cleanup crew and entertainment. Robert always insisted, "You cook the meal, we clean up the kitchen." That's how it was. On practice nights, it was poems, politics and ping-pong. On work nights I'd have to turn in early, but I slumbered off to the sweet sounds of guitar and autoharp. And once in awhile I'd hear the occasional sour note, followed by Robert's "Dammit!" — always the perfectionist.

BRAD KILLION:

I first met Robert in the Summer of 1981 at the LaConner Tavern (now the Pub) in Washington. We were introduced by my college friend, a native of LaConner, Don Huddleston. Robert, a lanky, gray-haired and bearded, Gandalfian presence was shooting pool with great enthusiasm (the same enthusiasm I would come to learn he used in all competitive endeavors). Upon him closing out the game with the sinking of the 8-ball, his opponent remarked, "You play a good game of pool," to which Robert boldly replied, "It's more than just a game." A pool enthusiast myself, I was intrigued to say the least.

During subsequent games and sporadic conversation thereafter, Don mentioned to Robert I played the guitar and he graciously invited me to get together and play music anytime. I left the Pub that day convinced I had met a rather interesting individual.

A year later, Don and I canoed to his shack on the river. It was early afternoon. We knocked a few times, waited a bit and were about to leave when the sleepy-eyed hermit opened the door to address his new visitors. We were eagerly invited in. The next few hours filled with discussion, laughter and poetry. Again we talked of collaborating musically. I left the shack that day convinced even more I wanted to better get to know this person. As a former Chicago suburbanite, I couldn't help but feel honored to have been in that rustic, secluded river shack with such a fascinating human being.

In the Fall of 1987, roughly five years later, out of the blue, Boni, my now wife, and I decided to visit him. He graciously invited us in and a genuine friendship well beyond anything I ever could have imagined was born.

So, when I was asked to write a piece on Robert Sund, I was besieged with reluctant anxiety. Should I focus on the hundreds and hundreds of hours playing music together? Should I talk about the bike rides, our ten-state vacation to the Southwest, our (his) whimsical carpentry projects, our cribbage and ping-pong mortal combat? Should I share my appreciation for his bigger-than-life poetry readings, his exceptional hospitality, his unique wisdom, his engaging sense of humor? How do I sum up the man who's character I could go on and on about the ensuing fourteen years upon which our friendship grew ever stronger?

Yes, at times he could be obstinate and dismissive about various aspects of life. Compounding matters, his increasing health problems most certainly got in his way. Yet, to many who knew him well, graciousness and enthusiasm are among his finest and most enduring hallmarks. How do I put into words how much I miss him? (Oh, how he could help us navigate through these dubious times.)

Fortunately, I don't have to miss him alone. The wonderful friendships and acquaintances I have made because I knew Robert are countless. These outstanding individuals have themselves, graciously and enthusiastically strove to keep his spirit alive. They are the anchor preventing my sentimental skiff from floating aimlessly out to sea.

ROBERT SUND:
La Conner Main Street
September 14, 1979. 7:30 P.M.

Monday evening, early September, school just open again -- two Indian boys stop me on Main Street sidewalk across from the bank. Tennis shoes and jeans and football-type sweatshirts, ten or eleven years old, maybe. One of them asks me: "Why aren't you over at the school anymore?"

I ask his name, I remember his face. He was in the third grade when I spent six weeks teaching poetry.

"John Stone," he says. His friend holding the football is "Ray Formsby." I ask where they live, and they point across the channel to the reservation.

They suddenly remind me of that time two years ago. I liked the children -- Indians, Chicanos, whites -- hated the atmosphere, felt uneasy with the administration, and felt sorry for some of the teachers.

So I said "John... John Stone?"

"Nathan John Stone," he says, a friendly boy. And he wants to know why I'm not teaching at the school any more.

At last I say: "Oh... you know... they don't want bums like me over at the school."

We part and the boy with the football tosses it into the air and goes running under it, and catches it, and turns to say:

"You're not a bum! You were *good!*"

Then they head down the street, and I head for the tavern.

ERICA PICKETT:

One of Robert's most salient traits was his great generosity of spirit. He really seemed to love people of every description. When he named the eleven board members for the Trust the attorney was startled at the large number of people but Robert would have had more of his friends on the board had the attorney not intervened. And those of us named were somewhat surprised at the diversity of backgrounds in the board and that we didn't all know each other. Yes, there was Tim McNulty and Chip Hughes, both poets. Then came Jeff Winston, successful entrepreneur and musician and Brad Killion, guitarist and comedian. Joan Cross is a former LaConner City Council member and the late Barbara Cram was the founder of the homeless shelter, Friendship House, in Mt. Vernon. Tom Skinner taught school in LaConner and Andy McConnell is a carpenter. Barbara Hathaway inspects bridges for a living and makes pottery and the late Arthur Greeno ran a cafe/frame shop in New Mexico. There were many views at the meetings, never a bad thing.

MARISA PAPETTI:

While most children are forced to spend time with a "weird babysitter" at one point or another, I was fortunate in that my babysitter was actually an inspiration to my life. In 1980, my mother and I moved to La Conner, Washington. It was there that my nanny—whom I called "Uncle Bob"—let me into his world for a few hours a day. When most children were playing with blocks, army men or dolls, I played with watercolors and fine-haired brushes. When most children ate tuna sandwiches with the crust cut off; I ate fresh local pears and fine cheeses. In later years, I would understand my babysitter was the revered Pacific Northwest poet, artist and musician Robert Sund. But as a child, he was simply my "Uncle Bob" and I was his "Misa Moo."

I grew up and watched as Uncle Bob began to fill in his Aura. For those who knew him personally, they will understand this. But for those who did not, I will do my best to explain.

Robert touched all of our hearts. His Aura filled the room five seconds before he walked in.

He was charismatic, simple, caring and brimming with hope and inspiration. Everything he did—his actions, his work—reflected this. When you spoke, Uncle Bob listened carefully. When you sang out of key, he would say "Not bad." And when he did his calligraphy, drawings, poems, woodwork or played the autoharp, the results were always infused with these special qualities.

Everything he believed in came out for the world to see, feel and experience.

Uncle Bob was without a doubt the most amazing person that I have ever had the pleasure of knowing. If you missed the opportunity to know him, don't worry. You still have time; his work will bring you there.

I miss him very much, but he is still with me in my heart. After he passed away, I visited his cabin in Anacortes. It still holds the scent of his spirit.

Enjoy your life. That is what he would wish upon us all.

ARJUNA (DIANE) BARTON: Recollections of Robert Sund

Essentially, I was little more than a full-grown child when I met Robert, though of course, I did not know that at that time. Full of ideas and wonder, tasting my first freedom, Robert was one of the first people I met with a similar inner world. Robert was a wise man, a wizard, a poet, a genius, fun, and creative. He was an older person who liked and understood me. He was the first person to introduce me to astrology and many other mystical subjects. Through all of our various adventures and situations, Robert was able to keep writing and dreaming, making us a part of his vision. Here are some stories he told at different times of his life before any of us knew him.

Somewhere in Robert's history, he lived in a boarding house in New Orleans. It was the kind of "affordable" place where no one asked any questions and complaints were the same as an eviction notice. Robert described the landlady as a big, stout woman with a hard edge and a sharp eye for troublemakers. She was a smoker who never removed the cigarette from her mouth. Every day as she stood stirring the large soup pot, the cigarette ash got longer and longer, amazingly long. Then in a blink it would be gone with no trace of its whereabouts and no change of expression on her face. The landlady was a far cry from his mother on the farm in Elma.

Did you know that Robert Sund took his pants off in Zsa Zsa Gabor's bedroom? This story is from New York City. He must have been staying in a fairly swanky place because this 60's sex kitten was staying there as well or maybe he was working there. Being a true poet, Robert's pants were in need of mending. Zsa Zsa's maid noticed the problem and offered to fix them. She told him to go into the bedroom, take off his pants, and hand them out to her so she could mend them. Though he was pantless in her bedroom, Robert was Zsa Zsa less as well, but it made a hell of a good story and was a lot more than many other men could claim.

As I search back through the hours and hours spent talking, dreaming, creating, scheming, and laughing with Robert, there are a few stories that stand out.

At Lorenzo Milam's houseboat where the photos were taken, I witnessed the most powerfully fought game of Monopoly ever to be played. As a lightweight, I was easily gobbled up in a couple of rounds, leaving the three heavyweights to take on each other. Lorenzo took on the role of capitalist with pleasure and with a "what are you going to do about it" tongue-in-cheek humor. His joy in irking Robert and Charlie was tremendous. Charlie was looking for the quick, clever, young genius upstart win by an upset. So he too, had his secret smirk. Robert, dear Robert, took the high road, looking down on these two morally corrupt Monopoly players and was sure he would win because he had his principles and was doing the "right" thing. As the game went along, I believe Lorenzo was winning on the board, at least. Allegiances formed and shifted. Arguments over rules and accusations of cheating escalated to judgments and character assassinations. Robert, in top form, gave several speeches worthy of being spoken from the pulpit. As the game had moved on from just a board game, it could never be decided who won, but there was big thunder in the heavens that night.

On a rainy November day in La Conner, one of many days in a row, where it had just poured and poured down, making us feel like we would never be dry again, Robert said we should go to the Waterfront Café for a cup of afternoon coffee. He handed me an extra set of fishing rain gear that he had that were somewhat my size. We sloshed on down to the main street, entered the café, and ordered two cups of coffee. "Take a seat, I'll bring it to you," said Mildred Potter, the owner. "Oh no," Robert said with that poet's twinkle in his eye, "We'll be taking it out on the deck." So we sat out on the deck in full rain gear in the pouring rain laughing as the raindrops splashed into our cups of coffee. The farmers who sat talking at the big round table because their fields were too flooded to work, saw only a pair of fools. Robert and I were on top of the world.

LE KAI WEN (CHUCK LUCKMANN):

Dreaming Robert Sund

Robert smiles, laughs, sings
As shamans do at Shi Shi Beach:

Marbled murrelets, tufted puffins
Bob in Pacific breakers;

Three days, three nights
Rapturous notes, hermit thrush;

Cormorants strut breeding plumage,
Hold wings high atop sea stacks,

Swoop down from nests,
Skim swells licked frothy white.

Robert shouts pure joy,
Transforms into sea otter:

Grins, floats on furry back,
In tumultuous surf, eating shellfish.

Later he builds driftwood fire,
Drinks cup after cup green tea,

Reads Wei Ying-Wu aloud,
Full moonlight.

GEORGIA JOHNSON:

Some Moon

Remembering the poet Robert Sund

Some moon,
caught by lingering light from the west
reflects back as a shard of broken garnet.
Refusing to blink the light changes and the shape with it,
ripe picked apricot, buttery bronze pear.

I catch that breeze from across the valley bringing
fresh cut alfalfa mixed with
beet flower and peas.

Overcome by all this sweetness, about the time dew begins
to cling to my shirt
the moon a quarter way up the sky teases a dimpled sandbar
across the field, rumbas across the tin roof of a fallen down fishing
shack, turning it silver as an old poet's mane.

For the rest of its nightly journey
it becomes the dust that lies at the bottom of two ceramic jars
sitting
on my table.
One jar holds a bit of my husband's father,

the other about the right amount to imagine it
the boney finger of Robert Sund.
Each celebrated the luck of a windfall pear
And spoke the old language of barred owl and coyote.
They sit at my table advising me about the night and the eastern
sky.
They tell me to court the dark to find my way through it.

BILL YAKE:

Animism, Buddhism, Friendship & Autoharp Melodies: Some Thoughts About Robert Sund's Work

What is it that gives me a special joy each time I come back to Robert Sund´s poems? The surprises, clarity and craft; his fresh and accurate eye; a playful and illuminating sense of humor; and the revelations. Revelations from a life pared down to what he found most important: attentiveness, art, friendship, and the land.

It is something like traveling to land where the light (the crystalline night as well) makes the things of this world full and round; subtle with hidden dimensions. These seem to exist without proof. There is little, if any, irony.

Sund's fundamental themes: friends, calligraphy, art, handmade artifacts, spirit, poetry, meditation, Buddhism, & the autoharp.

His landscapes stand as powers, teachers, and elders. They seem to inhabit him every bit as much as he inhabits them. The tradition of long occupation is honored.

Sund's animist vision: the wind, mountains, snow, sunlight, skunk cabbage, boxcars and coyotes, each with a quickened senescent spirit that skirts the territory of frank anthropomorphism, coexist within a sort of native Folk Buddhism.

In Taos Mountain weaving is a recurrent theme. And weaving is recurrent. Similar materials are used and reused as they would be in weaving a blanket or rug: sky, mountain, memory, night, a star, song, the recurrent days. The rhythm of successive horizons: sunrise and sunset; layers of day and night breathed successively, waking and dreaming, all horizontal weft woven through a vertical warp.

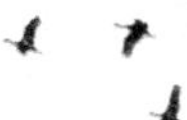

"Men that undertake one district are much more likely to advance natural knowledge than those that grasp at more than they can possibly be acquainted with: every kingdom, every province, should have it's [sic] own monographer." – Gilbert White, English naturalist. October 8, 1770. Letter VII to Daines Barrington.

Repeatedly, his poems teach us that old lesson -- the one we keep forgetting -- that when we are attentive, poems (and their revelations) spring from every place and every moment.

Places are as responsible for their artists as the artists are for their art. Places, in their long evolving lives, summon artists and breathe life into their work. Inspire. In Sund's notes, one can almost hear his thoughts emptying out and filling with the river and the estuary air. His rhythms becoming tidal flood and ebb, seasonal, migratory. Or cracked and surprising as refractions of waves, daylight breaking through a cloud, a weasel stalking swallow eggs, and "a small piece of dust" lit by slanting sunlight.

ANDY MCCONNELL:

In his memoir, *The Accidental Collector,* Wesley Wehr wrote that Robert never revised his "rather pneumatic poems... filled with lofty feelings" considering his first words to be the most authentic. This was never the Robert I knew. He was always editing his work, paring the words down to the essential. While he had a gift for oration, he was not someone who could inspire a listener by reading the telephone book aloud. His poems were carefully crafted and even his published work had notes and revisions written in his personal copies. He was never fully satisfied with his work, whether they be Bashō translations or his own poems.

Much of our time together was spent rummaging thrift stores, picking up stones on the beach, working in his garden, playing cribbage, or watching a Sonics game on his tiny television. I used to feel a bit guilty, for I was getting college credit to study poetry with Robert, yet we hardly spoke of it. Meanwhile, whatever I wrote and shared with him was met with correction. While at first, I felt a little hurt by his lack of compliments, I came to see his comments as prodding me not to be too easily satisfied. I began to notice that he lived his life in that way: choosing just the right stone from the beach, spoon from the silverware bin at the thrift store, plant for the garden...everything had to be just so. We shared a disdain for people that cut corners.

I had the good fortune to have never been chewed out by him but given a few more years, I probably would have been over some errant misunderstanding. Many people set Robert off, often well meaning close friends and occasionally a spiteful acquaintance. It wasn't uncommon for Robert to respond with a sharp, incisive letter, honed for days on his writing desk before being fired to the recipient, solely to carve them a new asshole. Had he been alive to read Wesley's comments on his writing, I'm sure that Robert would have turned him inside out with a little ink and a single piece of 8.5"X11" paper. He was not to be trifled with.

Conversely, with what little he had, he was always a generous host. There was always coffee or tea on the hotplate, a few cookies in the jar, a simple split pea or lentil soup on the stove and a warm welcome awaiting most any visitor (after 1pm or so, as Robert was mostly nocturnal). Time at his table was spent conversing in a way that is rare today. There was no hurry, and as much as he loved to tell a story, he was a curious listener. And no one left Robert's empty handed. He always sent a guest away with a calligraphy, a broadside or a chapbook, carefully packaged in cellophane or paper bag, a short commemoration of the visit inscribed on the gift inside.

While I wasn't in a classroom, the lessons came all the same. And although ostensibly I was studying poetry, we'd laugh and say it was actually the "Poetics of Useful Form" as we moved plants around in his small yard, worked on his fence or bought a loaf of bread at the local bakery. As we worked or did errands, he'd tell me this and that about growing up on his family farm, or life on the river. Less about poetry than *living*. His stories always called me back to a time I missed without ever knowing, to a world that had already been paved over. I yearned for the kind of knowledge he learned working behind a team of horses; living in a shack above the Skagit River; being from a different time.

Once, we were in his car, traveling between Mt. Vernon and Anacortes, the blur of green fields whipped past us as we rolled along. Passing an old, well used barn, I told him that I'd have loved to grow up on a farm, like him, and complained that the things kids learn in suburbia were kind of superfluous. I wished I could have learned things that *mattered.* He was silent, and looked ahead, considering what I had just said. Pointing out the window at a hand painted sign, identifying the crop behind it, he said, "That's asparagus." In that moment, I saw that while there was a great distance between what I wanted and what I had, the way to close the gap was to focus on what was right in front of me.

Oddly, in spite of what little time we spent writing or even talking about it, I learned more about how to do it well by simply kicking around with Robert than in any classroom. And while I don't spend much time writing these days, I notice his influence in every creative endeavor I take on, whether I am painting, working on a sculpture or even doing carpentry. To balance what little importance we gave the rules of writing, our dialogs around beauty and *selection* continue in my mind to this day.

EOWYN GREENO:

My memories of Robert are a series of images from my early childhood growing up in LaConnor. Robert, tall and graceful like a willow; his long grey hair growing ever closer to the ground. Him rowing to his shack on the river . . . flowing with the water, shades of the grey-blue and green surrounds reflected in his faded clothes. The sun and salt-water bleached wood of the shack, the same blue-grey as his frock. The simple pleasures and warm austerity of the cabin itself. A flower placed just so, in a window, peace. Seeing for the first time "Bald Island" and realizing I'd seen it many, many times before as the master's covered tracks on his pages, in fact the only part of the pages I could take in. A raucous bonfire party on the top of Bald Island, gypsies and hippies rejoicing and prancing to harpsichord resounding. Riotous nights after the Tavern closing, the party continuing in the room beneath my bed. The most infamous of those left drunken scrawls from Clyde on our dining room ceiling. A visit to a bohemian house in Seattle, Robert resident artist among many. Robert's were the first tears of joy I ever witnessed. Shed in gratitude for a debt forgiven. A dim and most distant memory of a cozy A-frame, above the mountains of driftwood at Shi Shi, eating a wonderfully sticky pineapple upside-down cake my mom and Robert conjured from a wood burning stove. Later memories of Robert and my dad preparing for a show at Price's palace in Inverness, CA. Robert taking a break to teach me to use his brushes with the gouache. A painting hangs in my hall today which Robert painted for my mom as a focal point for my birth. I've loved it ever since I knew it. Once I told him he should give up all the current stuff and go back to the tight symmetric mandalas of that painting. My advice was considered but rebuffed. It may be because of Robert that I first knew there was another language, that itself had a name with a mysterious world and reality attached. Perhaps a casual explanation from someone who knew what he'd said was a word in Yiddish. When my sister was two, he loved to recite the Sandburg poem:

"Why did the children
put beans in their ears
when the one thing we told the children
they must not do
was put beans in their ears?"

Robert leading the way to a muddy, stinky hot spring on Mount Baker, a reward for an afternoon drive in the Greeno family VW van. I missed his Taos days, it was my vacated room he occupied. Whether he told me himself (during a rare call home from my high school year in Moscow), or my parents shared it afterward, I heard he enjoyed the collection of image and print inspirations posted on my teenage self's bedroom walls. And then time, and distance, and young adult life stepped in and I never saw him again in person. News of his reunions with my dad and sister after she moved to Seattle were all. Until the phone call, received in Taipei, my dad heartbroken to lose a best friend. A part of our universe departed and those left behind adrift. Then losing my own dad and gathering the gang at Shi Shi for a formal farewell. Many gathered having made the trek not so many years before to consecrate Robert's ashes to the sea. Now, with a giant mandala created from what our hands gather along the beach, we formed a circle, shared a toast and read many Sund poems as we waited for the tide to take Arthur's ashes and join him with the beyond. A poem from Taos Mountain read at my sister's wedding in Eastern Washington, a reminder for me (who knew him not for his poetry or his art, but as a part of a community providing definition and reference to the next generation) that our elders had gifts that linger and continue to connect.

ERIK AMBJOR:

I met Robert in the fall of 1977. I moved into a house in the U-District and Robert had come to town to bid farewell to Autumn Scott and Chuck Easton who were leaving town in the dead of winter in a beat up VW bug to Boston. Robert had come for the celebration and farewell party and he ended up staying for the winter. Not an uncommon story I'm sure. We became fast friends and spent a lot of time together both in the city and on the river. Robert was the first real poet I had met. Robert that night started reciting poetry and telling stories and he recited the "Two Bums in One Boxcar" poem and it was the first time I had ever experienced poetry. As Robert was relating the riding the rails, I began to feel the clickety-clack of those rails in the rhythm and the cadence of his voice. I think his voice was what made the poems so real because his teacher Theodore Roethke instilled in him the discipline to memorize all of his poems, all of his stories. And so whenever he read in public, he really recited from rote memory and could then breathe into the poems and take you to a new level and every time was a magical experience. He told a story about when he was teaching in the Seattle school district, the poet in the schools program, a boy had come up to him after class and said, 'I never met a poet before. I always thought poets were dead in books.' You could never say that about Robert. Even now. He'll never be dead in a book.

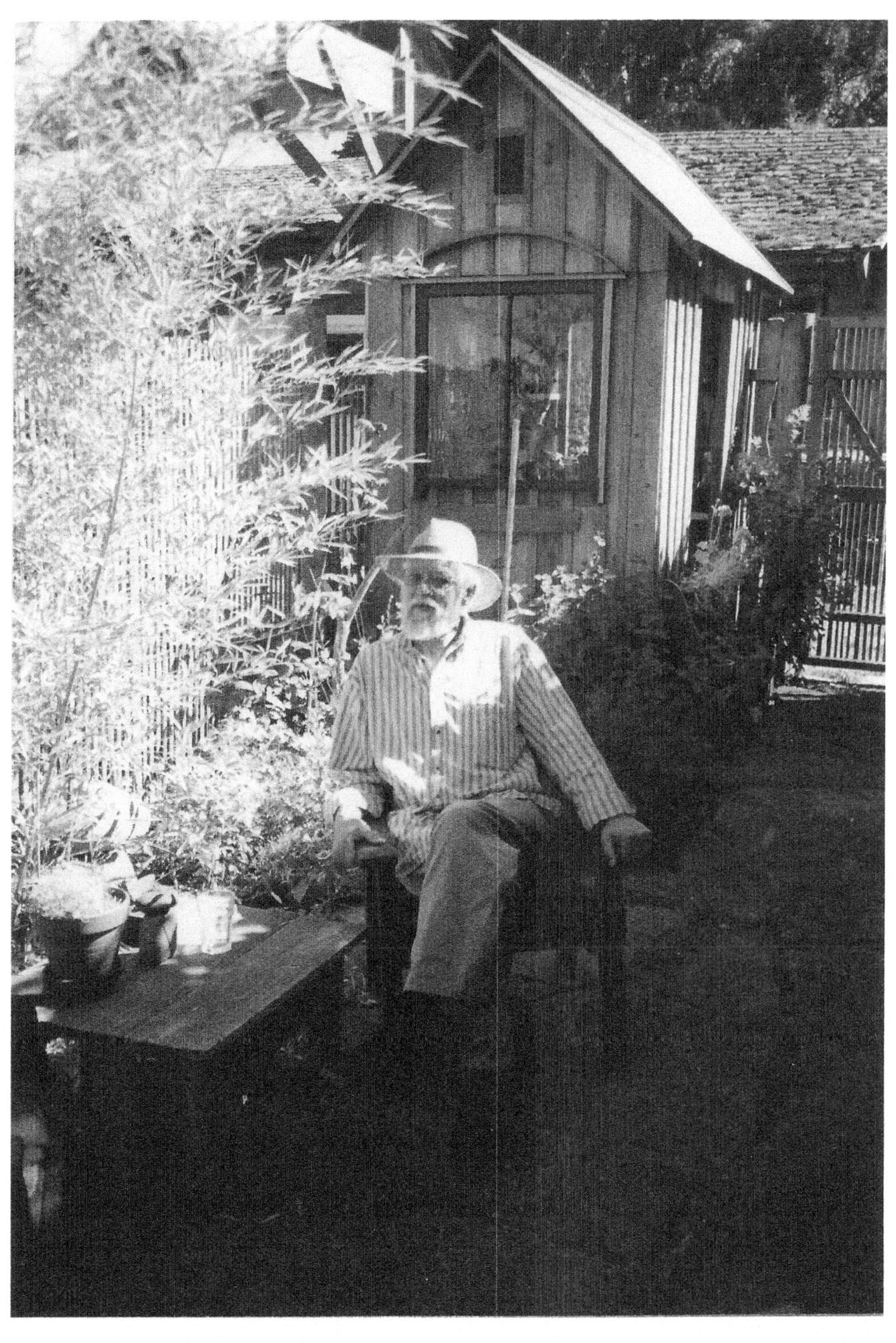

Photo by **Doug Spence,** *August 1997.*

CONTRIBUTORS:

At the end of my life,
I will lie down in
a little boat,
and float out on
the sea of
these friendships

ERIK SCHWEISS AMBJOR met Robert in 1977 and was an original member of Cloud House on 8th Avenue NE in the Seattle U-District. Over the years, his photography has graced the covers of several of Robert's book of poems, including *Ish River* and *Notes from Disappearing Lake.* He currently resides in San Francisco and is the owner of Sonoma Forge, a specialty producer of designer faucets.

ARJUNA BARTON: At my heart, I am a healer who does my work in my many ways. From massage and energy work to a Buddhist practice and a kind word or smile, I seek to make this world healthier and happier on a deeper level. I am a shy writer who keeps my words in page after page of unseen writings. Thank you for this opportunity to bring my voice forward.

WENDELL BERRY is an American novelist, poet, environmental activist, cultural critic, and farmer. He stresses simplicity of life and a strong sense of place. He is author of over fifty books.

JAMES BERTOLINO taught creative writing for 36 years, and retired from Willamette University in Oregon. His volume of poetry, *Every Wound Has A Rhythm,* was published by World Enough Writers in 2012, and *Ravenous Bliss: New & Selected Love Poems,* by MoonPath Press 2014. He's received several national awards and lives near Bellingham, Washington.

ROBERT BLY is one of the major poets of the Twentieth Century. He championed surrealism and political activism, urging poets to become involved in anti-war protests and activities. He was one of the early provocateurs of the Men's Movement, and was widely known for his book *Iron John,* a New York Times bestseller. He is the author of nearly thirty books of poetry, sixteen books of translation, and numerous anthologies and nonfiction works. He won the National Book Award for *The Light Around the Body.* Sund praised Bly, "He knows that the purpose of poetry is not to learn more about poetry, but more about life."

JOAN CROSS: I first met Robert at the 1890s Tavern when I first moved to La Conner in 1978; then attending poetry readings in La Conner at the bookstore, Garden Club and eventually he read poetry at my office building in La Conner at an event that celebrated the opening of a labyrinth that Maggie Wilder and I had painted on the parking lot. I loved his very accessible poetry and insights into a simpler life than I was leading. Then he moved in next door and became my neighbor on the hill in La Conner. When he got hungry, he would invite me to a sale of his art or calligraphy. We became friends for many years and I often visited him in Anacortes after he left La Conner.

MICHAEL DALEY is the author of four poetry collections, most recently, *Of a Feather* (Empty Bowl, 2016), from which his poem for Robert Sund is taken. His poems and essays have been widely published. He's received support from Seattle Arts Commission, Artist Trust, National Endowment of the Humanities, and Fulbright. He lives in Anacortes, Washington.

CHUCK EASTON is a native Washingtonian, having grown up in Mt. Vernon. Both parents were music teachers, so it was natural for him to play from an early age. He started on violin then switched to bass in high school, playing classical music in the orchestra and also trombone in the band. He slowly became aware of jazz, which has now become his major focus, although he still plays bass in the Pt Townsend Orchestra and various classical groups. After a stint in the army, where he got to play electric bass and electric guitar, the electric guitar won out, becoming from then on his primary instrument. Chuck graduated from Boston's Berklee College of Music in 1980. He has played many different styles of music over the years, but bebop-influenced jazz is his favorite. Chuck has been teaching private music lessons at Crossroads music in Pt. Townsend since 1995, with students of all ages on flute, trombone, saxophone, guitar, bass, piano and clarinet. For many years he has been on faculty for Centrum's Jazz Pt. Townsend and the Elderhostel NW Big Band. He continues to play locally on guitar, bass, flute, saxophone and occasionally Eb tuba and trombone. Chuck and his wife Autumn live on five acres south of Chimacum.

ALLEN FROST: On a night in Seattle around 1990, under the lights of the monorail, I'm sure I encountered Robert Sund. Who else could it have been with poems and his autoharp? Then, years later, Fred Owens showed up at the library one day and gave me a copy of *Bringing Friends Over.* That was my official introduction to Robert Sund.

SAMUEL GREEN was raised in Anacortes, Washington. He is co-publisher, with his wife, Sally, of Brooding Heron Press. His newest collection of poems is *All That Might Be Done,* from Carnegie Mellon University Press. A prose memoir, *FIRST UP: Barnstorming for Poetry,* about his two years as the first Poet Laureate of Washington State, is available from Chuckanut Editions, Village Books, in Bellingham.

SALLY GREEN—poet, printer, book designer, calligrapher, homesteader—is from Port Orchard, in Puget Sound. She is co-publisher, with her husband Sam, of the award-winning Brooding Heron Press, which published Robert Sund's poems in *Eleven Skagit Poets* and *Hands, Joining.* Sally's collection of poems, *Full Immersion,* from Expedition Press.

ARTHUR GREENO was a long-time friend of Robert's. He owned a frame shop in LaConner and founded the LaConner Arts Foundation. He was a fine promoter of Skagit art.

EOWYN GREENO was born in Seattle, WA in 1973 to Ginny and Arthur Greeno. Ginny and Arthur met while living on Shi Shi Beach during the summer of 1970. The Greenos lived in Eastern Washington and Boulder, CO before moving to LaConnor in 1980 shortly before their younger daughter, Margaret, was born. The family lived in the Skagit Valley until 1985 and then moved to Taos, NM after traveling in Europe for a year. Eowyn took up the family wanderlust with gusto and studied abroad in the Soviet Union during her senior year in High School. She earned her BA from Pitzer College and studied abroad twice more, in Zimbabwe and Nepal. She holds an MA in International Education from the School for International Training. She has worked in various International Education roles at Pitzer College, HESS language schools in Taiwan, UC Berkeley, Stanford, Brandeis, SIT Study Abroad, and will soon be joining the staff at University of Puget Sound. She lives in Seattle with her husband and daughter.

SAM HAMILL: An interest in the Beat Movement brought Hamill to California, where he studied with Kenneth Rexroth. A poet, teacher, editor and translator, he co-founded Copper Canyon Press and founded Poets Against the War. He has published fifteen volumes of poetry including a translation of Bashō's *Narrow Road to the Interior.*

BARB HATHAWAY: I was born and raised on the west coast, and arrived in Seattle with my family at 11 years old. I graduated from the University of Washington with a BS in Geology. I married and then worked around the western US doing some mineral and petroleum exploration. When my son was 4 years old I moved to Anacortes in Skagit County, Washington where I worked in civil engineering for 22 years at both the Skagit County Public Works Department and the Washington State Department of Transportation. I have enjoyed my life hiking and camping around the NW. After retiring I mostly do studio work as a ceramist. When Robert Sund died in 2001, he appointed eleven of his friends to be on the board of a trust to take care of his vision and intellectual property, and I am one of them.

STEVE HEROLD began studying to be an astrophysicist in those Sputnik days, but was converted to the palaeography and calligraphy side of history by a great teacher. Graduate school at the UW was so easy he spent most of his time in civil rights work and running his famous Id Bookstore, where activists, intellectuals and artists gathered. Charley Krafft and Robert Sund gathered him into the Asparagus Moonlight Group and residence in Fishtown, where he lived a life of simplicity, art and poetry. In the 1980s he was a pioneer in the creation of digital graphics and design, and in the 1990s he helped make the Internet what it is now. In recent years he has been doing research on manuscripts and antiquities and making both collections and books for libraries and museums.

GARY HICKENBOTTOM: I met Robert at Shi-Shi Beach in the summer of 1971. I was amazed at what was going on out there and later on in the fall, after the summer residents had all left, moved out there myself and lived in Roberts' shack until March. I hung out with Robert in Seattle a lot that spring, shooting pool most nights at the Central Tavern. We ended up in Boulder, Co. in May and after a long visit with Arthur and Ginny had our incredible boxcar trip back to the Northwest. The summer of 1972 we both moved back to Shi-Shi and I lived beside him in the 'miners shack'. This was a pivotal time for me and I treasure all the nights spent with him around the campfire....... I ended up getting married and raising a family in the Okanogan highlands where I lived for the next 40 years but visiting Robert was always on my travel circuit. It seemed magical to hang out in Fishtown and I would borrow Bo's boat and float down the Skagit River to Roberts' place in the delta. Later on, I enjoyed seeing him in LaConner and Anacortes and he always sent me home with a poem. He was a good friend, a gifted artist, and an inspirational poet.

GLENN "CHIP" HUGHES is the author of two poetry chapbooks, *Sleeping at the Open Window* (2005) and *Erato* (2010), both published by Pecan Grove Press (San Antonio). Since 1977 his poems have appeared in national literary journals such as *Poetry Northwest, Poetry East, Prairie Schooner, Poets West, Atlanta Review,* and numerous other publications. He enjoyed a thirty-year friendship with Robert Sund. Since Sund's death, he has edited *Taos Mountain: Poems and Paintings,* by Robert Sund (Poet's House Press: 2007); and with Tim McNulty, co-edited Sund's collected poems and translations, *Poems from Ish River Country* (Shoemaker & Hoard, 2003) and *Notes from Disappearing Lake: The River Journals of Robert Sund* (Pleasure Boat Press, 2012).

For the past 20 years PAUL HUNTER has published fine letterpress poetry under the imprint of Wood Works, currently including 26 books and over 60 broadsides. His poems have appeared in *Alaska Fisherman's Journal, Beloit Poetry Journal, Bloomsbury Review, Iowa Review, North American Review, Poetry, Poetry Northwest, Prairie Schooner, Raven Chronicles, The Small Farmer's Journal, The Southern Review, Spoon River Poetry Review* and *Windfall,* as well as in seven full-length books and three chapbooks. His first collection of farming poems, *Breaking Ground,* 2004, from Silverfish Review Press, was reviewed in the *New York Times,* and received the 2004 Washington State Book Award. A second volume of farming poems, *Ripening,* was published in 2007, a third companion volume, *Come the Harvest,* appeared in 2008, and the fourth from the same publisher, *Stubble* Field, appeared in 2012. He has been a featured poet on *The News Hour,* and has a prose book on small-scale, sustainable farming, *One Seed to Another: The New Small Farming,* published by the *Small Farmer's Journal.*

STEVEN R. JOHNSON: I graduated Western Washington University in 1969 and knew Robert back then. I visited him at Shi Shi when he was building his Carl Gustav Jung cabin in 1970 or so. It was the spirit of Shi Shi that talked to us and told us to do something to save the integrity of that coastal wonderland, as the clear cut logging was getting dangerously close to the Arches and Shi Shi. Shi Shi sent me on an epic journey down the coast to research land ownership, interview owners to see what their plans were, mostly loggers, and Indian Reservations, and then to the capitol in Olympia to get help as to how to save the last unroaded and unprotected land on the coast of Washington, and to Mexico!, except for Shi Shi, Point Of The Arches, and Lake Ozette. That was the beginning of 5 years, plus 5, of dedicated and obsessive grass roots ecology work, soon after graduation from Western. It put my degrees of art, photography, and cartography-geography to good use!

BRAD KILLION: After growing up in the suburbs of Chicago, Brad found his "home" in the Pacific Northwest in 1977. Brad is a lifelong musician who lives and works in Skagit Valley. He is a devout agnostic who loves his wife, family and friends. He says he will never be a politician because he has written way too many letters to the editor.

BONI KILLION is a native Washingtonian, mother and grandmother of fascinating children and is married to a wacko musician. She has been an English teacher for 28 years at Mount Vernon High School teaching: creative writing, poetry, humanities, journalism, and multicultural studies. She enjoys writing, poetry, music, cooking, and gardening. She thought about being a politician, but she says she will never be a politician because she's read too many letters to the editor.

CHARLES KRAFFT is a native of Seattle, WA. At age seventeen he ran away from home to become a beatnik poet in San Francisco, but was remanded back to WA where he ended up focusing on visual art. His reputation in the world of contemporary American fine art and crafts was made after he took the prosaic Dutch Delft tradition of blue and white china and turned it into a vehicle for biting sarcasm about war, street violence and the egregious manipulation of news and history. A self-taught artist in the tradition of the mystic painters of the "Northwest School," Krafft hitched his wagon in mid-career to the Pop Surrealist legacy of the crackerjack American hot rod hero Von Dutch and to the dense postmodern retro-avantgardism of Slovenia's NSK collective. This odd mix propelled him beyond regional respectability into international visibility. Krafft wrote a lively art gossip column ("That Ain't Art!") for a local rock music newspaper and published in a variety of literary and life-style journals during the heyday of the 'zines. In 1985, novelist Tom Robbins presented him with a coveted Darrel Bob Huston Literary Award.

LE KAI WEN (a.k.a. CHUCK LUCKMANN) lives in Bellingham, WA with his wife and son. A daughter lives near Robert's shack on Shit Creek. While teaching at Beijing Foreign Studies University, colleagues there gave Chuck his Chinese name: the three characters denote "happy," "successful," "literary." He's the co-author of *Voices along the Skagit.*

FRANCES MCCUE: Poet, Writer and Arts Instigator Frances McCue is a Senior Lecturer in the English Department at the University of Washington. The selection in here is taken from her latest book, *Mary Randlett Portraits,* a finalist for the Washington State Book Award. Her other books include *The Bled, The Stenographer's Breakfast* and *The Car That Brought You Here Still Runs.*

ANDY MCCONNELL is an artist and carpenter living in Seattle. He studied poetry with Robert through an independent study project at Fairhaven College during the mid nineties.

TIM MCNULTY is a poet, essayist, and nature writer. His most recent poetry collection, *Ascendance,* was published by Pleasure Boat Studio. McNulty's poems, essays, criticism, and articles on nature and conservation have appeared in numerous publications, and his natural history writings have been translated into German, Chinese, and Japanese. He has received the Washington State Book Award and National Outdoor Book Award, among other honors. He lives with his wife in the foothills of the Olympic Mountains.

BO MILLER: Walking thru the woods by candlelight. In the spring of '71, just out of the Army, I visited old college friends living north of the UW. I had been staying there for 4 or 5 days and sensed there was an unseen person also living in the house. It was Robert. He would come out of his basement room after we had turned in for the night and build a fire, drink tea and work until dawn. We became friends and I'd drive him around in my Hudson Hornet him ensconced in the back seat with knit scarf and white beard. He suggested we go out to Shi Shi Beach. We drove Hudson to the end of the road past Neah Bay and began a dark walk thru the woods. By candlelight we negotiated the mud wallows and made our way down to the beach for a starry walk to Petroleum Creek and the summer.

FRED OWENS: I write the *Frog Hospital* newsletter with up-to-the-minute news from Shit Creek, Fishtown, and the World at Large. Once Robert and I rowed out to his cabin on the river and he had not been there for some time, so we started a fire and got warm to make tea. Taking the lid off the honey pot, we found three dead mice, embalmed in the sweet honey. What a way to go! Robert is gone and Fishtown is gone, but wherever rivers run to the ocean, there be some of that spirit. I moved down to California five years ago, near the beach in Santa Barbara. I spend a lot of time walking on the beach, watching the birds and listening to the waves.

MARISA PAPETTI was raised in Skagit County and Germany, spending her summers in Bellingham, "Uncle Bob" was always on the must see list. She is a successful entrepreneur, raises vegetables, chickens, bees and Corgies. Married her soulmate and now lives in Bellingham.

ERICA PICKETT has long been interested in poetry. She currently serves as treasurer of the Robert Sund Poet's House board and is a member of the Anacortes City Council.

PAUL PIPER: I was born in Chicago, lived for extensive periods in Montana (where I received my MFA in Creative Writing) and Hawaii, and am currently a librarian at Western Washington University in Bellingham who spends more time than I should writing. I take my lead from Luis Borges. My work has appeared in numerous literary journals. I have five published books of poetry, the most recent being *Dogs and Other Poems.* I've had the privilege of being included in the anthologies *The New Montana Story, Tribute to Orpheus, America Zen, Shadow and Light.* I have also co-edited the books *Father Nature* and *X-Stories: The Personal Side of Fragile X Syndrome.* I await the world's next move.

MARY RANDLETT is a renowned Seattle-area photographer who specialized in photographing Pacific Northwest artists, writers, architecture and landscapes. Her work is notable for her documentation of the artists who created the Northwest School—Kenneth Callahan, Morris Graves, and Mark Tobey.

CHARLES REINSCH was drawn to radio station KRAB in the mid-1960's. Between 1965 and 1977 he worked at KRAB in a variety of roles, from volunteer program guide stapler to staff station manager. It was there that he first heard and met Robert Sund. In later years Reinsch served as controller or chief financial officer for several non-profit social service and health care organizations in Seattle and California. He retired from the University of Washington in 2010 after working there for 13 years.

BOB ROSE traveled cross-country from Boston in 1970, landing on north Whidbey Island. He's lived within 60 miles of that spot ever since. Rose spearheaded the effort to create the Anacortes Community Forest Lands. He then had a long career in land conservation at the WA DNR and Skagitonians to Preserve Farmland. He now farms oysters on Similk Bay.

JIM SMITH & JANET SAUNDERS: Jim (b. 1940, Ashton SD) and Janet (b. 1942, Weymouth MA) met in Clear Lake WA in the late 1970s, both drawn by the beauty and "hippiness" of the area. They moved to La Conner in 1980, finding a nice rental house near the sleepy downtown. Jim had met Robert Sund in Pioneer Square years before when Robert had just published "Bunch Grass." They resumed their friendship in La Conner. Jim found work with kids in the Swinomish Tribal Community; Janet taught ESL at Skagit Valley College. Both are retired.

BILL SLATER was a Skagit Valley painter who began his career in New York City as an assistant to Jasper Johns, who along with other Abstract Expressionists influenced his work. He was also a builder of fine wooden boats.

GARY SNYDER is a highly influential and celebrated California poet who along with Kenneth Rexroth and Ezra Pound is responsible for introducing Asian poetic aesthetics to American poetry. In addition to poetry, Snyder is known for his involvement in Zen Buddhism, environmentalism, and cultural geography.

ANN SPIERS is Vashon Island's inaugural poet laureate. The Peasandcues Press (Vancouver WA) recently printed her poem "Rain Violent" as a letter-press broadside, designed by Joseph and Marquita Green. Her chapbooks includes *Bunker Trail* (Finishing Line), *What Rain Does* (Egress Studio), *Long Climb Into Grace* (FootHills), *Herodotus*

Poems (Brooding Heron).

JOSEPH STROUD is the author of five books of poetry, the most recent *Of This World* (Copper Canyon Press) was awarded the Poetry Center Book of the Year. His work has earned a Pushcart Prize and a Witter Bynner Fellowship from the Library of Congress. In 2011 he was given the Award in Literature from the American Academy of Arts and Letters, and in 2014 the Lannan Lifetime Achievement Award in Literature.

GLEN TURNER lived in LaConner during its heydays (60s and 70s) and in the Skagit Valley for fifty years. Robert Sund lived with Glen and Ellie for extended periods, during which he was finishing *Bunch Grass* (wow!) and learning to play the autoharp (ouch!). Glen taught English at the Universities of Idaho and Oregon and Skagit Valley College. Glen met Robert through Charlie Krafft, exceptional artist and writer, who was in one of Glen's classes. Glen got Robert readings and a visiting poet's job at Skagit. Glen is the author of three collections of poetry: *Butterfly Dreams, Lemonade Days,* and *Moon Juice.* He now resides in Bellingham with his wife, Lynn.

PATRICK J. TWOHY is a Jesuit priest who has lived with and served the Native Peoples of the Pacific Northwest for 36 years. His life as a minister to the Native Peoples is Father Twohy's primary devotion and purpose. He has authored and published two books: *Finding A Way Home: Indian and Catholic Spiritual Paths of the Plateau Tribes* and *Beginnings: A Meditation on Coast Salish Lifeways.* Both works reflect his poetic style and his deep reverence for Catholic and Native tradition and beliefs.

CHRISTINE WARDENBURG-SKINNER is an artist/teacher living in Edison, WA with her husband, Tom Skinner.

FINN WILCOX worked in the woods of the Olympic and Cascade Mountains with a crew that included poets, Tim McNulty, Mike O'Conner and Michael Daley for over twenty years. From the mid-seventies through the early nineties, he was an editor for Empty Bowl Press. He is co-editor, along with Jerry Gorsline, of *Working the*

Woods, Working the Sea: An Anthology of Northwest Writings. His other works include, *Here Among the Sacrificed, Nine Flower Mountain,* and *Lesson Learned.* He lives with his wife of forty years in Port Townsend, Washington.

MAGGIE WILDER is a painter, filmmaker living in Skagit Valley.

WILLIAM CARLOS WILLIAMS was a major Twentieth Century American poet who was hugely influential both in his use of imagism, and his later experimental poetry and writing, particularly *Kora in Hell* and *Paterson.* He promoted writing in American language, rhythms and cadences. His numerous books include *Spring and All, The Desert Music and Other Poems,* and *Pictures from Brueghel and Other Poems.* He lived in Rutherford, New Jersey and was a practicing physician for much of his life.

JEFF WINSTON grew up in Connecticut, parents had extensive Scots-English and Scots-Irish heritage, going back to the original tobacco colonies of the Carolinas and the Irish immigration of the 19th century on mother's side. Three generations of railroad workers on father's side, travel is in the blood. Having come west in '69 after graduation, Jeff started the coffee shop Toad Hall in Bellingham, first encounter with Robert Sund and many other poets. Further chapters include sculpture in Seattle, then moving to Guemes Island in '71. A 20-year career of house design/building was followed by manufacturing Art Stamp and Crafts supplies as CLEARSNAP in Anacortes, resulting in world travel and the acquisition of 4 languages. Robert moved from LaConner to Anacortes in the '90s and we reconnected closely until his passing in 2001, he was a refuge from corporate struggles. Since then the Robert Sund Poets' House Trust has been dedicated to publishing his work and honoring his life with our annual gatherings. Jeff's "vanity career" of music production followed sale of business in 2006 and now a return to carpentry roots. There are many good friendships made via Robert, notably Erica Pickett and Brad Killion, Jeff's music partner. Robert was very sweet with our kids when they were young. His legacy of poetry and philosophy has always been very important. He brings us all together, even to this day.

THOMAS WOOD: For four decades Thomas Wood has worked as an artist in the Pacific Northwest, finding the cultural and natural surroundings to be a great source of inspiration for imaginative landscapes and mythological images. He sketches and paints out of doors while camping in Cascade Forests or sailing on Puget Sound. At home in Bellingham, in his backyard studio, he continues painting and prints etchings. His classic printmaking techniques are founded on studies of, and an appreciation for, the traditions of European printmakers of past centuries. The subjects are drawn from the Northwest landscape, from his garden, from mythology, and dreams.

BILL YAKE: Robert Sund belonged to the generation that shaped mine, although that recognition came late. The influence of those born in the 1920s—writers, teachers, scientists, and artists—largely accounts for why I was drawn to devote attention to the environment (25 years with the Department of Ecology) and put together poetry collections focusing on water, critters, and the spirit of the wild.

CREDITS:

Many thanks to all Robert Sund's friends who shared their memories, stories, poems and artwork. This book has been a unique opportunity to create a sort of biography of Robert in your words. We also wish to thank the Robert Sund Poetry House for all their support on this project.

Robert Sund, "Poem for Betty" first appeared in *The Beloit Poetry Journal* Vol 3 Number 3, Spring 1953.

Robert Sund "Letter to William Carlos Williams" and "March Morning: For William of Pasaic" Yale Collection of American Literature, Beinecke Rare Book and Manuscript Library.

Mary Randlett photographs, University of Washington Libraries, Special Collections, Negative numbers UW 37047, 37045. 37046, 37048.

Broadside advert, *The Collegian,* Western Washington University, Bellingham, WA, Friday, July 21, 1967.

KRAB radio guide 1965, image courtesy of Chuck Reinsch. KRAB FM radio excerpt also courtesy of Chuck Reinsch and the amazing www.krab.fm.

Robert Sund "Basket Bay, At Anchor, Near Midnight," published in *Northwest Passage* (Bellingham, WA) Vol.1 #12 October 7, 1969.

Robert Sund, introduction to *The Sullivan Slough Review,* The Sullivan Slough Press, Number 1, Spring 1969.

Bunch Grass review, *The Western Front,* Western Washington University, January 27, 1970.

Robert Sund "Passages from the Notebook of Douglas R. Redwood" published in *Northwest Passage* (Bellingham, WA) Vol.2 #2, November 4, 1969.

Thank you to Steven R. Johnson for use of his photographs at Shi Shi Beach, 1971.

Robert Sund "Two Bums in One Boxcar" University of Washington Libraries, Special Collections, Robert Sund papers, Acc. 5740.

Frances McCue "Robert Sund (1929–2001)" from *Mary Randlett Portraits* University of Washington Press, 2014.

Tim McNulty "Up Shit Creek" from *Ascendance,* by Tim McNulty, Pleasure Boat Studio, New York, 2013.

Poetry and Stories of Robert Sund, Memorial Celebration November 2001, a 2 CD recording by Poet's House Trust. Excerpts from Pat Twohy, Brad Killion, Jeff Winston, Tim McNulty, Gary Hickenbottom, Mike Price, Eric Ambjor are reprinted with permission of The Robert Sund Poet's House.

Michael Daley "Notes from Disappearing Lake Review" originally appeared in *Pacific Rim Review of Books,* Issue 17, Vol. 8 No.2 2012.

Jim Bertolino "Returning to the Poetry of Robert Sund" first published by Egressstudio.wordpress.com, May 2012.

Thank you to Erik Ambjor for use of his photographs throughout.

Fred Owens "Robert Sund's Soliloquy", Chapter 12 from the *Fishtown Blues.*

Robert Sund, from *The Newsletter paid for by the Committee to Elect Robert Sund Mayor,* published October 30, 1983.

La Conner Regional Library, thanks for the photocopies.

Robert Sund unpublished *Taos Mountain* extracts, edited by Glenn Hughes, printed with permission by the Robert Sund Trust.

Windletters courtesy of The Robert Sund Poet's House.

Robert Sund "Where the Animals Wear Shoes" University of Washington Libraries, Special Collections, Robert Sund papers, Acc. 5740.

Mary Hedlin from *In the Hall of Light,* The Robert Sund Poet's House Trust, 2010.

Ann Spiers "You Say, 'Remember Me'" Published in *What Rain Does,* Egress Studio Press, 2012.

Robert Sund "Autumn Equinox" from *Poems from Ish River Country* (2004) Shoemaker & Hoard, Washington D.C.

Paul Hunter "As Migratory Birds" was published in the 2002 Skagit River Poetry Festival's anthology *This Should Be Enough.*

Michael Daley, excerpted from *Of a Feather* published by Empty Bowl Press, 2015.

Marisa Papetti "Growing Up with Uncle Bob" *Bellingham Weekly,* December 2-8. 2004.

Thanks to Western Washington University Library, Special Collections, for sharing your Robert Sund collection.

ROBERT SUND WORKS:

Poetry Collections:

Bunch Grass, University of Washington Press, Seattle & London, 1969. 2nd edition, 1973

Ish River, North Point Press, San Francisco, 1983
(received the Washington State Governor's Writers Award)

Poems from Ish River Country: Collected Poems & Translations, Shoemaker & Hoard, Washington, D.C., 2004

Taos Mountain, Poet's House Press, Anacortes, WA, 2007

Notes from Disappearing Lake: The River Journals of Robert Sund, Pleasure Boat Studio, New York, 2012

Poetry Chapbooks:

Ish River Poets in Folio, (self published) 1965

In Praise of My Ink Bottle, (pamphlet) Double-Elephant Press, Seattle, 1971

Why I Am Singing for the Dancer, Poets Press, Olympia, Washington, 1978

The Hides of White Horses Shedding Rain, Copper Canyon Press, Port Townsend, Washington, 1981

How the Dancer is Carried into the Hall of Light, Sagittarius Press, Port Townsend, Washington, 1982

This Flower, The Great Blue Heron Society, La Conner, Washington, 1982. (From the dedication page: "To Kenneth Rexroth recalling his poetry reading Labor Day, 1980, La Conner")

As Though the Word Blue Had Been Dropped Into the Water, Sagittarius Press, Port Townsend, Washington, 1986, 2nd edition 1989, 3rd edition 1996

Shack Medicine: Poems from Disappearing Lake, Tangram Press, Berkeley, 1990 (reissued by The Robert Sund Poet's House Press, La Conner, 1992)

Home: A Prayer for the World Where You Found It, (pamphlet) Tangram Press, Berkeley, 1991

Bringing Friends Over: Haiku by Issa, Buson, Bashō and Friends, Tangram Press, Berkeley, 2002

Editor:

The Sullivan Slough Review, Number 1, Spring, 1969

CD Sound Recordings:
Poetry and Stories of Robert Sund: Memorial 2001, Robert Sund Poet's House Trust
The River with One Bank: Shi Shi Poems, Robert Sund Poet's House Trust 2015

DVD:
In the Hall of Light, Written and Directed by Maggie Wilder, Robert Sund Poet's House Trust, 2010

Guiding a stray bee
out of the house —
Enough work for one day!

Robert Sund
1999 —

GOOD DEED RAIN

Saint Lemonade, Allen Frost, 2014. Two novels illustrated by the author in the manner of the old Big Little Books.

Playground, Allen Frost, 2014. Poems collected from seven years of chapbooks.

Roosevelt, Allen Frost, 2015. A novel set in July 1942 when a boy and a girl search for a missing elephant. Illustrated by Fred Sodt.

5 Novels, Allen Frost, 2015. Novels written over five years, featuring circus giants, clockwork animals, detectives and time travelers.

The Sylvan Moore Show, Allen Frost, 2015. A short story omnibus of 193 stories written over 30 years.

Town in a Cloud, Allen Frost, 2015. A three-part book of poetry, written during the Bellingham rainy seasons of fall, winter, and spring.

A Flutter of Birds Passing Through Heaven. A Tribute to Robert Sund. 2016. Edited by Allen Frost and Paul Piper.

Coming Soon:

and light, Paul Piper, 2016. Poetry in a number of styles written over the past three years.

At the Edge of America, Allen Frost, 2016.

& the sequel to *Roosevelt.*

Lightning Source UK Ltd.
Milton Keynes UK
UKOW07f1807050716

277761UK00020B/396/P

9 781944 786809